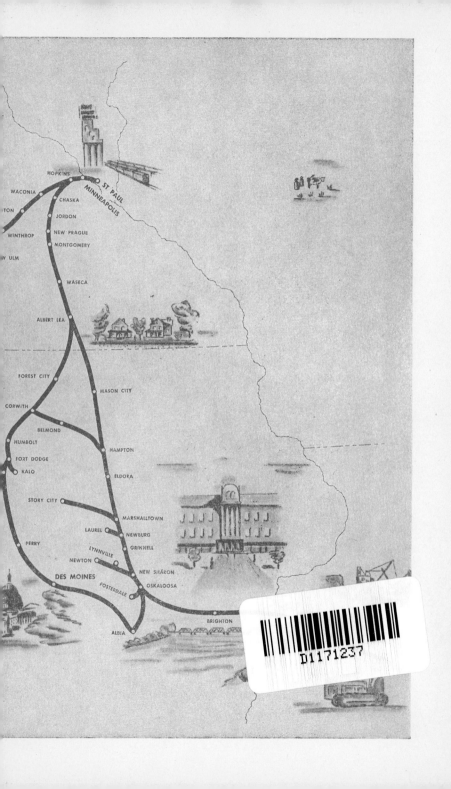

HOPKINS
WACONIA
ST PAUL
MINNEAPOLIS
CHASKA
TON
JORDON
NEW PRAGUE
WINTHROP
MONTGOMERY
W ULM

WASECA

ALBERT LEA

FOREST CITY

MASON CITY

CORWITH

BELMOND

HUMBOLT

HAMPTON

FORT DODGE
KALO

ELDORA

STORY CITY

MARSHALLTOWN
LAUREL
NEWBURG
PERRY
LYNNVILLE
GRINNELL
NEWTON
NEW SHARON
DES MOINES
FOSTERDALE
OSKALOOSA

BRIGHTON

ALBIA

MILEPOSTS ON THE PRAIRIE

BY THE WATERS OF MINNETONKA — With Lake Minnetonka in the background and the green lawn of Lake Park Hotel in the foreground, the train crew poses for the camera at Tonka Bay in 1886. Baldwin-built No. 8 was scarcely a decade old at that time and as good as new. Left to right in front of the tender are Brakeman Samuel A. Dunn, Baggageman E. R. Hogan, Conductor D. J. Maloney, Engineer I. Verdeaux and Fireman A. L. Nelson.

Mileposts On the Prairie

The Story of the *Minneapolis & St. Louis Railway*

By FRANK P. DONOVAN, JR.

SIMMONS-BOARDMAN PUBLISHING CORPORATION

NEW YORK

First Printing

Copyright 1950, by Frank P. Donovan, Jr.

Design and Typography by Elaine C. Farrar

Manufactured in the United States of America

TO THE MEN AND WOMEN WHO HAVE
BUILT AND WORKED FOR
THE MINNEAPOLIS & ST. LOUIS
RAILWAY
1870-1950

CONSIST

	List of Illustrations	viii
1.	Resurrected Railroad	3
2.	Minneapolis Looks Afar	9
3.	The St. Louis Road	21
4.	The Skally Gets Control	33
5.	Washburn Regime	45
6.	Enter the Rock Island	63
7.	Truesdale and Trying Times	79
8.	House of Hawley	91
9.	The Hook and Eye	105
10.	"... & Pacific"	123
11.	High Back Seats and Electric Lights	137
12.	The Clover Leaf and the Alton	151
13.	Retrenchment and Reorganization	159
14.	Bremner Takes Hold	173
15.	Doctor of Sick Railroads	187
16.	"Oh No, Day Kan't Do Dat!"	199
17.	Sale and Salvation	213
18.	Peace and Prosperity	225
19.	Men of M. & St. L.	237
20.	From Woodburners to Diesels	247
21.	On Rolls the Louie	259
22.	Time Freight 20	263
	Acknowledgments	279
	Family Tree	286
	Bibliography	288
	Index	297

ILLUSTRATIONS

Frontispiece—By the waters of the Minnetonka

First Section of Illustrations—Between pages 54 and 55.
Henry Titus Welles and William Drew Washburn.
Falls of St. Anthony; view of Minneapolis.
Manchester American-type locomotive; Albert Lea station.
Scene along the St. Croix.
River boats and Lake Park Hotel.
Minneapolis' first skyscraper; Washington Avenue station.
The Central Iowa's No. 26; an Iowa Central mixed run.
Marshalltown blacksmith shop; grain elevators at Boyd.
Edwin Hawley, William Haynes Truesdale and William Hep-
    burn Bremner.
LeBeau, S. Dak., station; stern-wheeled ferry and rotary plow-
    ing in the blizzard of 1917.
Old M&St.L and Iowa Central timetables.
North Star Limited; passenger train at Peoria.
Ten wheeler and Mogul locomotives.
Consolidation, Mikado and other locomotives.
Pacific and Mikado doubleheading; gas-electric motor car.

Second Section of Illustrations—Between pages 182 and 183.
Lucian Charles Sprague.
The Old (Motive power, roadbed, gondolas).
The New (Motive power, roadbed, all-steel box cars).
Semi-streamlined Mikado; three-unit Diesel; Grinnell depot.
Albia-Albert Lea motor train; blizzard of 1936; Keithsburg
    bridge.
Railway Transfer yard; Middle yard; Cedar Lake shops.
Extra freight in Scott county; local freight No. 70.

Sugar beets at Hopkins, Minn.; No. 20, flagship of the time
    freights.
All time map of the Minneapolis & St. Louis Railway.
Redwood, Minn., station; Madison station.
Mixed freight extra; No.19 coming into "Osky."
Olds, Iowa, from the cab of a Diesel; Monmouth-Peoria way
    freight.
Pacific, two-unit and three-unit Diesel locomotives.
Passenger and freight cars.
Diesel road switcher; Diesel shop at Cedar Lake, Minneapolis.
Offices of the past; new offices under construction.

Map of Lake Minnetonka 71
An early advertisement 138
Advertisement of the *North Star Limited* 142
Sammy Dunn and the company ad 145
Map of dispositions proposed for M&St.L lines . . . 201

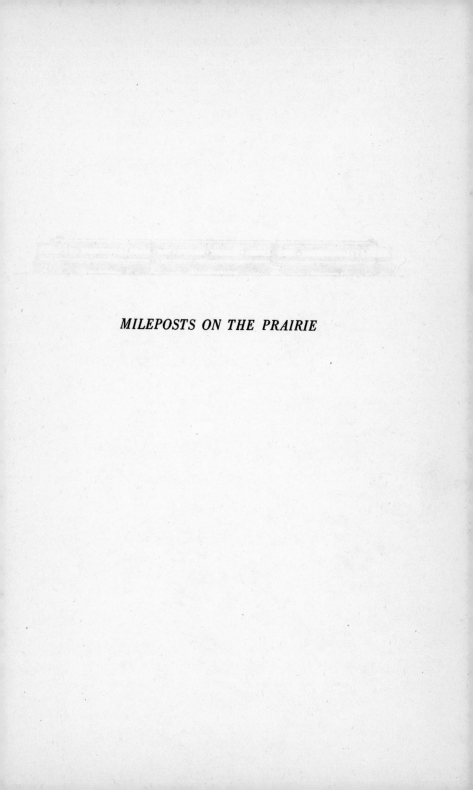

MILEPOSTS ON THE PRAIRIE

1

Resurrected Railroad

The selling of the Minneapolis & St. Louis Railroad got to be a joke. Several times a year the road would be put on the block, and each time there were no takers. The procedure was always the same: Special Master Howard S. Abbott, appointed by the court to sell the bankrupt road, would go to the company's Cedar Lake shops to dispose of the property. Each time he would stop on the balcony at the east entrance of the office and inform a non-existent audience that a final decree of foreclosure had been entered and the sale of the company's property ordered. Then he'd announce to the trees and hills that the sale would be adjourned to the superintendent's office.

Once inside the building, Abbott went to the chief clerk's desk and started reading aloud some forty pages of legal matter. The property was divided into eight parcels, and each one had to be offered separately. After describing a parcel at length, the Master would look up and query: "Do I hear any bids?" Except for the pounding of typewriters and the brief conversation of office employees, all was quiet.

"No bid," observed Abbott.

Meanwhile, the clerks and stenographers continued working without taking the slightest interest in the sale. Abbott would then drone through the next parcel. It took about two and a half hours to read the voluminous papers incident to the sale. This went on year after year. The Master never took short cuts and religiously carried out his duty. After constant practice, however, he came to know the verbose proceedings almost by heart and succeeded in cutting down the selling time to approximately two hours.

Nobody wanted the M&StL.

The 1,600-mile Class I railroad was the laughing stock among Midwestern carriers. Its roadbed was in poor condition, its cars battered and decrepit, and its wheezy locomotives scarcely able to handle the declining traffic. The employees' morale was at low ebb. People called it the "Midnight and Still Later," the "Maimed and Still Limping," and other uncomplimentary nicknames. Trainmen, remembering the old slogan "The Road That Runs," added, "for Coal and Water." Shippers used the line only as the last resort, and passengers shied clear of its creaky wooden coaches and unpredictable schedules. One could depend on the road in only one distressing particular: that it would lose money, constantly and with unswerving regularity. For most of the receivership period deficits piled up to the tune of 1 to 3 million each year. The road had been in the court's hands since 1923, and was destined to stay there for a total of twenty years and four months — the longest receivership of any Class I railroad now in existence.

Experts predicted that the M&StL was headed directly for the junk pile. "It starts nowhere and goes nowhere," they said. One prominent authority expressed the opinion that the road was indulging in a form of "self-cannibalization" and that it would eventually eat itself up. The road would have to skimp maintenance to keep operating un-

4

til it would gradually cease running. Employees began to keep a weather eye open for new jobs, and some took up correspondence courses to prepare for the day when the "Louie," as they affectionately called the road, would fold. Forty-two times the M&StL was put on the block and forty-two times there were no bidders. Then Walter W. Colpitts of the engineering firm of Coverdale & Colpitts was made chairman of the Reorganization Committee late in 1934, and informed the bondholders' committee that he had found a man to run the railroad. That man was Lucian Charles Sprague. Eight years later the forty-third attempt to sell the railroad succeeded.

Today the M&StL is a debt-free railroad paying substantial dividends on a modern plant. From probably the most run-down Class I carrier and the least profitable, it is now one of the most efficient, well-managed, and lucrative of properties. Thanks to the Sprague administration, a complete rehabilitation has taken place.

Light rail and gravel ballast on the main line have given away to 90- and 100-pound steel laid on a firm crushed-rock foundation. In place of antiquated, over-age steam locomotives, the road has modern motive power now nearly 100 per cent Dieselized. Whereas the yards were formerly cluttered with bad-order equipment, today's terminals sport all-steel boxcars, new 50-ton gondolas, and closed-top hoppers tailored to meet the shippers' needs. "Time" freights, which were a travesty on the name, now fully live up to their title. Big three-unit Diesels speed tonnage between Minneapolis and Peoria, clipping better than seven hours off the old schedule.

5

Traffic managers throughout the land know of the Peoria Gateway Line. In eastern cities such as New York and Boston, in southern communities like Birmingham and New Orleans, in the Midwestern gateways of Chicago and St. Louis, from Dallas in the heart of Texas to Great Falls in Montana's mountains, to say nothing of the coastal ports of Seattle, San Francisco, and Los Angeles, the M&StL representatives are on the job. It is a midwestern carrier with some twenty-seven off-line offices for nation-wide coverage. A popular bridge line between East and West. A local road with a continental mission to expedite freight through non-congested portals from coast to coast. That is the present-day M&StL.

Ledger-wise the road is as solid as the rock ballast on which its long freights roll. It is one of the comparatively few railroads with no bonded debt. Equipment obligations are slightly under seven million dollars, a moderate figure for a road which has practically replaced all its old rolling stock with modern cars and locomotives during the past fifteen years. The road's capital stock, like its rolling stock, brings in a comfortable net income, which in 1948 amounted to $3.69 on a share. Net income for that year was over two million as contrasted with an average yearly deficit of approximately the same amount during most of the receivership period.

Operating in four Midwestern states, the M&StL has become a fast, dependable freight carrier, run more efficiently, more economically, and with better equipment than ever before. Starting as an independent outlet for Minneapolis and Minnesota, it is still an independent railroad with the same name and the same general function. Minneapolis was its headquarters then; and today, on its eightieth birthday, the general offices are still in that city. The need for an independent outlet in the seventies laid the cornerstone for the thriving bridge line and the strategic local carrier that is the Minneapolis & St. Louis today. With this in mind, let us turn back to the city by the Falls of St. Anthony, back to when the M&StL was born.

...now is the time to resolve that a city with so many splendid material advantages shall no longer be isolated...

Minneapolis *Tribune*, February 19, 1870.

2

Minneapolis Looks Afar

Great things were happening in '69. America was pushing back the frontier, and by May 10, of that year the
last spike was driven, linking the East with the West. By
telegraph all the country knew that the Union Pacific had
met the Central Pacific on the barren prairie at Promontory, Utah. General Ulysses S. Grant succeeded Andrew
Johnson in the presidency the same year, and a feeling of
confidence swept the land. American enterprise and initi-
ative began to assert itself as never before.

In the Northwest, St. Paul was an important community, having a thriving river traffic and railroads running from the city like spokes of a wheel. The town
fathers had succeeded in getting the Lake Superior &
Mississippi Railroad to connect their growing city with
the largest of the Great Lakes. Already her citizens were
making plans for the completion of the road the following year. St. Paul, being the capital of Minnesota, had
considerable prestige and not a little civic pride. Minneapolis and St. Anthony were separated by the Mississippi,
although some people suggested they unite, for their
interests were similar. And they were, in a measure,
united by a fine suspension bridge—the earliest structure
spanning the main channel of the river from its source
in northern Minnesota to the Gulf of Mexico.

If water *transport* was the prime factor in giving St. Paul her initial development, it was water *power* which in equal measure assured the growth of her twin, Minneapolis, and her neighbor, St. Anthony. Long before the two villages came into being, the Government built Fort Snelling at the junction of the Mississippi and Minnesota rivers, just south of the present city of Minneapolis. The Falls of St. Anthony were utilized to provide power for a sawmill in cutting lumber for the fort, and in 1822-23 soldiers erected a small gristmill near the same site. It soon became apparent that the Falls were an admirable source of power for both lumbering and the milling of flour. In 1869 lumbering operations were carried on in these two adjacent towns opposite the Falls, with milling as a close runner-up. Sawmills and "flouring" mills clustered about this source of water power on both banks and on the islands between. Minneapolis and St. Anthony were wholly dependent on the Falls, and, indeed, it was impossible to think of the two towns without reckoning with their God-given source of power.

How dependent the twin communities became on the cataract was forcefully brought out in October, 1869, when the swirling Mississippi started to flow under the limestone rock forming the "falls." The cry spread like wildfire: "The Falls are going out!" Panic struck the communities. Cool heads, however, managed to check the unruly river, although it was not until about seven years later that complete and permanent control was effected. The St. Anthony Falls Water Power Company, which exploited the east side of the river, and the Minneapolis Mill Company, having control of the west, both spent large sums of money safeguarding this source of their very lifeblood. They contributed financial aid, and the

10

Federal Government also lent a hand in controlling the river. Before the task was completed nearly a million dollars had been expended.

That was the crisis of 1869. Another, perhaps not so much a crisis as a loss of economic independence, was the Minneapolis transporation situation which came to a head the same year. Before discussing this problem, a glance at the river and rail picture, as it affected Minneapolis and St. Anthony, will help in giving a background of the problem.

To begin with, very little river traffic ever came as far as the Falls of St. Anthony; it generally stopped short at St. Paul. The capital city had better harbor facilities than her up-river competitors, and the Mississippi was not very easily navigated beyond St. Paul. The railroad set-up was better, although not satisfactory.

The only road to the East was the Milwaukee & St. Paul, having a line from Minneapolis south to Mendota and Austin, thence through Iowa to Prairie du Chien, Wisconsin. Here it tied in with the older part of the system running to Milwaukee and Chicago. Its *Eastern Express* had sleeping cars from Minneapolis to Chicago, and it was advertised as "The only All-Rail Line, and the only route by which Baggage is checked THROUGH to Milwaukee, Chicago, New York, Boston and all Eastern points." The so-called Short Line to St. Paul was not in existence, nor was the River Division via Red Wing and Winona over which the *Hiawathas* speed today.

The other railroad serving Minneapolis was the historic St. Paul & Pacific, which, incidentally, was the first line to operate in Minnesota. Its famous locomotive, *William Crooks,* pulled the earliest train into St. Anthony over the ten-mile route from St. Paul in 1862. Seven years later the road extended northwest to Sauk Rapids with another line running westward about sixty-five miles where it stopped at Litchfield. Eventually this company formed the nucleus of the Great Northern under the able administration of Jim Hill, but in the late sixties it was not well managed and hardly earned its operating expenses.

It can readily be seen that the Milwaukee & St. Paul was the most important carrier, as far as lumbermen and millers were concerned. But this powerful road favored Chicago and, quite naturally, Milwaukee, the city of its birth. Freight rates were predicated to aid Milwaukee and the Windy City rather than Minneapolis. Meanwhile, the businessmen in Minneapolis and St. Anthony had high hopes for a line from the Falls to Shakopee as an independent outlet to the South, with connections to the East. The St. Paul & Sioux City road had a land grant for just such a line, but it lost interest in the Minneapolis extension after building from St. Paul to Mankato along the Minnesota Valley.

Cut off from an independent outlet to the South, the lumber and milling interests sought to have the Lake Superior & Mississippi road, then being constructed to Duluth, make Minneapolis or St. Anthony its southern terminal. It was not to be, for St. Paul won out, although the Falls' towns put up a good fight. The two communities at the cataract had all the available water power they needed; but the finest mill, if it lacks easy access to raw materials and a ready avenue for its finished product, is of little use. The rapid and steady growth of Minneapolis and St. Anthony, due to their natural source of energy, was seriously jeopardized by the lack of independent transportation outlets.

It was rumored, in effect, that Minneapolis had missed

the boat. Try as they would, the towns by the Falls could not make the Mississippi a strong arm of commerce. Moreover, they lost out on a direct railroad to Duluth, where Lake Superior had unlimited possibilities for water transport all the way to New York.

Minneapolis, indeed, had missed the boat, literally and figuratively.

Enough of hoping, of wishing and of waiting. The situation demanded action. Lumbermen, millers, and civic-minded businessmen resolved they would build their own railroad. For communities with a combined population of a little under 18,000 (the U. S. Census put the figure at 18,079 in 1870) this was a bold decision. The two towns in those days, however, had staunch pioneer stock—folks mostly from New England, whose forebears came over to this country to seek religious freedom. Their children, in turn, were an independent-thinking lot, beholden to no man.

It was these transplanted New Englanders, together with a few up-state New Yorkers, who determined to get their own railroad. It would, they declaimed, do precisely what they hitherto had been unable to accomplish in the way of independent transportation. Their aim was two-fold: first, to establish a link for the millers and lumber manfacturers with Duluth, so they could have cheap water passage to the East; second, to provide a line extending south toward St. Louis, affording an all-year market down the river from that city to New Orleans. The road to St. Louis would not only insure a market when Lake Superior would be closed to navigation in the winter but would have the additional advantage of crossing east-and-west trunk lines, promising independent routing to Chicago and other eastern points. Apart from this, they reasoned, there was coal in Iowa, which is just what Minneapolis lacked, and she in turn would forward flour and lumber to the Hawkeye State.

The two leading men in promulgating the north-and-south link were Henry Titus Welles and William Drew Washburn. Many others helped in getting the project under way, but none did more than these two far-sighted men.

Welles was a practical, energetic man, schooled in law, politics, and business. Born in Glastonbury, Connecticut, April 3, 1821, he, as a lad, worked on his father's farm and studied law. Later he was admitted to the Connecticut bar, and became interested in politics, and at twenty-nine represented his native town in the legislature. Coming west in 1853, Welles entered lumbering at St. Anthony and later turned to real estate, in which he built up an ample fortune, and at the same time reentered politics. When the village of St. Anthony was incorporated, Henry T. Welles became its first mayor. He subsequently moved across the river and again pioneered in city government, this time becoming president of Minneapolis' first town council in 1858. No novice in railroad affairs—having served as a director on the St. Paul & Pacific—it was only natural for him to foster the "St. Louis" line. Being acquainted with many prominent citizens, having a knack of making friends and getting along with others, he was an ideal person to solicit aid for the home road. Moreover, he tackled the job with gusto, speaking here and there, arousing public interest, raising money.

Different in many ways from Welles was "General" William Drew Washburn. "W. D." also came from New England. Born in Livermore, Maine, January 14, 1831, he was the youngest of eleven children, of whom seven

14

were boys. This is of particular significance because most of his brothers achieved considerable fame, and William was expected to uphold the family tradition of success. As a boy, he was nicknamed "Young Rapid" because he usually had many projects going at one time. Shortly after reaching his majority, brothers Cadwallader, Elihu, and Israel were in Congress representing Wisconsin, Illinois, and Maine, respectively, and, curiously enough, all at the same time. They had a head start on Young Rapid, but he lost no time in striking out for himself when he was graduated from Bowdoin College in 1854.

"W. D." pursued law at Orono and Bangor in Maine for a time, then went to seek his fortune in Minnesota. The youngest of the Washburns soon found employment in the Minneapolis Mill Company, of which Cadwallader was an organizer. Later "W. D." branched out into land work and became Federal surveyor-general for Minnesota. He was on the early board of directors of the Minnesota Valley Railroad, the forerunner of the St. Paul & Sioux City, and was one of those who helped launch the Minneapolis *Tribune* in 1867.

"General" Washburn dabbled in many things, with varying degrees of success; but when it came to railroading, he rolled the ball straight down the middle of the alley. He believed in railroads with all the vigor of his stubborn Yankee constitution. William Drew Washburn became well known as a lumberman, miller, and senator, but his greatest permanent contribution to Minnesota were his roads of steel.

Having aroused sufficient interest in the proposed line, Welles and Washburn sought a charter. They found one in the almost-forgotten Minnesota Western, one of the earliest railroads incorporated in the Territory. A brief

15

digression may be in order, tracing the development or, rather, the lack of development of the road.

The Minnesota Western Railroad Company was chartered in the Territory March 3, 1853, five years before Minnesota became a state, and nine years before a railway was actually built in the state.

The company was empowered to construct a railroad with tracks running "from some convenient point to be selected on Lake St. Croix, or St. Croix River, thence running to the town of Saint Paul and the Falls of Saint Anthony on the Mississippi River...by the most feasible route to the western boundary of said Territory, [Minnesota] at such point as shall be determined most expedient ...with a branch to the Red River...and also a branch running to a point to be selected on the St. Louis River if deemed advisable by said company."

Of the thirteen original incorporators Franklin Steele is best remembered, for he was an early settler in the Territory and a leading figure in the development of Minneapolis and St. Anthony. Becoming sutler of Fort Snelling in 1838, Steele later aided in the development of the Falls, built the first suspension bridge connecting the two towns, actively engaged in lumbering, real estate, and many other occupations. There was not much this doughty pioneer did not attempt, from banking to helping benevolent institutions. Furthermore, Steele was a rough, canny individual, more than ready to match his wits against anyone the Territory had to offer.

Other incorporators are remembered by the Minnesota counties of McLeod, Rice, and Wilkin, named in honor of Martin McLeod, member of the territorial council; Henry M. Rice, U. S. senator; and Alexander Wilkin, territorial secretary. Still others famous at the time were

16

Socrates Nelson, merchant and later state senator; Morton S. Wilkinson, lawyer and subsequently U. S. senator; and Henry Z. Hayner, chief justice of Minnesota. The remaining incorporators were Benjamin Allen, Joesph B. Doe, Otis Hoyt, A. Hyatt Smith, Robert J. Walker, and N. Greene Wilcox.

"Frank" Steele was elected to the chair at the first stockholders meeting January 27, 1854. George L. Becker, later state senator and an ardent supporter of railroads, was appointed secretary, and Alexander Wilkin, treasurer. The directors were Abram M. Fridley, an enterprising farmer; William Hollinshead, lawyer and business partner of Becker; Joseph M. Marshall, banker; William P. Murray, member of the territorial legislature; John Rollins, early settler and lumberman; and Roswell P. Russell, the first storekeeper in St. Anthony and a pioneer of pioneers. Steele, of course, was on the directorate, along with Walker and Wilkin of the original incorporators.

No rail was ever laid by this company, although the charter lingered on. It was one of over a score of pioneer "railroads" incorporated but never built. Some of these "paper" roads were formed in the hope of getting eastern capital or of securing land grants. Congress did pass a bill carrying a generous land grant to the Territory in 1857; however, the panic of that year put a quietus on any construction. The Five Million Dollar Loan approved by the state in 1858 enabled about 240 miles of roadbed to be graded, none of which ever saw a rail. The special bonds of the state making the loan possible so depreciated in value as to become nearly worthless. Indeed, the Five Million Dollar Loan turned out to be a huge fiasco, embarrassing to Minnesota until the redemption of the bonds took place some two decades later.

The tattered old Minnesota Western minute book tells of a committee appointed to prepare a memorial to the Senate and to the House of Representatives of the United States "praying for a grant of land to aid in the construction of a Rail Road from .... to ...." Here the minutes stop until a meeting of the board on August 26, 1869, is recorded. In the September 4, stockholders meeting record one finds that Welles and Washburn held a considerable number of shares and that things were beginning to pick up. After that there were peppery meetings and many changes of board directors. It is hard to picture "W. D." sitting around waiting for a land grant as, indeed, it is difficult to imagine him waiting very long for anybody or anything. He wanted results and he achieved them, for a resolution was passed on May 26, 1870, changing the name of the Minnesota Western to the Minneapolis & St. Louis Railway Company. Minneapolis looked to the markets of St. Louis and the South.

*But to do this thing of laying off and building
a leading line of road, is no child's play...*
Minneapolis *Tribune*, February 19, 1870.

3

The St. Louis Road

The Minneapolis & St. Louis from the time of its formation on May 26, 1870, to the present day has had its original name and original function. Other lines serving Minneapolis and Minnesota have undergone changes in names and objectives, but the St. Louis Road, formed to provide an independent outlet to the South and East, is operated primarily for that purpose today.

It took a good measure of courage to build a road beginning in a comparatively small community and extending through the backbone of the undeveloped Midwest. And yet the projected line to St. Louis struck public fancy even before it had been formally organized. For months the Minneapolis *Tribune* called for a north and south line, reminding its readers that such a road would mean "that blessed boon—*commercial independence.*" The papers carried maps, covering almost a page, showing the St. Louis Road in relation to other lines in Minnesota, Iowa, and Missouri. During the early seventies hardly an issue left the presses that did not have some mention of the Minneapolis & St. Louis or the need for an independent line "out into the great world, north and south."

The necessary changes were made in the company's charter, enabling the M&StL to construct a line south to Albert Lea. The road's engineer, Col. Joel B. Clough, was soon in the field sighting his transit, setting stakes, negotiating for right-of-way. No dillydallying for land grants, no visionary plans to build all over the state, no nonsense. Step-by-step progress, conservative financing, and steady construction would see them through.

By June 23, 1870, the *Tribune* was reporting that fifty men in crews divided into five squads had started building the new road. July saw "about one hundred men" employed, and the paper for September 28, jubilantly proclaimed "more than ten miles of grading completed." All this construction went on between Minneapolis and Sioux City Junction, on the first lap of the line to Albert Lea.

The original plan of the Minneapolis & St. Louis included a line to provide an outlet by way of the Great Lakes. This portion of the road was surveyed to run from what is now East Minneapolis to White Bear Lake, where it would meet the Lake Superior & Mississippi, making a short cut to Duluth. It so happened, however, that the M&StL could not advance the funds for immediate construction of the thirteen-mile segment. To expedite building the link, the M&StL issued two thousand shares of special stock to W. D. Washburn and H. T. Welles. These two men then formed the Minneapolis and Duluth Railroad Company, incorporated May 16, 1871. Washburn and Welles became president and vice president, respectively, as well as directors. Other board members of the company, who, incidentally, bought large blocks of stock, were William G. Moorhead, S. M. Felton, and Frank H. Clark, all Philadelphia bankers.

While dirt was flying on the M&StL, construction began on the White Bear Lake line. Nearly everyone referred to the Lake extension as part of the St. Louis Road, which it was in practice if not in name. The two were operated together, using a common terminal in Minneapolis, and both were a vital factor in the town's development.

The friendly rivalry between the twin cities of Minneapolis and St. Paul which exists today, was, in the 1870's, one of bitter jealousy. If St. Paul's *Pioneer* and *Press* said uncomplimentary things about the community at the Falls, the Minneapolis *Tribune* retorted in kind. The *Tribune* naturally played up the White Bear line, looking upon it (in the issue for February 18, 1870) as a way "out of the sink, which leads upward something like one hundred and thirty-two feet to the mile"—meaning the steep grade out of St. Paul to the north. The *Pioneer* and *Press* minimized the importance of the White Bear road and pooh-poohed the whole project.

Grading on the Minneapolis and Duluth, nonetheless, went on apace; and on May 31, 1871, the first rail was laid near White Bear Lake. President Washburn proudly drove the first spike and Chief Engineer Clough hammered home the second. Others tried their hand with the maul, and then the party repaired to the hotel for dinner and ended up with a sail on the lake.

Meanwhile, things were not so idyllic in Minneapolis, where the M&StL was laying its rails for both roads down to the depot site at Second and Marshall (now Fifth Avenue South) Streets. The M&StL, alas, had run its tracks directly in front of the approach to the suspension bridge. The county commissioners maintained that the puffing engines scared the teams and endangered the lives of citizens. They forthwith served an injunction on the road to prohibit operation across the busy thoroughfare. They achieved no results. Another injunction was served; this time on "General" W. D. Washburn and Hon. H. T. Welles. Still no results. The locomotives

23

continued to chuff to and from the bridge without let or hindrance.

The bald truth was that the executives were too busy getting the White Bear line in shape for the first official train and could not be bothered with petty injunctions. As a matter of fact, on July 21, the day after the second writ had been issued, they were felicitating Col. Clough on his rapid completion of the Minneapolis and Duluth. The Colonel was presented with what the *Tribune* in its July 22, issue called "an elegant gold stem-wind American watch, valued at $200," inscribed to him by the "Engineer and Construction Departments, July, 1871." Col. Clough was a man of experience and competence. It is not surprising that he was so rewarded, for he labored long and hard on both the main stem and the White Bear line. Originally hailing from Massachusetts, Clough had had a varied career surveying railroads, from the Mobile & Ohio in the deep South to the Vermont Central in New England. He had helped construct the Cleveland, Painesville & Ashtabula road in the Midwest and had served as construction engineer with the army of the Potomac in Virginia during the Civil War.

The excursion to White Bear on July 22, 1871, was the inaugural run on that line and a prelude to the grand opening on the main stem some two months later. About five hundred people from Minneapolis and St. Anthony boarded an eight-car special, which according to the *Tribune* "started from the end of the injunction bridge at precisely 8:55 o'clock." The train was drawn by Lake Superior & Mississippi engine No. 12 with R. L. Cone at the throttle and Conductor A. Tyler taking up the "deadhead checks." Music was provided by Turner's Brass Band.

The party rode to White Bear Lake in a holiday mood,

and from that station they coupled on to the Lake Superior road's train for Stillwater. A delegation of citizens and the local band met them at the depot. After a trip down Lake St. Croix the visitors boarded the cars for White Bear Lake. Here they disembarked and strolled to a "very pleasant grove on the lake shore" where half a dozen tables were "laden with a generous collation." Having downed a hearty meal, the crowd moved to the lawn in front of the hotel. The speech-making was true to form, with leading citizens, statesmen, and rail officials one after another addressing the multitude. After a half dozen orators had had their say, the gathering called loudly for "General" Washburn. Said he:

"...In the fourteen years which I have spent in Minneapolis, I have never felt a prouder day than this. This road is everything to us. It will make Minneapolis the great railroad and commercial center west of Chicago..."

He then explained how he had had the assistance of "Philadelphia men," who had invested their money in the Lake Superior & Mississippi, and stated, "They helped us, and they are going to help us to build it to Carver, and then on to the state line. We shall transfer the road to them, and I can assure you gentlemen, that they will run it on liberal principles."

Regular service commenced August 7, with four trips each way to and from White Bear Lake. Further to accommodate travelers, all trains, except for one round trip, carried through cars between Minneapolis and Stillwater or Duluth in conjunction with the Lake Superior road. Apparently, traffic did not come up to expectations, for service was halved a few days later.

Meanwhile, there were fresh injunctions and writs. The day after regular operation began Sheriff Johnson was

25

serving a writ on Conductor Tyler of the Minneapolis and Duluth and on Hon. H. T. Welles, ordering them to show cause for disregarding the injunction. By this time the White Bear trains had ceased running below the bridge. Enough was enough! After much wrangling, the injunctions were dissolved. The road, however, was ordered to stop its trains before crossing the approach, and to limit the speed to four miles-an-hour in the vicinity of the bridge. Furthermore, the authorities required that adequate warning signals be erected to protect man and beast.

While the necessary caution signals were being installed the White Bear trains used the St. Paul & Pacific's depot in the northern part of the town. Since the St. Paul & Pacific had already given the Minneapolis and Duluth running rights over the Mississippi and over a couple of miles of track east of the river, this arrangement was a simple matter. On August 18, the *Tribune* announced that the signals were erected. It added, "They are neither handsome, ornamental nor valuable, but will probably answer the purpose for which they are intended." They did. Before a fortnight had elapsed the trains were gingerly running down by the suspension bridge on their way to the new depot on Second Street.

Once service was begun to White Bear Lake and the injunction business out of the way, attention was focused on the road south. The slightest morsel of news concerning the Minneapolis & St Louis called for an article and frequently an editorial. If a contract was let for a station, that was news. Finally, in its August 29, issue the paper stated with frankness: "From headquarters *this* time the report comes that track laying *has* been commenced on the St. Louis road between this city and Carver.

This is the third time we have started this work, and nothing can prevail upon us to state the fact again."

As the road was being "ironed" there were the usual right-of-way fights with other roads. At Chaska both the Hastings & Dakota (now the Milwaukee) and the M&StL raced for the crossing. After a great deal of controversy each road agreed to pay one-half the cost of installing and maintaining the crossing frogs. To this day the agreement is still in effect.

In all fairness to the road, the fact should be brought out that building the M&StL was infinitely harder than completing the short cut to White Bear. There were deep ravines and lofty hills near Eden Prairie, a costly trestle at Baker's Hollow 75 feet deep and 350 feet long, and an elaborate drawbridge over the Minnesota River at Carver.

While construction was progressing out on the line, plans were being made for the new station in town. Meanwhile, temporary quarters were set up, and on August 9, 1871, the *Tribune* informed its readers, "...Newton, the new and good looking agent, presides with grace and dignity in his box-car office." August 27, the paper announced that the "new depot on Second Street is almost ready for occupancy...similar in architectural design to the Milwaukee depot but smaller. The inside is being neatly painted and grained in imitation of black walnut and oak."

It is doubtful whether the present generation ever looked with greater anticipation for a new automotive model than the folks in Minneapolis sought word of the inaugural run on the "home" road. Interest heightened on November 14, when the city council and the officers of the company made an informal tour to inspect the line. Thanks to the arduous labors of Engineer Clough and

Roadmaster Tom Brennan, the line met the councilmen's approval, and the $60,000 bond issue was authorized.

The way was clear for the grand opening on November 25, 1871.

On that auspicious day Minneapolis was agog with excitement. That very morning a special train from Stillwater, White Bear Lake, and other points pulled into the city by the Falls of St. Anthony for the festival. Many of these out-of-towners had witnessed the White Bear opening, but it was evident that the M&StL's celebration would outshine all others. The Minneapolis and Duluth's engine Number 1, bedecked in evergreens and banners, was ready to pull its eight-car train on the inaugural trip. Rippling in the breeze were flags bearing the names Stillwater, Carver, Chaska, and Duluth surrounding that of Minneapolis. In the coaches sat the invited guests, some 350 strong, eagerly awaiting the highball from the Lake Superior road's Conductor Crawford.

At 9:45 a.m. the official train chuffed out of town and headed for Carver and Sioux City Junction. The special arrived at Carver near noon and after a brief stop to pick up townsmen puffed across the Minnesota River toward the Junction. In this sparsely-settled locale, where the M&StL met the St. Paul & Sioux City line, a pleasant incident awaited the visitors. An employee of the road made a brief talk extolling the character of Roadmaster Thomas Brennan and then, in behalf of his fellow workers, presented him with a "beautiful American Gold Watch." The construction boss was so taken back he was at loss for words; and after he had made several futile attempts to express his appreciation, "General" Washburn responded for him. Later Brennan, who was a favorite with the men, was handed a sixty-dollar piece of jewelry for his wife.

After this brief interlude the inaugural train returned to Carver, adding two more cars of local people, and then steamed northward. Around two o'clock the long, full train slowed down for Minneapolis. Here the special was met by a delegation of citizens and Turner's Band. The main part of the celebration was just beginning.

While the inspection party had been on the line, prominent men from St. Paul and other parts of the state had gathered in the historic Nicollet House, ready with a speech, a good word, a friendly handshake. Probably this was the first time the leading citizens of St. Paul and Minneapolis had come together as men of goodwill, forgetting petty rivalries and exchanging sincere felicitations. Among the notables present were General Henry H. Sibley, the first governor of the state, and Horace Thompson, president of the First National Bank of St. Paul. The rail executives were represented in the persons of E. F. Drake, president, and Col. J. L. Merriam, vice president, of the St. Paul & Sioux City, together with Hon. William L. Banning, ex-president of the Lake Superior & Mississippi. Incidentally, Franklin Steele and former U. S. Senator M. S. Wilkinson, both of whom were among the original incorporators of the Minnesota Western, took part in the occasion.

The procession, led by Turner's Band, made quite a spectacle as it marched down the streets to Harmonia Hall. Here the women folk had an elaborate meal spread for about four hundred people. Hardly had the guests been seated when "General" Washburn arose and addressed the gathering. He spoke with pride of the St.

Louis Road—"the first section...which has been formally opened to-day ... the first railroad ever built in Minnesota without a land grant, and built unaided, except by local or municipal donations from the village of Carver and our own city..." The "General" waxed enthusiastic when he spoke of reversing the old channels of trade, of opening the vast empire southwest of the rich Minnesota Valley, and of placing the city, "by the full carrying out of the enterprise...on the Through Trunk Line from the head of the great inland sea of America to the head of winter navigation of the Father of Waters at St. Louis."

Then came the toasts, nine in all, representing various localities, institutions, and railroads. Number one on the list was that of Hon. William L. Banning of St. Paul, "father of the Superior Railroad system." He stressed the importance of the Great Lakes and also urged Minneapolis to "strive hard for the St. Louis connection." Other toasts were offered by E. F. Drake, president of the St. Paul & Sioux City; Morton S. Wilkinson, representing the Minnesota Valley; General Sibley, the first governor of Minnesota; and Levi H. Griffin, a spokesman from Carver.

Chaska's representative, Henry Young, averred that the coming of the railroad made race and nationality give way to American citizenship. He observed there were "no more Dutchmen, no more Norwegians, no more Frenchmen, no more Irishmen, no more Yermans, no more Yews, noding but Amerigans."

Next day regular passenger service began with two trains each way between Minneapolis and Sioux City Junction. The St. Louis Road was off to a good start.

The Minneapolis & Duluth railroad is to have
a camel-back ladies' car to connect with the L.
S. & M. R. R. at White Bear Lake.

Minneapolis *Tribune*, June 11, 1872.

4

The Skally Gets Control

The vitality and "push" of early-day Minneapolis was exemplified in the early board of directors of the M&StL. Around the board table in 1871, were the men who had built the city and its industries, men who are remembered today as educators and statesmen. Before going on to the rapidly-moving events in connection with the operation and policies of the St. Louis Road, a look at the gentlemen who directed the affairs of the company may be in order.

At the head of the table, figuratively and perhaps literally, was President Welles. It is not hard to imagine Vice President Washburn at his side taking an active part in all that was going on. Judge Isaac Atwater from up-state New York was secretary and transcribed the minutes of the meeting. The judge, formerly associate justice of the State Supreme Court, doubled as solicitor for the road when not copying records. He is remembered today for his comprehensive *History of Minneapolis,* recounting the early development of the city. Nearby sat Treasurer Rufus J. Baldwin, another easterner who hailed from the Empire State. Baldwin, who was educated for the law, later turned to banking and became prominent in local finance. In addition he had a hand in developing the Minneapolis Mill Company, and was a state senator in the early sixties.

33

Around the table were the millers, men who did much to make the city the world's largest flour center, in the eighties. None was to achieve greater prominence than John Sargent Pillsbury, who had just finished two terms as state senator. A native of New Hampshire, he came to St. Anthony in his late twenties and entered the hardware business. During the time he served on the M&StL's first directorate he became interested in milling. A distinguished career in public service was yet to come. Three successive terms as governor of Minnesota were to be high-watermarks in good administration. Pillsbury, in his long period as regent of the University of Minnesota, helped to lay the groundwork for the high standing of the modern "U." Today his name is perpetuated in the famous Pillsbury Mills, of which he was a co-founder.

Another New Hampshire-born miller was William W. Eastman, a spare man of nervous temperament and decisive manner. He, along with his state-of-Maine partner, Paris Gibson, also on the board, built the Cataract Mill in 1859. It was the first privately built mill on the site of Minneapolis, west of the river. Somewhat older than these two men and the only original incorporator of the old Minnesota Western to serve on the board was Roswell P. Russell. He left his native hills of Vermont as a lad of sixteen to go west. Landing at the frontier outpost of Fort Snelling, he was ultimately to become engaged in lumbering and milling.

Likewise of importance in the early 1870's were the lumber interests, who, of course, were represented on the board. Prominent among them was Capt. John Martin, another Vermonter, who had left the paternal farm to become a steamboat captain. When the gold rush of '49 came along, he quit his seafaring life to follow the throng to California. Somewhat wiser and poorer, Martin came back to the rocky Vermont countryside only to find life there too drab for his adventuresome soul. Once more he headed westward, this time to settle in St. Anthony. Using his savings to buy timber lands, Martin soon became very much engrossed in lumbering, and in later years turned to milling. Equally prominent on the board as a lumberman was an ex-Pennsylvanian, William P. Ankeny who, like many of his associates, eventually turned to milling.

The remainder of the pioneer directorate were either bankers or professional men. Outstanding in finance was R. J. Mendenhall, an orthodox Quaker, plain in dress and quiet in manner. He was one of the town's leading bankers and interested in everything pertaining to the community's growth and the welfare of its people. The other financial men sitting on the board were Jacob K. Sidle, organizer and president of the First National Bank of Minneapolis, and W. P. Westfall, cashier of the National Exchange Bank.

It is curious to note that while most of the directors came from New England, the three bankers hailed from North Carolina, Pennsylvania, and New York, respectively. Finally a lawyer, William W. McNair, and a physician, Dr. Levi Butler, rounded out the board. McNair had come to Minnesota at the age of twenty-one and had built up a substantial clientele in Minneapolis. Dr. Butler, the only director from the then western state of Indiana, had performed distinguished service as a surgeon in the Third Minnesota Regiment during the Civil War. A versatile man of considerable attainments, he afterwards turned to lumbering and politics.

Here, then, were the board members of Minneapolis'

own railroad. Out-of-staters all, they were solid citizens who had cast their lot in Minnesota and had prospered. They were willing to take chances, but none were, in the modern term, speculators. Nor was their railroad in any sense a speculation. It had definite objectives, and the directors hewed to these objectives with all the tenacity of pioneers.

Now that the fanfare was over and twenty-eight miles of difficult construction had been completed on the St. Louis Road, the cry was: "On to the state line!" It was only eighty miles further from "end of track" at Sioux City Junction to Albert Lea, miles that presented no great difficulty in the gently rolling countryside of southern Minnesota. Indeed, Welles and Washburn had an understanding with the Central Railroad Company of Iowa, looking toward a traffic agreement and ultimate consolidation. The Iowa road was rapidly building across the Hawkeye State from Albia near the southern border to Northwood, virtually on the Minnesota line. The two roads would work together to mutual advantage, forming a strong north and south avenue of commerce. Nothing seemed impractical or too roseate about this. As a matter of fact, consolidation did come—*about forty years later.*

Meanwhile, what looked like a quiet, well-ordered future for the M&StL turned out to be a hectic, uncertain period. During that period there were changes of control, a bitter and long-drawn-out rate war, bankruptcies, and the panic of '73. The St. Louis Road emerged like a ship tossed on the rocks by a storm, much in need of repair —but still seaworthy.

The Philadelphia men who partly financed the M&StL were bankers closely associated with Jay Cooke, who had raised money to build the Lake Superior & Mississippi and the Northern Pacific. They in turn underwrote the St. Louis Road and the White Bear line. Hence, from the start, the fortunes and objectives of the Welles and Washburn roads were closely allied with those of the Lake Superior line. It is not surprising that Minneapolis interests felt that control by the Lake Superior & Mississippi would be advantageous in strengthening the chain of independent railroads, in reducing freight rates, and in opening new gateways. Thus it came about that the Lake Superior road leased the Minneapolis and Duluth on June 5, 1871, and the Minneapolis & St. Louis, on October 24, of the same year. This explains the presence of Lake Superior crews and rolling stock on the inaugural runs of the White Bear Lake and Sioux City Junction trains. Before three years elapsed, however, these seemingly snug leases for the Welles and Washburn roads were changed. On the other hand, the close relationship and almost indiscriminate mixing of the companies continued for decades. This calls for a brief description of the Lake Superior & Mississippi, later known as the "Skally."

The Skally?

An odd name, to be sure, which came about in an odd manner. There are many stories concerning the nickname's origin, but the following has a ring of truth to it. In those days the construction and maintenance crews were predominantly Swedish. In those days, too, the section men's pay was low, considerably lower than the pay for work on the Great Lakes. As a result, the Swedes worked on the tracks while Lake Superior was frozen and then looked to Duluth as soon as navigation began in the spring. Just a word or rumor that boats had started running, and the Swedes would drop picks, shovels, and lining bars, and strike out for Duluth. More often than not, they quit work *en masse* upon hearing that the ice was breaking up. A trainman would shout at a departing sectionman:

"Where you goin', Ole?"

"Skally go hoot!" would be the clipped reply—at least that's how it sounded to American ears. Actually it was: "Skall gå till Duluth!" meaning, "I'm going to Duluth!" Constant repetition of this phrase made an impression on the railroaders, until they began calling the Lake Superior & Mississippi and its successor, the St. Paul & Duluth, "the Skally." To this day older trainmen still refer to it as the Skally.

Like the St. Louis Road, the Lake Superior & Mississippi was built to secure lower freight rates and to compete with the monopolistic control of traffic held by Chicago and Milwaukee interests. Unlike the M&StL, the Lake Superior road received an extensive grant of pine lands. Hardly had the road been completed in 1870, from the Mississippi to Lake Superior, when a fierce rate war was waged between it and the only road going to the East, the powerful Milwaukee & St. Paul. When the Lake Superior road leased the Welles and Washburn lines, it was in the thick of the fight for traffiic, a fight which was eventually to plunge the company into receivership.

On a strict cost basis, the rail-and-water route by way of Duluth would command a large share of traffic to eastern markets. But the Milwaukee & St. Paul had no intention of letting the newcomer get much of the highly lucrative grain. By an arbitrary ruling, the Milwaukee & St. Paul reduced the distance, tariffwise, of all stations on its Chicago route to a maximum of 156 miles from St. Paul. This was the length of the "Skally." It mattered not (during the navigation season) that Chicago was over four hundred miles away. It took the same rate as St. Paul -Duluth traffic, which moved over little more than a third of the distance.

Alexander Mitchell, who dominated the Milwaukee & St. Paul's directorate, placed buyers at many stations of independent lines leading to St. Paul, ordering them to purchase all wheat, regardless of price. The Lake Superior road retaliated by carrying trainloads of wheat to Duluth without collecting any revenue. Small wonder that after two seasons of this cut-throat competition, the Lake Superior & Mississippi went into receivership.

However low the Lake Superior road had sunk financially, it was still potentially valuable property. The Cooke interests had a large stake in the road and an even larger holding in the Northern Pacific. The upshot was that the NP leased the Lake Superior line, thus bringing the Welles and Washburn properties under the hand of what was to become the first of the northern "transcontinental" systems.

The service to White Bear Lake and to Sioux City Junction apparently changed with the fortunes of the Lake Superior and/or the Northern Pacific roads. At any rate, every month or two brought a revised schedule—adding trains for a time, then curtailing them when revenue declined. The double daily-except-Sunday round trips to both points were frequently trimmed to a single train each way. The White Bear line, especially, had its fluctuations, not only in regard to number of passenger trains operated but to type of equipment as well. It ran the

39

gamut—from mixed trains in daylight service to Pullman Palace cars on night runs. But the overnight run to Duluth only lasted for a short time during 1872, and then fell under the ax of retrenchment. In spite of somewhat erratic service, the White Bear line proved to be a strong competitor to the all-rail route to the East. Trains from Minneapolis met boats at Duluth going to or from Detroit, Cleveland, Erie, and Buffalo. In July, 1872, the Union and the Atlantic, Duluth and Pacific steamboat companies advertised eleven steamers in operation, calling at the "Zenith City" daily except Saturday and Sunday. New gateways, reduced rates, and independent routings applied to passengers as well as to cargo. There is no gainsaying the fact that as far as the people of Minneapolis were concerned, the new railroads had proved their mettle.

In those days a fruitful source of revenue came from excursion business, and it is not hard to picture trainloads of picnickers swarming into the Second Street depot. Appearing in the newspapers were notices of the "Baptist Sunday School excursion," the "Congregational friends," and other religious groups going to White Bear for fishing, a picnic, and a sail on the lake. "Fare: 50 cents" or a "round trip including the use of boats: 75 cents."

Meanwhile, one may ask, what was being done to further the "St. Louis connection"? What, in short, were they doing below the little village of the Sioux City Junction? The answer is: nothing. The lessor was hard-put to keep the trains running and to meet the payroll. The importance of the latter event called for an excerpt in the Minneapolis *Tribune* for February 2, 1872: "The employees of the Lake Superior and Mississippi road are being made happy. The pay car is on its rounds again." In an effort to pare expenses, the Lake Superior road announced in its

40

newspaper advertisement of March 3, that Minneapolis trains would arrive and depart at the St. Paul & Pacific station instead of the Second Street depot. The slow, tedious run down by the "injunction bridge" henceforth would apply only to freight service. At the same time the notice added that the Sioux City Junction trains would operate to and from St. Anthony.

The year 1872 was drawing to a close, with no work done in extending the St. Louis Road to Albert Lea and and the Iowa state line. Problems aplenty confronted the management. Trying to keep the trains on time, in face of reduced maintenance and curtailed repairs, called for all the resourcefulness the railroaders could muster. A-gent Newton's dictum, in response to complaints of tardy operation, that "trains will go on time every time," fell far short of fulfillment.

On the White Bear branch the trestle over the "big swamp" about midway between Minneapolis and White Bear Lake caused no end of trouble. Shortly after the road had been opened, the bridge sagged in the quick-sand and derailed an evening train. The structure was rebuilt, but still the timbers quaked and sagged. Watch-men constantly had to inspect the bridge. In the olden days brakemen riding the car tops would notice the train dip in the middle as it crossed the swamp. On occasions one rail would be six inches lower than the other after a freight had passed over the bridge.

When the author passed over the road in a sectionman's motor car in 1949, the trestle was nowhere to be seen. Yes, the section foreman remembered the old bridge and how it was constantly getting out of line. "How do they go over the swamp today?"

"We don't," observed the trackman with a smile. "We

41

go *around* it." Then he pointed to a sharp deflection in the route, just enough to sidestep the swamp. Seventy years of fighting the morass, and then the railway engineers decided that discretion is the better part of valor and in this case more economical. It is one of the few cases in which a railroad gave up a fight, tearing out a direct line in favor of a circuitous route without the advantage of a better grade.

What was the future of the M&StL under Northern Pacific management? No one could say for sure, either in the front office at Duluth or at the fluted-pillared headquarters of Jay Cooke & Company in Philadelphia. Ununbridled competition had almost ruined the Lake Superior road. The Grangers were promising to make things difficult by a flood of restrictive legislative bills. The money market was tightening up as overexpansion ran its course. The familiar Minneapolis & St. Louis and Minneapolis and Duluth names on timetables in the newspapers were replaced with Lake Superior & Mississippi's bold letters. Finally, only an impersonal "Northern Pacific R. R., Lake Superior & Mississippi Division" headlined the timetables.

For a time the M&StL lost its identity and became a mere branch of the rapidly expanding Northern Pacific. But the panic of '73 was to change all this. With the failure of Jay Cooke & Company, the NP's leased lines were to be turned back to their owners. The St. Louis Road and the White Bear branch were once more to become local roads in name and actuality.

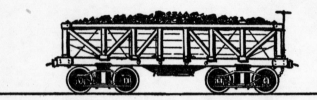

I propose to be loyal to Minneapolis interests first, last and all the time.

      W. D. Washburn before the Minneapolis Board of Trade, January 6, 1873.

5

Washburn Regime

When the Minneapolis & St. Louis was handed back to W. D. Washburn and its local officers in 1874, Minneapolitans sighed with relief. The St. Louis Road, in which the citizens had immense pride, had not been run very well. The newspapers asserted trains were operated at inconvenient hours on indifferent schedules at the whim of executives in Duluth. It is true, however, that the Northern Pacific had inaugurated some improvements, such as through sleepers to the "Zenith City," although this luxury was of short duration. When hard times came to Jay Cooke's "Banana Belt," as the NP was called, the road naturally looked after its own property first. Next in turn came the Lake Superior & Mississippi, and, finally, the funds that were left went to the stepchildren: the White Bear line and the road to Sioux City Junction. When fortunes were low on the parent company, the St. Louis Road received the cast-off equipment and trundled along as best it could.

A first-hand account of a ride from Minneapolis to Duluth appeared in the Minneapolis *Tribune* September 24, 1873. The writer, a lady taking a trip from Minneapolis to Duluth, stated quite frankly that "from Min-

45

neapolis to White Bear everything seemed shackly and out of repair, and all our startings, and stoppings sent a shock through the entire train; indeed sometimes throwing passengers from the seats. Once on the main line, however, and all was smooth and well ordered."

Such was the condition of the White Bear branch and presumably the Sioux City Junction road when "General" W. D. Washburn assumed active control. Heretofore "W. D." had held the presidency of the Minneapolis and Duluth only, but in 1874 he became head of the M&StL proper. As a matter of fact, in previous years Welles frequently referred to the "General" as the "executive manager of the road" and attributed the early completion of its first (Minneapolis-Sioux City Junction) section to the "energy and enterprise" of Washburn.

It was with great satisfaction that Washburn announced that all the engines and cars would be adorned with the name, Minneapolis & St. Louis. True, the only locomotives the company owned were two 4-4-0's, or American types, which were formerly the property of the Minneapolis and Duluth. But the company made arrangements for a five-year lease of $100,000 worth of engines and cars from the Northern Pacific. Then they moved the offices, lock, stock, and barrel, to the station "opposite the Milwaukee depot" on Second Street. The community-owned road would be community-operated right from the center of Minneapolis.

Meanwhile, the train schedules were immediately shifted so that the early morning departures were moved up to more convenient times. The wee-hour-of-the-morning operation was one of the chief grievances the folk of Hennepin, Carver, and Scott counties had against the former management. By strict economy the "excess of expenses over earnings," which as of August 31, 1873, had amounted to $39,772, was whittled down to $2,087 the following fiscal year.

President Washburn had ready-made plans for speedy completion of the line to the Iowa border. The immediate problem, however, was one of keeping the trains running and the road solvent. The panic of '73 played havoc with Minnesota's railroads, as it did with carriers throughout the country. Times were hard and money scarce. There also was the "grasshopper plague," actually an invasion of Rocky Mountain locusts in 1873, and for four years thereafter. The hoppers ruined vast areas of crops, although the brunt of the attack was generally to the west of the M&StL.

Even more disconcerting than monetary setbacks and the grasshoppers were the "Grangers." Never before or since has there been such a flood of "anti-railroad" legislation as that brought about by the National Grange of the Patrons of Husbandry during this period. This organization formed lodges or "granges" to aid the farmer. Its originator, Oliver H. Kelly, a Bostonian, at first settled on a farm in Sherburne County, Minnesota. After a long time behind the plow, Kelly was appointed clerk in the Department of Agriculture in Washington and was later given a clerkship in the post office of that city. While in the nation's capital he interested other employees in the fraternal order which he formed in 1867.

By 1871, when the Grange had a large following, it began to campaign vigorously for railroad regulation. What started as a mild educational movement became a crusade and political organization of telling influence. No sooner had the M&StL been turned back to its owners than the Grange helped enact the Railroad Law of 1874, which created a board of three railroad commissioners. These men could prescribe rates within the state and revise schedules whenever they saw fit. In a word, the commissioners could hamstring the roads by dictating their tariffs. There was no doubt that the roads up to this time had virtually no regulation, and probably because of the utter lack of outside jurisdiction, discrimination and rebating took place. On the other hand, the extreme regulatory measures were often ill advised and carried out by men with slight knowledge of tariffs and practical rail operation. Washburn himself said he believed in regulation, but along the lines of sound thinking and not as a result of rabid "anti-monopolist" prejudice.

The attitude of the farmers toward the railroads during the heyday of the Grangers is shown in the following verse:

> Near the track of a railway newly laid,
> A farmer leaned on his earth-worn spade;
> While his taxes were high and his crops but slim,
> The charges for freight played the deuce with him;
> So he growled a growl at the train's sharp din—
> "I'll gather you in; I'll gather you in!"
>
> "I have borne you long, and here I vow
> Your railroads to beat, some way, or how;
> I will get up a law, by the great horned owl!
> To cut down your profits and make you howl;
> And but little or nothing, I'll ship from bin
> Of hoarding corn, till I've gathered you in!"

The upshot was that until the hasty, overnight legislation was repealed, eastern capital shied clear of investing in Minnesota railroads, as it did in Wisconsin and other states where Granger-laws were rampant. From 1873 to 1875 not a mile of new railroad was built in the state. Indeed, with the exception of the Milwaukee's river road, the Minnesota lines were all losing money, and some were in the hands of the courts. This latter condition, however, was due not so much to the Grangers as to the general business recession.

In 1874 the company strengthened its position in the milling district by laying new spurs to keep pace with the "flouring" industry. Extensive experiments were made in testing the Bates, Pettengill, and Wilson automatic car couplers, looking forward to the elimination of the link and pin. But that period was probably best known for the introduction of the Sunday excursion to White Bear Lake. Only weekday trains had operated in regular service up until this time, and these Sabbath specials to the lake caused no end of comment. One day the papers would carry letters to the editor decrying Sunday excursions and the next day would run lengthy epistles praising the road for giving the working man an enjoyable outing. While the battle raged the road went on carrying as high as six hundred people on a single train up to the lake and back.

For the most part, however, 1874, 1875, and 1876 were years of belt-tightening. Economy, retrenchment, and conservative management were the order of the day. All this irked Washburn. But he himself was in financial straits and much of his personal property had to be sold to pay debts on his Anoka lumber mill. Still, there were blue skies in the offing. Business was improving. The money market was slowly turning for the better. The Burlington, Cedar Rapids & Northern (BCR&N), a road which

49

cut across eastern Iowa from near the southern rim on the Mississippi to the northern border south of Albert Lea, was under new management. Due to the impetus of the redoubtable John I. Blair, it aggressively sought an outlet to the Twin Cities. If the M&StL would not build south to meet it, there was every reason to believe that the "Blair" road would construct its own line, at least part of the way, and by trackage rights gain entry into Minneapolis and St. Paul.

The old cry "on to the State Line" kept recurring to "W. D." like an echo to haunt him at every turn. It was he who so vociferously advocated early completion to the Iowa border for the vaunted through-route to St. Louis. Had it not been for the panic, the Northern Pacific would undoubtedly have spanned the gap for the M&StL. Now the NP was out and "General" Washburn was in. Would the local road under local management complete its mission? The Minneapolis city council had $94,000 in bonds salted away if and when the St. Louis Road whistled into Albert Lea.

Washburn thought of the bonds, of the BCR&N, but most of all of Minneapolis. This man, whom some people considered aloof and opinionated, was in reality one of of the best friends the city had. Few men before or since ever looked after its interests so consistently, so sincerely, so whole heartedly. The truth was, the "General" had never forgotten his trust. Just as soon as conditions improved he had surveyors sighting their transits from "tracks end" down to the pretty village of Albert Lea. He had agents dickering with villages for rights-of-way, for depot sites, and for financial help of one sort or another. One day the energetic M&StL president would entreat the city council to hold the bonds, and the next

50

he would confer with BCR&N officials for an all-out effort on the part of both companies to meet at Albert Lea.

At last the job was done, and in good season, too. On November 12, 1877, the mayor and representatives of the common council, along with other invited guests, about sixty people in all, rode the first official train. It rolled out of the St. Paul & Pacific station at seven in the morning, and whistled for the partly completed depot at Albert Lea a little after high noon. The party then continued through town, steaming along the new rails laid by BCR &N men to the much sought state line. The Minneapolis *Tribune* of the following day recounts how they stopped "with one car in Iowa and the other in Minnesota."

Returning to Albert Lea, the group went to the Hall House where a lavish dinner awaited them. There were the customary speeches of which the reader will be spared the details. Mayor John DeLaittre responded for Minneapolis and E. C. Stacy spoke in behalf of Albert Lea. Yes, and true to form, "W. D." declared it was the "happiest day" of his life. The expression seems hackneyed to us, yet it can verily be believed the occasion was even more gratifying for him than the previous "happiest" days, when the White Bear branch was completed and again when he opened the main stem to Sioux City Junction.

The M&StL was at last shaping up into a strategic little carrier. It had the shortest route, in conjunction with the "Blair" road and the St. Louis, Keokuk & North-western, to St. Louis. Moreover, all through-freight from southwest points on the St. Paul & Sioux City to Minneapolis was shunted over its line from Merriam Junction (formerly called Sioux City Junction) to the Mill City. In addition, a traffic alliance had been made with the Hastings & Dakota (now the Milwaukee Road) to route H&D goods bound for Minneapolis over the M&StL via Chaska. In 1878 the company reported net earnings of $138,666. Thanks to the company's aggressive policy in improving its sidings in the mill district, the road that year shipped about half of the flour manufactured in Minneapolis.

In 1878 the company boasted thirteen locomotives, mostly, if not all, of the popular "American" type. They were all wood-burners, and the majority had five-foot drivers and were capable of fast running, as speed was reckoned in that day. Nine cars in passenger train service took care of the increased riders and augmented mail and express, which poured in from connecting lines. Some 281 freight cars attested the importance of the company's freight traffic. Judging from the statistics of that year—apparently the earliest annual report still preserved—grain and lumber products were the chief commodities hauled.

That year, nevertheless, is chiefly remembered for the tragic catastrophe in the mill district. Early in the evening of May 2, after the day workers had returned to their homes, a roar was heard down by the C. C. Washburn's "A" mill. Belching long columns of black smoke and darting flames, the building "exploded" and was totally destroyed. Two other mills, the Diamond and the Humboldt, standing nearby, also collapsed. In addition, five M&StL box cars and one flat were burned by the fire. Eighteen lives were lost in the worst of the young city's disasters, and damages were estimated at over a million dollars. The "A" had been the largest flour mill in the country, and a prolific source of revenue for the M&StL. With its destruction, along with other structures gutted by explosion or by fire, the road's income was sharply curtailed. The stockholders' report estimated the loss in revenue, caused by the mill explosion, along with hot July weather which destroyed the wheat crops, at $100,000. The mills were subsequently rebuilt, but the loss of life which had resulted from the grain-dust explosion, brought sadness to the community for a long time thereafter.

The end of the seventies and the early eighties saw a haphazard development northward which included some owned, some leased, and some jointly operated mileage. Moreover, the type of control seemingly changed with the seasons. After the M&StL was returned to his owners, it leased the Minneapolis and Duluth, and in May, 1881, it purchased the thirteen-mile line. Next year, however, the Minneapolis and Duluth was leased to the St. Paul & Duluth; and finally in 1901 it was bought by the Northern Pacific.

While the White Bear line was changing hands at the drop of a hat the St. Louis Road was laying rails further north in Minnesota. In 1880 the M&StL, in conjunction with the Taylors Falls & Lake Superior Railroad, built a scenic twenty-mile line linking the hamlet of Wyoming with Taylors Falls. Under a contract signed that year the M&StL had running rights over the Skally, as the St. Paul & Duluth was called, from White Bear Lake through Wyoming to Duluth. This made possible through-train service on the St. Louis Road from Minneapolis to Taylors Falls, and also to Duluth.

It was a common sight to see M&StL-operated trains of wooden coaches, packed with excursionists bound for a day at Taylors Falls. They came to explore the many caves, to gaze at potholes in the rocks, and to watch the rapids. Not a few took a waiting steamer down the St. Croix to Stillwater and Hastings, while others preferred

53

a shorter canoe trip on the river, returning in time to catch the night train back home.

After the Taylors Falls line was opened, the M&StL operated it jointly with the St. Paul & Duluth until it was taken over entirely by the latter company. In 1883 the St. Louis Road also gave up its trackage rights on the St. Paul & Duluth. When the Northern Pacific absorbed the Skally in 1900, the Taylors Falls branch continued to do a land office business in tourist traffic. Gradually, after the coming of the automobile, service disintegrated to one mixed train "daily except Sunday" until the colorful line was abandoned in 1948. This in brief is the saga of the M&StL north of Minneapolis.

Along with the building of the road north came the extension of the main stem down into the corn country of Iowa. The first objective was the flourishing town of Fort Dodge, the second the booming coal land in the vicinity of Angus. By June, 1878, track layers had reached the Iowa border on the new road running southwest out of Albert Lea. Another company, styled the Minnesota and Iowa Southern, under M&StL sponsorship, pushed the road to Livermore by the end of the decade.

In the meantime a farmers' railroad was struggling up from Fort Dodge to the northern rim of Webster County. Originally incorporated as the Fort Dodge and Fort Ridgeley Railroad and Telegraph Company, July 22, 1876, the "and Telegraph" was stricken out two years later and it then began to build the line in earnest. It was hard-going from the start, even with county bonds and acres of swamp land thrown in as a bonus. The company was obligated to have its trains operating across the county line by January 1, 1879, with a stipulation that they maintain a speed of at least fifteen miles an hour while crossing

Right — HENRY TITUS WELLES — First president of the M&StL (1870-1873), businessman, banker, philanthropist and first mayor of St. Anthony, Welles was a prominent figure in early-day Minneapolis.

Left — WILLIAM DREW WASHBURN — Second president of the road (1874-1882), miller, lumberman, congressman and senator, Washburn did much to foster the development of Minneapolis. When he resigned as chief executive of the M&StL, the road extended into Iowa and westward to Morton, Minn. Washburn later headed the Soo Line.

The Falls of St. Anthony as they looked at the time the M&StL was formed. Water power was responsible for the early growth of Minneapolis.

View of Minneapolis from the Winslow House across the Mississippi in St. Anthony. Photo taken in 1870 when the M&StL was born. The sawmills in the foreground were burned three years later.

Outshopped in 1882, No. 66 was one of seventeen American-type engines purchased from Manchester Locomotive Works in 1881 and 1882. Note diamond stack, characteristic of the Manchester group.

Albert Lea station in 1884. The hotel in the depot was first named the Bunker House and later the Winslow House. It featured four-course meals for 50¢, and its cuisine was famous all along the Albert Lea Route.

YESTERDAY ALONG THE ST. CROIX — Train in the 1880's climbing the grade out of Taylors Falls for the run to Wyoming, Minn., on the main line of the old St. Paul & Duluth Railroad. The M&StL built part of the branch and for a time operated it. From the beginning of the 20th century until its abandonment in 1948, the scenic 20-mile line was owned by the Northern Pacific.

Collection of S. D. Dimond

Reputed to be the finest boat built in western waters, the *City of St. Louis* was reminiscent of the heyday of Minnetonka. Originally owned by W. D. Washburn and operated to connect with M&StL trains, this stately side-wheeler was later sold to the Lake Miinnetonka Navigation Co.

Lake Park Hotel at Tonka Bay as it looked in 1905 when owned by the M&StL. On its broad, airy verandas strolled socially prominent visitors from Kansas City, St. Louis and New Orleans. In the Elegant Eighties Minnetonka was the most fashionable watering place in the Midwest.

Collection of Ward Burton

Collection of S. D. Dimond

Largest boat on the lake and a formidable rival to the *City of St. Louis* was James J. Hill's *Belle of Minnetonka*. The sight of the two steamers racing across the waters with passengers cheering from their three decks is part of the Tonka tradition. The *Belle* was subsequently taken over by the Navigation Co.

The first skyscraper west of Chicago! The twelve-story Guaranty Loan Building, now known as the Metropolitan Life Building, was an architectural wonder in the 90's. Crowded excursion trains brought thousands to Minneapolis to view the city from its lofty observation tower. For many years the M&StL occupied the two top floors.

Minneapolis Public Library

Washington Avenue station after abandonment. From 1892 to 1919 thousands of people boarded trains at this old Minneapolis landmark for points in Minnesota, Iowa, Illinois and South Dakota. Hourly, also, came and went Minnetonka locals. The M&StL now uses the Great Northern station further downtown.

Beautiful freshly-painted Mason engine ready for delivery to the Central Iowa Railway. Named *Charles Alexander,* in honor of the road's secretary, No. 26 was built in 1880 and for years was a familiar sight down in the corn country.

Collection of Robert Milner

Iowa Central train at Oskaloosa in the 1890's. The running board and cupola on the combination baggage and passenger car indicates that it was also used as a caboose on what is patently a mixed run.

A reminder of yesteryear, the old Iowa Central blacksmith shop at Marshalltown even today shows little sign of wear. For eighty years this community was, and is, the headquarters for car repair, first on the Hook and Eye and later on the M&StL. All Iowa Central motive power was manitained here.

Looking west at Boyd, Minn., before World War I. The severely plain depot in the background and the wooden grain elevators in the foreground were typical prairie-country structures around the turn of the century.

Collection of R. C. Haynes

EDWIN HAWLEY — As president or chairman of the board (1896-1912), Hawley greatly expanded the M&StL and was instrumental in getting the Iowa Central and the Des Moines & Fort Dodge under its control.

Underwood & Underwood

WILLIAM HAYNES TRUESDALE (Left) — President (1887-1894) and also receiver of the M&StL, Truesdale nursed the road back to health in the rate-cutting era of the late '80's. WILLIAM HEPBURN BREMNER (Right) — For nearly two decades (1917-1934) Bremner headed the M&StL as president or federal manager. For eleven years he also was receiver and it was his lot to pilot the road through war, bankruptcy and the Great Depression.

Collection of R. C. Haynes

Looking down Main Street toward Railway Street and the station at LeBeau, S. Dak. A band near the depot is in the background. Ten-foot wide concrete sidewalks were laid a year or two after this photo was taken.

Cowboys loading cattle aboard stern-wheeled ferry boat *Scotty Philip* for fattening on buffalo grass across the Missouri River from LeBeau.

Collection of R. C. Haynes

Rotary plowing westward near Bradley, S. Dak., after blizzard of 1917. For weeks the West End was completely tied up by wind-swept drifts covering the prairies.

Collection of A. M. Kingsbury

Old M&StL and Iowa Central timetables.

Robert Graham

Pride of the Prairie: *North Star Limited* crossing Mississippi River in Minneapolis showing University of Minnesota in background. For three decades the *North Star* was a household word in the Midwest. Photo taken shortly before train was discontinued.

Typical of the old order is this American-type engine with a brace of cars at the Rock Island station in Peoria. Humble locals of this nature were once a familiar part of the Midwestern Scene especially on the M&StL and the old Iowa Central.

Paul Stringham

Paul Stringham

The well-kept 4-6-0 is polished and bright on this special train pictured at Water Street, Peoria, in October 1937. With its bell a-twirl and black smoke pouring from the stack the Ten Wheeler knuckles down to business.

"Caboose hop" at Morton, Minn., about 1905, showing Conductor Charles W. Haynes in front of the tender. Note retractable coupler on the pilot. In the early thirties, there were 44 Moguls on the M&StL. Second only to Consolidations, they were the most used freight locomotives during early decades of the century.

Collection of R. C. Haynes

Alco-built in 1912, No. 459 was among the last Consolidations to be purchased by the M&StL. At one time the road had 59 2-8-0's on the books, and for a score of years they were the predominant freight engine.

Builders photo of a Mikado ready for delivery in 1915. Large numbering on the tender once characterized M&StL motive power. A photo of a modernized 2-8-2 or "Mike" is shown elsewhere in this book.

Six-wheel switcher on the Minneapolis Railway Transfer, a busy M&StL subsidiary serving Minneapolis' mill district.

Robert Graham

Once an exceedingly popular type of locomotive, the American disappeared from M&StL rails in the 30's. For years the 100-class engines pulled the "Wooden Shoe", a fast, light passenger train between New Ulm and Minneapolis.

Paul Stringham

Up until the coming of the Pacific in 1921, the Ten Wheeler pulled named trains and other heavy passenger runs. This refurbished 227 was one of 36 engines of the same type on the roster.

Robert Graham

A late-comer and an early-goer on the M&StL, the Pacific had a comparatively short life on the road. The 502 shown as it looked before repainting and part-streamlining. All five engines of this type have been scrapped.

One of eleven gas-electric cars purchased between 1929 and 1931 to supplant steam passenger trains. Most of these units have since been rebuilt and converted to Diesel-electric power.

Time freight No. 94 doubleheading with a Pacific and Mikado on a chilly March day in 1936. The locale is Montgomery, Minn., before the advent of Diesels and rock ballast.

Gas-electric motor car on train No. 14 crossing trestle over Carsons Bay at Deephaven, Minn., on the shores of Minnetonka. The old wooden coach at the rear has given way to modern air-conditioned stainless steel cars.

the border. The type of motive power was not specified. From all accounts, the chief driving force behind the road was its treasurer and general superintendent, George R. Pearsons. He worked like a Trojan to complete the line, and finally fell sick from long hours of hard work and constant exposure to bad weather. Things looked bleak indeed for the local enterprise when a red-headed Irishman by the name of "Billy" O'Brien took charge. Then, with the luck of the Irish, the recovery of Pearsons, and three shifts of workmen, the job was completed—on time. Legend has it that six picked men passed over the county line pumping a handcar at a speed in excess of fifteen miles an hour while, watch in hand, Vice President George W. Bassett was eagerly clocking them.

An agreement was made by which the M&StL would acquire control as soon as the local road reached Livermore. This was soon complied with, and the Washburn company then operated through service from Minneapolis to Fort Dodge. The St. Louis Road, meanwhile, altered the local road's entrance into Fort Dodge and erected its own station.

To garner together all the varied and sundry lines of which the M&StL had control a new corporation was formed on April 20, 1881, called *The* Minneapolis *and* St. Louis Railway Company (of Minnesota and Iowa). This was a consolidation of the old M&StL, the Minneapolis and Duluth, the Minnesota and Iowa Southern, and the Fort Dodge and Fort Ridgeley.

The M&StL was now an aggressive carrier, a credit to Minneapolis and to the communities it served. Once the road was out of the financial doldrums, Washburn saw to it that it no longer marked time. He was in a sense, a dreamer with a knack of making dreams come true.

What is more to the point, he could pick good men—men, for example, like engineer W. W. Rich, who did much to expedite new construction. Rich proved to be an able successor to Col. Clough after the latter had resigned to become city engineer for Minneapolis while the road was halting at Merriam Junction. Washburn later took Rich with him to the Soo, and from that company the engineer went abroad to supervise railway building in China. Then there was E. W. Gaylord, a man liked and respected, who came up from the maintenance-of-way department to the superintendency.

It was characteristic of Washburn to complete a job he had started, and the Angus coal fields were on his list of unfinished business. The result was only a momentary halt at Fort Dodge. Then the trackmen could be heard hammering spikes in the hamlets of Dayton, Ogden, and, by January, 1882, Angus. That year William Drew Washburn resigned from the presidency.

Because the road south of Fort Dodge had practically no ballast, it was dubbed the Mud Line, and what is left of it today still goes by that uncomplimentary nickname. But the line is historically important, because for thirty years the town of Angus was technically the southernmost terminal on the M&StL.

What then is Angus like, or to be more exact, what *was* Angus like? And why, anyway, did an up-and-coming railroad make its terminus at a village which today has scarcely 250 souls? It is a common fallacy to judge nineteenth century achievements by twentieth century standards. The plan to make Angus a terminal in the eighties had considerable merit at the time. Angus coal fired M&StL locomotives, it turned the wheels of Minneapolis factories, and warmed many an Iowa and Minnesota home.

But to begin at the beginning one has to go back to the seventies when Angus was called Coaltown.

In the early seventies the historic Des Moines Valley Railroad built northwest from Iowa's capital city to Tara. It passed through Coaltown, which was later renamed Angus. The community showed promise as a mining center in its earlier days, and at the time the M&StL came into the town the mineral resources were being worked to the full. The St. Louis Road erected a roundhouse, a station, and terminal headquarters, to say nothing of yards and spur tracks to the mines. Long, heavy trains of coal groaned from Angus to Fort Dodge, Albert Lea, and the Twin Cities. We speak of "long" in the contemporary sense meaning fifteen or twenty cars, and "heavy" as referring to gondolas handling 28,000 pounds or nearly 15 tons of coal. In that day it was all the high-wheeled "Standards" could do to start a loaded train. For a time the road had that optimum achievement in railroading: two-way traffic. Coal went into Minnesota in exchange for lumber and flour for Iowans.

The first mine of any importance in Angus was sunk by John F. Dunscombe, who later sold his interests to the Climax Coal Company, in which James J. Hill was said to have had an interest. It topped the record with 80 cars loaded in a day, 53 of which were lump coal. Next in productivity came Standard, reputed to have mined 650 tons within twenty-four hours. Others sprawled out over the far flung community were Keystone, Moingona, Milwaukee, Panic, Dalbey, Ohio, and Armstrong—nine major companies.

In 1884, when mining was at its peak, Angus had the reputation of being the biggest coal town in Iowa. Its population, according to an article describing the growth and decline of the town in the *History of Boone County, Iowa,* edited by Nathan Goldthwait, was 3,500. From that peak year decline set in, slowly at first, and then with alarming rapidity. The long-drawn-out strike which began in September, 1884, and terminated in a riot in January of the following year, started the retrogression. Backed by the Knights of Labor, the miners walked out *en masse* when their demands for a pay increase were refused. The operators tried to recruit new men but were rebuffed on every hand. Whenever a trainload of imported workers came to town they were booted out of the community by the strikers. The situation became so tense the militia was summoned, and one company of armed troops stayed until the dispute was finally settled by arbitration. After that, however, Angus never regained its former prestige.

Some of the shafts closed, many miners went to coal operations elsewhere or engaged in other occupations. The M&StL, however, did considerable business for several years thereafter. As less coal rumbled down the chutes trains ran more infrequently and sidings were no longer crammed with cars. Still, the *Tenderfoot,* a paper later re-named the *Iowa Times* during the lush days of Angus, predicted that an era of tremendous growth was just ahead. A year or so after its rosy prognostications the publication quit. The remaining journal, aptly titled the *Black Diamond,* struggled on. Its harried editor, Robert Lowrey, seeing the handwriting on the wall, concluded:

> ...the newspaper business in Angus has been dull. Appearances indicate that it will be much more so before the summer season is over. We have no reflections to cast upon our business men for not extending a more liberal support toward the paper. But to attempt to run a paper of any size, such as the Diamond is, and make a living out of it in Angus, is beyond the powers of anyone. We have

managed to make expenses, but we are not here for just that purpose, and when we begin to find the necessary expense incurred in running it not forthcoming, we'll lock up and put it on ice for the summer.

That was in May 27, 1887. Several weeks later the paper was "put on ice," where it apparently has remained ever since.

An attempt was made to revive the coal business in 1892. A weekly called the Angus *News* was also launched in January of that year. The spurt was only a flash in the pan, for after that winter had passed things took a turn for the worse and the *News* never lived to see its first birthday. In 1893 the local bank closed its doors. The "Cleveland panic" of that year just about decimated the population. For a pittance in that depressed era a buyer could get a warranty deed to a dozen houses and lots. The ground was not wanted, but the lumber in the half-vacated buildings was in demand. Consequently, structure after structure was demolished and the boards and rafters shipped to other towns, where they were used in building "new" homes. Angus went board-by-board, so to speak, to Perry, to Rippey, to Dawson, to Berkley, to—well, all over the state.

At this writing Angus is little more than a hamlet with only a sign, a siding, and an elevator. Where once the busy depot saw miners of many nations, where a roundhouse held engines ready for coal drags, where a terminal office hummed with activity—all is gone. The townsmen still remaining make their living from the soil. They or their forefathers were there before the miners came and they are there now that the miners are gone. Angus is not dead; but instead of a roaring town, it is a modest community, small and serene. The long stretches between the homes are reminiscent of other days when miners lived here in humble dwellings side by side. Where long rows of buildings used to be there now are acres of tilled soil, the stable livelihood of Angus today and tomorrow.

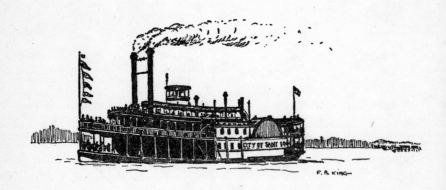

Western railroad men are in themselves a tower of strength. They stand for decision, action, and organization. They are indefatigable, constructive, and, above all, resourceful...

Frank H. Spearman in *The Strategy of Great Railroads.*

6

Enter the Rock Island

When Washburn stepped out of the presidency, Ransom Reed Cable stepped in. The new chief was an executive of the old school, an operating man, a little short, perhaps, on formal education but infinitely long on experience. At the time he went to the M&StL he was also vice president of the Rock Island. Indeed, the Rock Island was Cable -- and Cable the Rock Island.

For good or bad, the Minneapolis and St. Louis had a sweeping change in its executive personnel. Washburn stayed on the board a decade thereafter and a few of the other directors remained, but the men who ran the railroad were new. Vice President H. T. Welles resigned and was succeeded by A. B. Stickney. A. H. Bode, the veteran secretary and treasurer, who often doubled as superintendent, resigned. So did directors J. K. Sidle, who had been with the road ever since it started, and W. D. Hale, Washburn's man "Friday." The directors' meetings of 1882 showed virtually a complete turnover, a *carte blanche* for the gentlemen from the Rock Island.

It is interesting to reflect on the railroad strategy of the period. There was on the board, for example, W. R. Merriam, who along with the newcomer, H. H. Porter, represented the Omaha Road, of which the old St. Paul & Sioux

City was a part. By the end of 1882 only Washburn and W. W. McNair were left on the directorate as spokesmen for Minneapolis. The remaining directors all represented Rock Island interests—all, that is, except A. B. Stickney. Stickney was a kind of lone wolf. He lasted only about a year as vice president and director, and then went to build what is now the Chicago Great Western. He will come up again on the Iowa Central, which he later headed during his remarkable career in Midwestern railroading.

No sooner had R. R. Cable taken office when traffic alliances were speedily made or strengthened. Friendly agreements with all the roads in which the Rock Island had an interest became the order of the day. Cable built up the Albert Lea Gateway, in conjunction with the Burlington, Cedar Rapids & Northern. Cable arranged for through routing of freight, via Angus and the Des Moines and Fort Dodge, to the Iowa capital. Cable made the M&StL a strong arm of his beloved Rock Island.

By this time the M&StL was becoming more than a small local road. Besides building to the north and south the Washburn regime saw an extension westward via Winthrop to Morton, reaching the latter point in 1882. This branch skirted the southern edge of Lake Minnetonka and competed with the slim-gauge "Motor Line" which ran from Minneapolis to Excelsior.

In the eighties railroads were pushing their tracks everywhere in the Midwest. Not to be outdone, the Rock Island, which Cable headed in 1883, started on an expansion program of great magnitude. With money from the parent road he helped finance new lines in Minnesota and South Dakota and turned them over to the M&StL to operate. He was eager to reach the wheat fields and the West, to tap new resources, and to give his railroads variegated traffic. That accounts for the St. Louis Road serving the grain country today, adding bit by bit to what Washburn completed in 1882.

The story of westward expansion concerns that half-legendary road, the Wisconsin, Minnesota and Pacific. This line never had a foot of track in Wisconsin and fell short of reaching the Pacific by a half continent. To the best of the author's knowledge the rolling stock was borrowed, leased, or otherwise appropriated from the Rock Island, the Burlington, Cedar Rapids & Northern, or the M&StL. In so far as the records show, no cars ever bore the name or initials of the Wisconsin, Minnesota and Pacific. The road was a separate entity on the statute books although Rock Island was emblazoned on some of the day coaches and M&StL employees took up tickets and operated the trains. One party owned the road, another controlled it as the largest single stockholder, and a third tended to the operation. Moreover, the WM&P consisted of two distinct railroads, separated by some fifty miles, which were never connected. The eastern end, which was at one time the Cannon Valley Division of the M&StL, was the oldest section and the logical place to begin.

On February 17, 1865, the Cannon River Improvement Company was chartered to open up that waterway for commerce. Valuable grants of swamp land went with the enterprise as mile after mile of slack water navigation was completed. By the seventies, however, it was apparent that railroads would supersede river transport in that area. Meanwhile, the then-dormant Minnesota Central Rail Road, incorporated in the Territory May 23, 1857, showed signs of coming to life. In 1878 it purchased the Improvement Company and three years later commenced laying rails westward from Red Wing. A spirited battle ensued between it and the Milwaukee Road in the race for Northfield. After several right-of-way skirmishes, reconciliation came and the roads built into the town without further ado. From Northfield the Minnesota Central pushed on into Waterville, the M&StL connection, in 1883. On August 10, of that year the name was changed to the Wisconsin, Minnesota and Pacific Railway Company, anticipating expansion to the East and the West. The M&StL was operating the road as its Cannon Valley Division. It should be noted, however, that the Cannon Valley line was never owned by the Minneapolis and St. Louis.

About this time the WM&P became a reality in the West. Land was bought with funds provided by Rock Island interests to push construction of the "western end" from Morton, Minnesota, to Watertown, South Dakota, a distance of 122 miles. The rails reached Watertown in 1884, and operation was taken over by the M&StL. Thus there were two sections of the same railroad never connected, both of which were associated with but not owned by the Rock Island, and both of which were operated by the M&StL. Incidentally, the Cannon Valley line reached Mankato in 1887, and was still a long, long way from the "other" WM&P in western Minnesota.

Before leaving the Cannon Valley line, a word may be said about the schedule recently unearthed in the M&StL offices. It is "Time Card No. 1," effective May 31, 1885, on the "Minnesota & North-western Railway operated by the Minneapolis & St. Louis Railway Company between West St. Paul and Randolph, until further notice." From the above it is evident that the St. Louis Road operated the Minnesota & North-western to hook up with the Cannon Valley Division at Randolph. Nothing further has come to light on the "leased" road, and the Railroad &

Warehouse Commission's reports make no mention of it. This schedule shows one "time freight" each way, indicating the importance of "fast" carding even in those days. A "special rule" stating that "the maximum speed of all trains will be fifteen (15) miles an hour" is a gentle reminder of the limitations of yesteryear.

It is easy to picture the dynamic Rock Island president in these times stopping a few days in the Mill City to visit the Minneapolis and St. Louis office in the "Boston Block." In his capacity as head of the M&StL and the Rock Island he must have enjoyed seeing both roads so closely united. The St. Louis Road needed a strong ally for freight and passenger traffic in connnection with Chicago and St. Louis markets, and the Rock Island ardently wanted a friendly outlet to the Twin Cities. Thus, the M&StL and the Burlington, Cedar Rapids & Northern shook hands at Albert Lea, and both parties achieved their objectives. There was also another common point at Watertown. So far, things were going along nicely; perhaps some day the Rock Island would take over the M&StL...

Cable was an old hand at building up strategic railroads, short lines, and partly completed properties which are now part of the Rock Island System. He began humbly enough as an Ohio farm boy—born in Athens County, September 23, 1834—and later turned to railroading. For everyone at some time or another there is a golden opportunity. Young Cable's chance came when an uncle, P. L. Cable, owner of the Coal Valley, Illinois, mines, and a large stockholder in the Rock Island & Peoria Railroad, gave him a job. This was the first step in his career as a railroad man. Having sound business sense, Ransom Cable quickly learned railroading on the twelve-mile carrier, as well as the fine points of running a coal mine.

67

His varied duties as clerk, bookkeeper, and, sometimes, train conductor, gave him the rudiments of transportation and industrial management.

The knowledge he acquired was put to good advantage when he became superintendent and later president of the Rockford, Rock Island & St. Louis Railroad, a line now part of the Burlington. From the Rockford road he went to properties later associated with the Rock Island and, by 1879, Cable became assistant to the president of the latter system. Four years afterward he was in his boss's chair as head of that expanding railroad. When he became president, the company was operating 1,311 miles of line. When he resigned from that position in 1898 to take the chairmanship of the board, the "Great Rock Island Route" was embracing about seven thousand miles.

Obviously, much of Cable's work as chief executive of the M&StL had to be deputed. It was. His right-hand man became William H. Truesdale, a top-of-the-rail official, as popular as he was able. Right after Stickney's bob-tailed tenure as vice president, "Bill" Truesdale took over in the same capacity. He was also general manager, which is to say he ran the railroad. Cable apparently met Truesdale when the latter was clerking for the Rockford road. At any rate, the two made a good team.

With the coming of Cable, the M&StL could no longer be tagged as a local road. It had through cars to Chicago via Albert Lea and West Liberty, in conjunction with the Burlington, Cedar Rapids & Northern and the Rock Island. By 1882, thanks to running rights over the Northern Pacific between the Twin Cities, trains chuffed from St. Paul to Des Moines. This "only direct and first-class route between the capital cities of the great states of Minnesota and Iowa" went over the M&StL to Angus and thence over the rails of the old Des Moines and Fort Dodge to the Hawkeye city. Even earlier, through equipment was in service linking St. Paul and Minneapolis with St. Louis. Travelers went over the popular Albert Lea Route to Burlington, Iowa, thence via the St. Louis, Keokuk & North-western to the Missouri metropolis.

In the eighties and nineties there was hardly a person in the Twin Cities who didn't know about the St. Louis Road. There were fine limiteds on many lines to the East and West, but on the North and South axis, the "Louie," as railroaders called the M&StL, was second to none. In a word, Cable and Truesdale put the Minneapolis and St. Louis on the map.

So much for the physical aspects of the railroad, its construction, equipment and service. But there are intangibles, such as the spirit and tradition of a carrier, its role in the social life of the period which should not be neglected. All this leads foursquare to Lake Minnetonka, which is inseperably linked with the M&StL. If a man had wealth and standing in the late eighties and lived in Minneapolis, St. Louis, or Kansas City, it was fitting and proper that he take his vacation by the waters of Minnetonka. Easterners had Saratoga Springs, New Englanders had Bar Harbor, and Midwesterners had their Minnetonka.

For about fifteen years the Lake Minnetonka region was in its heyday, and what a grand period it was! The Minneapolis and St. Louis, being the first standard gauge railroad to serve the southern lake region, did much to make the once famous watering place accessible to all. In the elegant eighties, gay times were the rule out Tonka way and chapters could be written on the fun and frolic of these other years.

It began when the hotels came, three in particular, to lend prestige and social graces to this favored lake region. The first influx of tourists, however, arrived on the north side of Minnetonka with the coming of what is now the Great Northern to Wayzata in 1867. Then James J. Hill built Hotel Lafayette at Minnetonka Beach shortly after the GN completed the Spring Park branch. That took care of the northern side of the lake while the south was agog with excitement concerning the building of the M&StL westward from Hopkins. With the prospects of a railroad to Excelsior, other than the three-foot gauge "motor" line, two large hotels were erected. One was the Minnetonka Lake Park Hotel, later changed to Lake Park, and the other Hotel St. Louis.

When the St. Louis Road came to Excelsior it developed the southern Lake Minnetonka region even more than Jim Hill did the north side. A mile-and-a-half spur was soon constructed from the "Pacific Extension" at Manitou Junction to Tonka Bay—virtually on the lawn of the Lake Park Hotel. The road acquired half interest in the home-like inn, modern no doubt in its day, but contemporary pictures make it look as old-fashioned as a melodeon. White, wooden, and wind-swept, the odd-shaped structure stood at the head of Tonka peninsula, where breezes from the lake blew through the spacious verandas on three sides of the hotel.

Vying with Lake Park was Charles Gibson's Hotel St. Louis a few miles east of Excelsior. The M&StL built a station called Hotel St. Louis, and from it carloads of people poured forth during the summer season. While mentioning stations, a word may be in order concerning the stop on the trestle crossing Carsons Bay. The lake people were virtually brought up on the water, and when

MAP OF LAKE MINNETONKA.

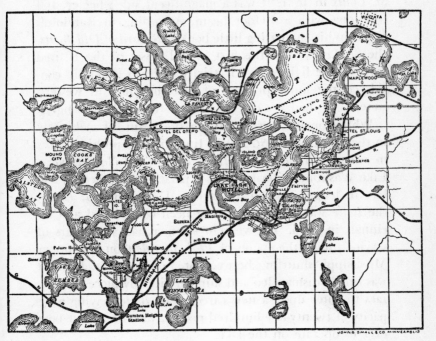

commuters found they could take a short cut across the bay from Cottagewood village to the railroad, the company obligingly put a station on the bridge. Later Cottagewood-on-the-trestle was moved to the firmer ground of greater Cottagewood by the side of the bay.

Among the high spots in the early days of Lake Minnetonka were the boat races between steamers owned by

71

W. D. Washburn and James J. Hill. Not content with competition on the rails, these two executives in their lighter moments turned to the lake to vie with each other in seamanship. "W. D." constructed his famous *City of St. Louis* in 1881. It was a magnificent side-wheeler, 160 feet long with a 40-foot beam. According to Randolph Edgar in his fascinating little book *A Record of Old Boats,* the *St. Louis* "was the first inland vessel of the United States to be lighted by electricity and was generally considered the finest product of boat building in western waters." It had a capacity of one thousand passengers.

While tourists were admiring the beautiful mahogany in the cabin of the *St. Louis,* Jim Hill was pushing plans to assemble his *Belle of Minnetonka,* the following year. Like Washburn's boat, it was a palatial side-wheeler, 300 feet in length and 60 feet across. Unlike the *St. Louis,* the *Belle* was not new, having been constructed at Cincinnati in 1866. The veteran steamer had seen years of service under the name of *Phil Sheridan* on the upper Mississippi, shuttling between St. Louis and St. Paul. It was finally dismantled and shipped piece by piece to Wayzata to enter upon a new career. The *Belle,* having a capacity of twenty-five hundred people, was the largest boat ever to operate on the lake.

The day came when they launched the *Belle of Minnetonka,* and fierce rivalry immediately took place between it and the next largest boat, Washburn's *City of St. Louis.* Both steamers met the trains at Wayzata, then raced across the lake to the "M&StL town" of Excelsior, and from there back to the Great Northern branch at Minnetonka Beach. Usually the *Belle* was in the lead, although the *St. Louis* put up stiff competition. It was great sport watching the boats, their twin stacks belching black smoke, the side

72

wheels churning the waters, and crowds cheering from all three decks.

Later the Lake Minnetonka Navigation Company took over the two boats and operated them as part of its scheduled fleet. Steamers of the Navigation Company called at Solbergs Point, Excelsior, and Lake Park on the M&StL, and many other ports, making connections with trains on both sides of the lake. People swarmed from depot to dockside, from veranda to ballroom, as Minnetonka became a fashionable resort.

One can readily picture the "great verandas" of Lake Park Hotel filled with summer visitors promenading to and fro like passengers on an ocean liner. Cooled by gentle breezes from the lake, gay balls and moonlit verandas attracted comely southern belles and their swains. The slower tempo of Dixie plus the gracious living of people of wealth and culture lent charm and atmosphere to the rather crude wooden structure.

Enough of dance and romance. For the fishermen there were pike, pickerel, bass, sunfish, and crappies awaiting the hook and line; for the sailor, boats of many shapes and sizes lined the docks; for the athletic-minded, swimming in the bay, hiking beneath the stately oaks, tennis on the hotel courts, roller skating in a nearby rink, and cycling all over the place. "And remember," one can almost hear the passenger agent say, "the M&StL will take you there. We have through trains from Chicago, St. Louis, Des Moines...with close connections from all points east, south, and west. Yes, ma'am, every room in the Lake Park opens out onto a veranda. Be glad to place your reservation."

To transport guests to Lake Park, the St. Louis Road ran shuttle service all day and part of the night from

Minneapolis to Tonka Bay. Residents in the vicinity still remember the old Seven Spot, one of the smallest "Standards" on the road, chuffing with its three or four coaches from town to park. They recall Bill Watson at the throttle, a peppery little man with a graying goatee. Bill always rode with his Scotch terrier seated behind him in the engine. Folks used to remark, on seeing them from a distance perched high up in the bouncing cab, that it was hard to tell the man from the dog. The care Billy Watson lavished on that old Baldwin! He was always shining the brasswork on its whistle, the handrailings, and the nameplate. There was no mistaking Engineer Watson when he blew for the Junction, the whistle was as distinctive as the man, the dog, and the old Seven Spot, a part of the Tonka tradition.

Is it necessary to add that the St. Louis Road did a spanking passenger business in that era? But other roads, eager for a share of the lush tourist trade, began construction towards the southern Minnetonka region in the late eighties. The Great Northern came first, building westward from Hopkins along the abandoned right-of-way of the "motor" line to Excelsior, and continuing on to St. Bonifacious and Hutchinson. The Milwaukee flung out a branch from Hopkins to Deephaven, virtually to the doors of the four-story Hotel St. Louis. The Elegant Eighties, however, were more profitable to Minnetonka than the so-called Gay Nineties. For one thing the panic of '93 put a crimp in the tourist trade. Another factor in the decline of the resort was the extension of railroads throughout Minnesota—and other states—to hundreds of lakes and vacation spots.

Now to digress a bit beyond the Cable and Truesdale administration to see how the hotels gave way to the cottages, the trains to the trolleys, and finally, the electric cars and boats to the ubiquitous automobile. By 1893 the once-busy Navigation Company had only two boats, the *Saucy Kate* and the *Alert,* in regular service to meet the trains. Most of the hotels were operating at a loss; former patrons either stayed at home or went elsewhere. Around the turn of the century the Great Northern quit Lake Minnetonka's south shore and extended its line from Spring Park along the northern side to St. Bonifacious. In 1905 Hotel St. Louis was torn down, and with its demise the Milwaukee ceased running into Deephaven.

Meantime the Lake Park was operating at a deficit and a new buyer was being sought by the M&StL, which no longer wished to stay in the hotel business. The company's equity in the inn was purchased by the Minneapolis & St. Paul Suburban Railway, under the leadership of the colorful Thomas Lowry. The trolley line also leased the short Tonka Bay branch so that its cars could reach the hotel. At the same time, the electric road built its own tracks from Hopkins to Manitou Junction, partly utilizing the Great Northern's right-of-way. It leased the Milwaukee's line to Deephaven, bought a fleet of boats, and constructed several more in its own Snelling shops at St. Paul. For two decades the yellow trolleys brought a multitude of people *to* the lake, and the yellow "street-car" boats, as the propellor steamers were called, carried throngs *on* the lake. The hotel, however, was razed, and by 1926 the "street-car" boats had ceased to run as part of the traction company's fleet. Six years later the trolley service was discontinued and the Minnetonka lines were scrapped.

The era of hotels, commuter trains, interurban cars, and lake steamers was ended and in its place came the homes and black-top highways. But the M&StL, the first standard-gauge railroad to tap the southern Minnetonka region, still operates there today as part of its road to the West. The Tonka Bay branch, however, is long since torn up, and shuttling locals no longer carry trainloads of tourists to wooded slopes and clean, sandy beaches "by the waters of Minnetonka."

*The physical condition of the Minneapolis &
St. Louis Railway has been maintained and will
compare favorably with the average of Western
roads; at the same time it is...managed with the
strictest economy...*

From William H. Truesdale's statement to
the bondholders, May 26, 1888.

7

Truesdale and Trying Times

As in the old song refrain, "I plays de banjo better now than him that taught me do," so William H. Truesdale outshone his teacher. Cable's understudy became Cable's successor. Truesdale was probably the ablest railroad man to run the M&StL until the coming of Lucian Sprague in recent years.

Large, bluff, hearty Bill Truesdale put his body and soul into guiding the destiny of the St. Louis Road when fate itself seemed against the property. Single mind on single matter, absolute concentration, that was the new president and, at the same time, the receiver of the M&StL.

Never a titan in the sense of a Harriman or a Hill, he nonetheless succeeded in running comparatively small or moderate-sized railroads in a big, competent, and commendable manner. Born near Youngstown, Ohio, December 1, 1851, and educated in the common schools of Rock Island, Illinois, Truesdale started his railroad career at the age of eighteen. His first rail job was clerking in the auditing department of the old Rockford, Rock Island & St. Louis. Later he rose to purchasing agent and subsequently to transfer agent at the road's overseas office in Frankfurt, Germany. In 1874 he came back to the States to become associated with a legal firm specializing in railroad matters. Two years afterward Truesdale was made assistant to the receiver of Logansport, Crawfordsville & Southwestern (now part of the Pennsylvania), and then general freight agent of the same road.

Opportunity, however, seemed more promising in the West, and in 1881 Truesdale went with the Omaha Road as assistant traffic manager. When in 1883 R. R. Cable was heading the M&StL, he sought a capable aide, and as a result, William Truesdale was summoned to the Louie as assistant to the president. Less than half a year later Truesdale became vice president, which due to Cable's many commitments on the Rock Island meant practically the acting presidency. By 1887 he *was* president.

Hardly had Truesdale assumed the mantle of that top position when the courts appointed him receiver. As a matter of fact, he advocated receivership in his characteristic blunt, frank manner. His report to the bondholders on May 26, 1888, contained no weasel words but, in his vivid English, forceful statements of conditions. In an era when railroad executives were not as forthright in stating the facts as they are today, Truesdale gave the public the unvarnished truth.

What was the matter with the M&StL?

To begin with, the net earnings in "the best six months of its business year, from July 1st, 1887, to December 31st, 1887, fell short of the interest accruing during that period [by] the sum of $39,609.98, and...since January 1st, 1888, the showing is still more unfavorable..."

"The earnings during the last half of 1887 are so unsatisfactory that under instructions of the board, the Company did not pay the interest ($120,000) due January 1st on the improvement and equipment bonds."

The reason for this gloomy report? There was no mincing of words here, either. To be sure, there were acts of

God; a very severe winter, and a sudden melting of snow, causing freshets and floods which tore down bridges and washed out the right-of-way. But more devastating were the acts of man, among which was the notorious rate war, on which Truesdale commented: "This wanton, aimless, causeless conflict covered an extent of territory and incurred losses which cannot be estimated but were enormous and in its every feature it stands without a parallel in the history of railroading."

Things had changed a great deal since the M&StL first started operation in 1871. Instead of one through route to Chicago from the Twin Cities there were now six. In addition there was the Soo, which W. D. Washburn was building from Minneapolis to Sault Ste. Marie, serving as another outlet to the East. Truesdale referred to this overproduction of railways as a "controlling" cause of the M&StL's plight.

"But the most important factor of all in the situation," he averred, "are the lines to Lake Superior, from the cities of St. Paul and Minneapolis." Two of these lines were in operation and a third was in process of construction. It was inevitable and necessary that the lake lines be built, but their effect on the intra- and interstate rates knocked the whole tariff schedule into a cocked hat. It was a repetition of the same thing that happened when the Lake Superior & Mississippi was first built. The effect, however, was much more widespread and harmful, not only to competing lines but to *all* the railroads in Minnesota and in a degree to those in bordering states.

How, it may be asked, could a couple of 150-mile lines upset the tariffs throughout the entire state? It all boiled down to the fact that at least two Twin City-Chicago lines slashed their rates on a 400-mile haul to approximately a 150-mile status. The latter mileage was about the distance from St. Paul or Minneapolis to Duluth. This affected the entire rate structure in the state, inasmuch as the carriers were prohibited from charging more for the short haul than for the long haul over the same route in the same direction. The M&StL, in common with other roads, had two alternatives and both were horns of a dilemma. It could meet the pared rates of the two Chicago roads or, on the other hand, set a tariff based on operating costs. Meeting the ridiculously low rate meant operating at a loss, but, if the charges were based on actual out-of-pocket costs, a large proportion of the tonnage would go over the rails of the two Chicago roads.

In those days the Interstate Commerce Commission was just beginning, and it had no power to increase rates nor authorize what was later known as "fourth section relief." This "relief" is simply permission to levy a higher tariff for a short haul than for a long haul due to unusual circumstances. In the absence of jurisdiction governing minimum rates, a powerful trunk line could freeze its less favored competitors into submission by lowering the tariffs at its pleasure.

Truesdale was particularly incensed at the rulings of the regulatory commissions, which he condemned as being "notoriously unfair and unreasonable." Said he, "The most charitable explanation of some of these rulings is, that by them they are best serving, or forwarding the political or private interests of the party, or some of its prominent leaders to whom they are indebted for the important position they occupy." This as well as his preceding quotations, are all from the bondholders report of 1888.

People did not always agree with the outspoken president of the M&StL, but they liked his honesty. Employees came to respect his forthright manner, and the stockholders admired his pluck and business ability.

Old timers on the road say Truesdale had one stock question whenever an improvement was broached: "How much will it cost?" At the same time, he advocated improvements, and while economy minded he was never niggardly. A radical change was necessary to keep the road afloat, and Truesdale was the man to bring about such a change. The M&StL's preferred stock was a drug on the market, selling from 9¾ to 12 cents a share; the road was was steadily losing money; it was short of equipment; and it had a deficit of more than $565,000 with no funds in the bank and little prospect of getting credit. The ax struck on June 28, 1888, when an order by the district courts of Hennepin County, Minnesota, and Webster County, Iowa, adjudged the road insolvent. On that day William H. Truesdale was appointed receiver.

Troubles, it is said, never come singly, and on the M&StL they apparently came by the carload. The city of Minneapolis was annoyed at the series of grade crossings along the St. Louis Road and demanded that the railroad depress its tracks and erect bridges across the right-of-way. The whole problem of crossing-elimination was further complicated by ownership of property: deciding what belonged to the St. Paul, Minneapolis & Manitoba Railway, and what constituted the Minneapolis and St. Louis.

In 1874 the M&StL leased "forever, the right to build, maintain and operate a single track of railway" between First and Sixth Streets North in Minneapolis from the St. Paul & Pacific. When the St. Paul road was subsequently acquired by the Manitoba, trouble ensued. It was alleged that the M&StL lease was not binding on the Manitoba company. The city suggested that the M&StL pull up its tracks on the property leased from the Manitoba, thus getting rid of a half-dozen grade crossings. It was further advocated that the M&StL run its trains over the rails of the Manitoba within the area in question. To this Truesdale retorted: "The demand is a monstrous one in every aspect."

The courts later held the M&StL lease valid, but the triangular controversy between the city and the two railroads continued. Then Truesdale went to the public and in a spirited pamphlet entitled *Statement of the Minneapolis & St. Louis Railway Co. of Its Position Relative to the North Minneapolis Crossing Controversy* he set forth his case. In it he reprimanded his opponents with the severity and directness of a Dutch uncle. He asserted that the M&StL was being "regarded as a charity child" and that to use the Manitoba's track "subject to all the delays and annoyances that a competitive company or the whims and fancies of a lot of switchmen...may impose upon us" was untenable. The screed makes exeedingly interesting reading even today.

"There is an element in this city," he snorted, "which on all occasions is seized with a violent fit of sneezing whenever snuff is taken by a certain St. Paul gentleman." In short, the M&StL would not be dictated to by James J. Hill or anyone else while Truesdale was heading the company.

The long and involved litigation between the three parties was finally settled when Judge A. H. Young of the District Court of Hennepin County acted as the mediator. In the annual report of 1890 Truesdale cheerfully stated that the agreement was "satisfactory to all parties" and at the same time "eminently fair and just to all."

Before the grade crossing project had been completed some three years later, it had cost the company over $200,000.

In 1890 the road moved its offices from the Boston Block to the fine new twelve-story Guaranty Loan Building, now known as the Metropolitan Life Building. The word "fine" is used advisedly, for it was the first skyscraper west of Chicago, and a remarkable structure in its day. Crowded excursions brought thousands to Minneapolis to see the architectual wonder of green granite and red sandstone. Tourists always made it a point to visit the roof pavillion—the forerunner of the modern roof garden—where a variety of flowers, palms, and shrubbery added to the novelty. On pleasant summer evenings string orchestras played to delighted audiences. In that era there was a top-floor restaurant which served food as delectable as could be found anywhere in the Twin Cities. In the Gay Nineties folks were as thrilled viewing the city from the "observation tower" of the Guaranty as visitors are today peering from the Empire State Building onto metropolitan New York. The M&StL had its offices on the eleventh floor.

The road which had been insolvent only a few years ago had its headquarters in the best building in town. Out on the line, improvements were also taking place, for all during receivership a large slice of income was going toward improvements. Truesdale restored the traditional M&StL morale of the employees and made trains adhere to schedule. Some of the veteran railroaders remember his trials with late connections of the Burlington, Cedar Rapids & Northern at Albert Lea. Finally in exasperation, they say, he bellowed to the BCR&N officials, "If you haven't got engineers to keep your trains on time, *I'll send you some!*"

To expedite the movement of the road's own passenger trains, particularly the locals to Excelsior, the receiver double tracked the main line from Kenwood to Hopkins. In 1892 a new station was erected at Washington Avenue just west of Third Avenue North by the Great Northern and leased to the M&StL. This replaced a smaller depot about a block away.

Meanwhile, the road catered to a brisk commuter clientele on the line to the west as far as Waconia. Like the famous "Main Line" on the Pennsylvania Railroad, which was built up principally because of frequent suburban service from Philadelphia to Paoli, so the Louie had its own commuter corridor. St. Louis Park was named after the St. Louis Road, and it thrived primarily because of the convenient train service to town. Kenwood was another community which owed much of its start to the shuttling locals on the M&StL. Many a monthly ticket was sold in the depot with its large overhanging roof resembling a pagoda, and yet the rounded cupola at one end definitely typed it as a railway station.

Again, like the Pennsy's Main Line with theatre trains carrying the socially prominent to see the latest stage successes, so the M&StL had its evening local for the legitimate stage. Some of the best people took the 8:08 Saturday night special from Excelsior to the Grand Opera House or the Bijou for an evening's entertainment. The resourceful passenger department sold special tickets including rail fare and a reserved seat at the theatre. A dollar covering the round trip from Excelsior and a choice box seat to boot. Eighty-five cents put one in the parquet circle, and for a mere six bits even the working man could get a thirty-five-cent balcony seat and transportation.

After the turn of the century suburban trolleys were

taking most of the short-haul traffic bordering on the city, and by 1910 the interurban had made a big dent in the Excelsior business. Commuter trains, however, were run until 1934, when the automobile and the motor bus made such operation unprofitable.

The color and romance were in the "varnish," as railroaders sometimes call the passenger trains, but even in yesteryear most of the money was in freight. One of the first things Truesdale did as receiver was to put the equipment in shape for increased tonnage and to buy new cars as quickly as finances permitted. The fiscal year which ended June 30, 1891, saw some 107 new (except for the trucks) freight cars and seven entirely new cars put into service. The next annual report finds two hundred new boxcars on the road and authorization for building fifteen stock cars at the Cedar Lake shops. The increased traffic necessitated buying two "heavy" switch engines.

By 1893 the last iron rail had been removed from the main tracks and replaced with steel. Several years previous to that the machine shop at Cedar Lake, "a wooden building and a dangerous fire trap," was replaced by a a sturdy structure of stone, brick, and iron. At this writing the shop is still standing and is in good condition although nearly sixty years old.

All things considered, the road did very well under Truesdale's stewardship. Net earnings rose from $338,958 for the fiscal year of 1889 (July 1, 1888 - June 30, 1889) to $798,432 in the boom year of 1892. The wise policy of keeping track and rolling stock in good condition made it possible for the company to handle the large increase in business with only a very slight increase in expense. The panic of '93 and its aftermath accounted for a downward trend in earnings of from $706,813 in fiscal 1893 to

$656,410 in the following year. Continuous improvements put the road in an enviable position for the reorganization which took place during the latter part of 1894.

When the receivership was terminated, the new company retained the same name, except that *Railroad* was substituted for *Railway*. Ex-receiver Truesdale then went to the Rock Island as vice president, and by the end of the century he headed the Delaware, Lackawanna & Western. In his place came William L. Bull, chairman of the reorganization committee, who represented Brown Brothers of New York. Bull's presidency was short, less than two years, but he succeeded in keeping the road at a high standard of efficiency. It is interesting to note that in 1894 just previous to Bull's administration A. L. Mohler came to the road from the St. Paul, Minnneapolis & Manitoba to serve as general manager. The new operating man did so well that when Bull left the M&StL to reorganize the Oregon Railroad & Navigation Company, he made Mohler president of the west coast road. Mohler later headed the Union Pacific.

But there was another executive—a quiet, laconic, unassuming man—who came to the Minneapolis and St. Louis at the time Bull headed the property: Edwin Hawley. No, he was not a talker, and to most of the road's officials he slipped in as vice president and as a director almost unnoticed. For the next eighteen years, however, Hawley was very much a part of the St. Louis Road, most of the time as its chief executive. Edwin Hawley and his regime are a chapter in itself, indeed several chapters, as will be seen.

I have played a lone hand and stuck to my job.
I have simply done two things—I have worked
and I have waited.

    Edwin Hawley in *Railway Age*, October 22,
1909.

8

House of Hawley

A lad of seventeen from Chatham, New York, went to Manhattan to seek his fortune, carrying a letter in his pocket from the political boss of Columbia County, addressed to an executive of the Erie Railroad. The official liked the country boy's looks and gave him a job as errand boy in the road's New York office at four dollars a week. That is how Edwin Hawley started railroading. Twenty-nine years later he became president of the M&StL, and when he died February 1, 1912, he left a fortune estimated at 30 million dollars.

For more than a dozen years the Minneapolis and St. Louis and the Iowa Central were known as "Hawley Roads." The Chatham-born financier, however, had many interests, being at one time or another active in the management of the Alton, the Clover Leaf, the Frisco, the Katy, and the Chesapeake & Ohio, to say nothing of the Colorado & Southern, which he sold to the Burlington. Hawley also had a substantial interest in the Interborough Rapid Transit Company of New York and was president of the Great Western Power Company, a large hydroelectric development on the Feather River in California. Moreover, he was a member of the New York Stock Exchange, which gave the firm of Hawley & Davis, of which

91

he was a copartner, its rights for interchange of business in the financial district. But the Louie and the Iowa Central were the first two companies he dominated, and as president of these roads Hawley personally guided their progress. He is to be credited with much of the success of the M&StL as well as a good portion of its shortcomings, although his successes far outnumbered his failures.

It was intimated in the last chapter, when Bull was president and Hawley vice president, that control of the company passed to the East. Prior to that time the St. Louis Road was a decidedly Midwestern concern, run by local men with scarcely any of its directors further east than Chicago. By the turn of the century, however, there was just one director hailing from Minneapolis, and he was vice president and general manager of the road. The rest of the board members made their headquarters in New York. It is necessary, therefore, to turn to Manhattan, as well as to Minnesota, for at least a decade to trace the fortunes of the M&StL. First, however, more about Hawley, who even to this day remains somewhat of an enigma in rail history.

Born in 1850, Edwin Hawley was a product of the nineteenth century, and his career in turn made a memorable impact on the twentieth century. He started in railroading during the period Jay Gould headed the Erie and Collis P. Huntington ran the Southern Pacific. Frugal habits and steady application to duty advanced Hawley to responsible clerical positions on the Erie. Later he switched to the Chicago, Rock Island & Pacific and soon became contracting agent for that road. In 1874 he gave up his job on the Rock Island to take a similar position with the California Fast Freight Line. Nine years afterward Hawley, at the request of Collis P. Huntington, became associated with the Southern Pacific, as general eastern agent, and for almost two decades was identified with that company.

The "innate nature of Hawley to make money," as his associate, W. B. Davids, puts it, soon asserted itself. Alertness in investment of his savings and ability to husband his profits soon put Edwin Hawley in the ranks of the well-to-do. In the nineties, prior to reorganization, the M&StL looked good to him, and he and his friends invested heavily in that property. When the great business boom occurred under President William McKinley, and the Republican gold standard and tariff succeeded the Cleveland free trade era and hard times, the value of Hawley's investments in the M&StL appreciated. As his fortunes soared with the times, Hawley tacitly convinced his associates of his genius, and they and he branched out into wider spheres of activity and power. It was Hawley's investment in the M&StL which gave him his start in the financial world and a high standing among his moneyed friends.

Shortly after Collis P. Huntington died, Hawley and Assistant Treasurer Frank H. Davis resigned from the SP. They preferred not to go with E. H. Harriman and the Union Pacific, to whom the Huntington interests were sold. Instead they formed the firm of Hawley & Davis, located first at 349 Broadway and later at 25 Broad Street, New York. For many years the latter address was that of the executive offices of the M&StL in the East.

In 1896, when Hawley was made president of the St. Louis Road, Frank H. Davis became its treasurer. As a matter of fact, Davis served in that capacity for some twenty-five years. Another veteran of the "House of Hawley" was F. M. Tompkins, who was secretary of the company for a long period. It is interesting to know that Tompkins—a neighbor of the Hawley family in Chatham —started to work for the SP at the age of fourteen as Edwin Hawley's office boy. Tompkins was, at the time of his death in 1948, the "dean" of the ex-directors of the M&StL. A few years ago, in being reminded of that fact, he just smiled and replied that he hoped Mr. Davids would live long enough to lift that crown from his weary brow. At this writing Walter B. Davids probably wears the "crown" as the oldest ex-director. Incidentally, he is a veteran M&StL man himself, having served for fifteen years as treasurer and as a director of the company.

One could go on talking about the officers of Hawley & Davis—men like former M&StL Secretary A. C. Doan and ex-Director Walter S. Crandell, from whom Crandall [sic], South Dakota, gets its name. There is little use, however, in laboring the point that Hawley and Hawley men managed the St. Louis Road. Indeed, during the Hawley regime the greatest expansion of M&StL mileage took place. Hawley had a substantial portion of his own fortune and the wealth of his associates invested in the road. It was his first real leadership as head of a railroad enterprise. In it he felt a deep personal pride and interest. He was then a man in his forties. Older and wealthier men were backing him in every move he made. He had much more to lose than his money and the investments of his friends, if the M&StL should become a failure. It would mean the loss of invaluable prestige, and he guarded this prestige with as much vigilance, if not more, than he guarded his bank accounts. The "Minnie" was to be a stepping stone in his vision of greater accomplishments.

The annual reports showed a steady although not spectacular improvement. Fifty- and sixty-pound rails were being replaced by seventy- and eighty-pounders, steel and stone were taking the place of wood on many bridges, and buildings were being kept in good order. New equipment was constantly coming into the picture, and Mogul-type locomotives were slowly replacing the "Standards" in freight service.

At the same time, roads associated with the M&StL, but not owned by it, were purchased outright, forming a closer-knit system. The Wisconsin, Minnesota and Pacific, extending from Morton, Minnesota, to Watertown, South Dakota, was deeded to the road January 20, 1899. On the other hand, the eastern end of the WM&P, linking Red Wing with Mankato, ceased to be operated by the M&StL after June 1, 1899. It was subsequently taken over by the Chicago Great Western, thus ending for all time the picturesque "Cannon Valley Line" as an operating unit of the St. Louis Road.

The twenty-mile Minneapolis, New Ulm and Southwestern was formally purchased February 9, 1899, and at the same time, funds were earmarked to extend the line south to Storm Lake, Iowa. The wherewithal to buy and build was secured by executing a First and Refunding Mortgage to the amount of $7,800,000. Of that sum $2,500,000 went to retire and cancel the company's First Preferred Capital Stock.

Of the many miles of new line built during the Hawley administration none posed more problems than the construction to Storm Lake. To cross the Cottonwood River just south of New Ulm a lofty deck-truss bridge was built, and a few miles farther down the line another structure spanning the Little Cottonwood was erected. To negotiate the grade between Estherville and Raleigh a horseshoe curve took the road through the rolling Iowa coun-

95

tryside. It was only about a half mile across by highway and approximately three times that length going around the "horseshoe."

The really rugged country, however, lay between Spencer and Storm Lake. Trestle after trestle carried the rails from eighty to over a hundred feet above river and ravine. Near Cornell there was a spindling three-deck bridge, built on a curve, which quivered every time a train crept over the wooden structure. This 135-mile line, known as the Southwestern Extension, was completed on August 19, 1900. The branch was intended to reach Omaha, but it was never extended beyond Storm Lake.

An observant passenger riding over the M&StL's main line today will note an abandoned roadbed first on one side of the track and then on the other, roughly between Hopkins and Chaska. This is the "old main line" which was relocated in 1902 and 1903, making it unnecessary to reduce tonnage on Chaska Hill. Hawley was not a man to spend money lavishly, but if an expenditure meant reduced operating expenses, he was the first to advocate the project. Indeed, during this time he relocated the Iowa Central between Searsboro and Oak Grove in much the same manner as was done with the M&StL. Hawley, by the way, became president of the Iowa road in 1900.

Up to this point no mention has been made of Edwin Hawley's understudy in Minneapolis, a man by the name of L Ferman Day. The financier met Day in traffic circles and was impressed by the latter's knowledge of railroading. As a result, when General Manager A. L. Mohler left the M&StL to head the Oregon Railroad & Navigation Company, Day was summoned to take his place. The new executive gave up the chairmanship of the Southwestern

96

Traffic Association to become Hawley's right-hand man. For over a dozen years the strange signature, "L F. Day," appeared on company stationery. His friends often called him Larry, but his first name was just plain "L" and he insisted that the letter be unadorned by a period.

Day was an able executive, although occasionally while out on the line he offered advice on problems in which he had little knowledge. The story is told of how he chanced to come upon a switchman trying to rerail an engine in the Kenwood yard. After observing that the rerailing frogs were placed in what seemed to be an awkward position he commented:

"You'll never get it on that way."

The switchman, one Roberts, not knowing who Day was and resenting the instruction, snapped back with,"I'll bet five dollars I'll get it back on the first pull!"

"Here's ten to your five you can't do it!"

After the greenbacks were produced, Roberts signalled Bert Theroux up in the cab and the engineer gently opened the throttle. The wheels climbed the frogs and then eased back on the rails.

As Roberts pocketed the fifteen dollars he inquired of the stranger, "Who are you anyway?"

"Day," was the reply.

"Good night!" exclaimed Roberts recognizing the general manager.

Things ran along smoothly on the St. Louis Road after the reorganization and up to about 1903. Regular dividends were paid, 5 per cent on First Preferred Stock and from 3 to 4½ per cent on the Second. When the First Preferred was retired in 1899, the remaining Preferred went on merrily bringing in 5 per cent for many years.

The Common, however, varied from 1½ to 5 per cent. After 1903, barring one exception, dividends ceased being paid on the Common for the remainder of the Hawley regime.

Naturally, one looks for the reason of dividend curtailment. It can be found, among other things, in an argument between Day and Vice President and General Superintendent Robert Williams, of the Burlington, Cedar Rapids & Northern. Just a simple matter regarding the schedules of Nos. 1 and 2, the "day" trains between the Twin Cities and Chicago, operated jointly over the M&StL, the BCR&N, and the Rock Island. "Larry" Day wanted that popular train on his rails at a time when Bob Williams thought it should be rumbling over the BCR&N. Whose fault it was will probably never be known, but the outcome was inevitable. The historic relationship between the two roads was severed, for the BCR&N built its own line most of the way to St. Paul, and the remainder was leased from the Milwaukee Road. That occurred during the fiscal year of 1903, the last time both M&StL stocks paid 5 per cent dividends.

How much traffic was lost by each road going its separate way is hard to say. A large amount of tonnage originated not only in Chicago for the Twin Cities but at stations in Iowa and the Southwest as well. Freight from Minnesota to destinations on the Rock Island was no small item. Largely because of this severance and bad crops, the road showed a net deficit of $51,922 for the fiscal year of 1904.

Meanwhile, Edwin Hawley had other plans for the M&StL. One can visualize him looking out of his luxurious office on the thirteenth floor of the Broad Exchange Building. In that day the twenty-story building compared favorably with the relatively few "skyscrapers" in New York. Hawley could get a clear view of the Bay, of Governor's Island, of the Statue of Liberty, and of the majestic Hudson flowing past America's largest city. He could see the country growing—bigger boats in the harbor, taller buildings in Manhattan, more railroad tracks sprawled all over the west bank of the Hudson.

Yes, Hawley was conscious of the nation's growth. More than that, he could hear what was going on from reliable and frequently very colorful sources. Hawley was a member of the so-called "Waldorf Crowd"—that strange mixture of the quiet and the flamboyant, of the grim and the gay. "Diamond Jim" Brady and "Bet-a-Million" Gates were in that group. So was the California millionaire, George Crocker. Others included Dan Sully, the cotton king, and Bernard M. Baruch, a promising young financier, now known as the "Elder Statesman." Of this heterogeneous gathering Hawley was in many ways an anomaly.

While others talked, he listened; while many spent their money lavishly, Hawley scrupulously saved. No long-winded messages of his ever went over the wires from the road's executive office in Manhattan to the operating headquarters in Minneapolis. They were all brief, clear, simple. A typical example, recalled by Davids, concerned the proposed merger of the Iowa Central and the Chicago & Alton. The correspondence, as he remembers it, was as follows:

Dear Day:

    I can get the Alton for the IC, what do you think?

                             E. Hawley

Dear Hawley:

    Don't think IC should get Alton.

Yours sincerely,
L F. Day

Economy in speech, economy in living, economy on the railroad—that was Edwin Hawley. Unlike Russell Sage, his contemporary, Hawley was not a miser, nor did he dress like a man trudging over the hill to the poorhouse. The thrifty M&StL president always wore good clothes, although they were never showy or extravagant. But he hated waste even more than did Calvin Coolidge. If a piece of soap was almost used up, the frugal railroad executive would stick it on a fresh cake, put it carefully away in the cupboard for a day, then bring it out when the two pieces were cemented together.

His associates would smile when the boss brought out a batch of unused envelopes from his day's mail which he had collected. He put the mongrel assortment on the oak board of director's table to arrange in piles according to size, to be used again. A return address printed on one of them? No matter, Hawley would carefully cross out the lettering, and the envelope would be regarded as good as new. A mutilated or torn unused stamp? If George Washington's head was clearly visible, it could be used—that was his criterion.

Out on the road his frugal instincts were just as evident. Once while out on an inspection tour in South Dakota, he saw some new ties being used for riprapping. Hawley made no comment, but a few weeks later he sent A. B. Cutter out to Minneapolis to assist L F. Day "in economizing."

But, as it has been stated, Edwin Hawley had plans for the M&StL. He saw, as others had, since the time the

100

first train rolled between Minneapolis and Albert Lea, that the St. Louis Road's very lifeblood depended on its connections. While his forbears dreamed and hoped and talked of mergers Hawley took the bull by the horns and brought about what in effect was a consolidation. He acquired a substantial interest in the Iowa Central, that orphan railroad that was wooed and jilted by interests from the Hawkeye State to Wall Street.

The two roads complemented each other and had much in common. It is hard to imagine what the M&StL would be like today without the Iowa Central and its Peoria Gateway. It is even more difficult to visualize a prosperous Iowa Central bereft of the St. Louis Road's valuable terminal facilities in Minneapolis. As long as each road had favorable traffic connections, things were all right. However, should new interests control connections or different policies emanate from their board rooms, there is no telling what would be the fate of the two local roads.

Hawley, having started railroading by way of the traffic department, was quick to comprehend the importance of Peoria as a gateway. His experience in freight solicitation convinced him of the utter necessity of having permanent, reliable connections for the M&StL. Time was running short. Already nearly all the independent roads had come under the dominance of major trunk lines. The Burlington, Cedar Rapids & Northern was virtually a Rock Island property, and it was not for sale. The Milwaukee Road and the Chicago Great Western were more or less permanently located. Only the Iowa Central remained unaffiliated. The railroad map of Minnesota and Iowa was jelling—the M&StL must buy or be bought. Rumor had it that the Rock Island or the Illinois Central would take over the St. Louis Road. Whether there was any foundation to these rumors is hard to say, but the possibility was there.

Edwin Hawley did the right thing at the right time. He invested heavily in the Iowa road, and by the turn of the century had become its president. With Hawley came L. F. Day, vice president and general manager of the M&StL, holding the same title on the Iowa Central. Before two years had elapsed, top ranking officials of the Minneapolis and St. Louis were holding similar jobs on the Hawkeye road. To all intents and purposes the two companies were operated as one railroad, although they were not officially wedded until January 1, 1912.

The old Hook and Eye, as the Iowa Central was nicknamed, is so important a part of the M&StL today that the entire next chapter will be devoted to it. The road is not big, as railroads go; but, mile for mile, it probably has more color and romance and folklore associated with it than many lines several times its size.

I came here broke
And it was do or die
So I hired out
On the Hook and Eye.

Rhyme of Iowa Central trainmen in the nineties.

9

The Hook and Eye

Most of the Hawkeye State's railroads are part of "transcontinentals" or other large trunk lines having their general offices in Chicago or St. Louis. But the Iowa Central was Iowa's own. It was conceived by Iowa men, run by native sons, and for thirty years had its headquarters at Marshalltown, right in the center of the state. Never a great money-maker, it nonetheless is deeply entrenched in the hearts of Iowans, especially those directly served by its lines.

"We're on the old Iowa Central!" That's a familar expression heard even today down where the tall corn grows. The older folk, in particular, remember how the road built up their farms; hauled grain, hogs, cattle to market; brought back merchandise and furniture from town.

They recall how a cattleman in Ollie (on the former route between Martinsburg and Brighton, now discontinued) used to charter a two- or three-car train to bring customers from Oskaloosa and nearby points to attend his blue-blooded cattle auctions held in the village. They'll reminisce on the good times of other years: Sunday excursions to Oskaloosa and those to Keithsburg-on-the-Mississippi, whence they went by boat down Ol' Man River to Fort Madison to tour the penitentiary. Yes, those

Sabbath outings by train were high spots in the social life of many Iowa towns. "With only a sandwich and a song we made a day of it!"

From one end of the continent to the other the Iowa Central was known to boomers—those itinerant railroaders of yesterday who went from road to road—as the Hook and Eye. There are many theories as to how the road acquired that nickname, but one look at an old timetable and the question is answered. On the title page of a schedule of 1874 vintage, when the line was called Central Railroad Company of Iowa, is a large "I" with two smaller "R's" having their straight lines on the "I". A "C" is placed on its back across the top of the "I". The "C" is the hook and the "I" the eye. The timecard contains ten pages folded accordion-like and is in the shape of an oversized hat check. Economy of space was evidently one of its chief virtues.

Plans for a north-and-south road across Iowa, however, were rife at least a decade before the Central Railroad Company of Iowa came into being. The dream of a great through route linking St. Louis and St. Paul via the Hawkeye State was envisioned prior to the Civil War. Indeed, on March 10, 1859, Josiah B. Grinnell was elected president of what the newspapers styled the Iowa Central Railroad. (The projected road, which was to include the town of Grinnell on its route from Missouri to Minnesota, should not be confused with a later company of the same name.) Josiah Grinnell's Iowa Central was never built, for the War Between the States intervened and the project was dropped.

When the conflict ended, a Quaker schoolteacher by the name of David Morgan from New Sharon, Iowa, revived the idea. He headed a company called the Cen-

106

tral Iowa Rail Road, chartered April 10, 1865, which was to run from Moravia through Albia, Oskaloosa and Toledo to Cedar Falls. Aided by Peter Melendy, who did much to stimulate interest in the northern end, considerable grading was done. But the "Grandest Railroad Project of the Age," as it was termed, never saw a train. Here again one should not confuse the partly graded Central Iowa Rail Road with the actually built Central Iowa Railway Company of the eighties. The Morgan-Melendy project never had sufficient financial backing to lay even a mile of track.

As is often the case, the beginnings of a comprehensive line frequently stem back to an avowedly local road having no aspirations to greatness. When the Eldora Railroad and Coal Company came into being February 7, 1866, it wanted no more than to build a sixteen-mile road to Ackley. After this new road was opened two years later, it enabled Eldora coal to be taken from the mines to the Dubuque & Sioux City connection at Ackley, and thence shipped to distant points. On September 1, 1868, a sweeping change in management took place when the Eldora line was sold to the Iowa River Railway Company. Charles C. Gilman headed the purchasing company, as well as the Eldora road, but most of the other executives were new.

The Iowa River Railway then started to build south to connect with the Chicago & North Western at Marshalltown, when the former in turn was taken over by the Central Railroad Company of Iowa on September 30, 1869. By the end of the year the rails had come to Marshalltown, and on January 7, 1870, a general celebration was held in the community to herald the formal opening of the road. The zeal of Messrs. Grinnell, Morgan, and Melendy in trying to foster a north-and-south road through Iowa was passed on to the Gilmans. The annual report of 1871 showed Charles Carroll Gilman as president and general superintendent; J. W. Gilman as local treasurer and general passenger agent; and John S. Gilman as a director.

Probably the ablest of the Gilmans was Charles Carroll, who was named by his parents after Charles Carroll of Carrollton, Maryland, the last survivor of the signers of the Declaration of Independence. The grand old man of Carrollton also laid the first stone on the Baltimore & Ohio Railroad, and in so doing said: "I consider this among the most important acts of my life; second only to my signing of the Declaration of Independence, if even it be second to that." How fitting it was that Charles Carroll Gilman was to be the man to survey and build the Central Railroad Company of Iowa through *central* Iowa virtually from one border of the state to the other. He realized the importance of railroads as did the renowned gentleman after whom he was named.

By the beginning of 1872 the entire road, from Northwood at the northern border of the state to Albia near the Iowa-Missouri line, was open to traffic. Between Oskaloosa and Albia much of the old grade of David Morgan's ill-fated road was used. The building of the Central Railroad Company of Iowa was so intermixed with construction companies that it is hard to tell precisely who built what. It is known, however, that a good part of the road north of Ackley was constructed by the St. Louis and St. Paul Railroad Company and much of the line south of Marshalltown was built by the Iowa River Railway Company. At any rate, Iowa's own railroad was managed and operated right from the heart of the state in Marshalltown.

The road suffered from financial reverses, changes in management, and insufficient traffic almost from the start. In the middle of the seventies Isaac M. Cate succeeded Gilman in the presidency, and in 1876 Josiah B. Grinnell was appointed receiver. This well known Iowa pioneer, preacher, and politician who had done so much for the state had little success in unraveling the road's financial entanglements. Two years later he resigned and was succeeded by H. L. Morrill, a railroad man of wide experience. On May 5, 1879, the Central Railroad Company of Iowa emerged from the hands of the court as the Central Iowa Railway.

So much for the north-and-south line. Meanwhile, developments were taking place on the east-and-west portion, which was shortly to be built from Oskaloosa to the Mississippi. This section of the Iowa road started very humbly as the New Sharon Coal Valley and Eastern Railway, incorporated January 29, 1880. Its name was changed to the Chicago, Burlington and Pacific Railroad on January 7, 1882, as construction advanced far beyond the confines of New Sharon. From New Sharon in a southeasterly direction toward Martinsburg some grading was done, the fills of which may still be seen. But the short cut to Martinsburg was dropped when the company decided to build east from Oskaloosa to the banks of the Mississippi opposite Keithsburg. The company was associated with the Central Iowa, and it is not surprising that it was sold to the latter road on April 1, 1882.

Before the line was finished, the construction crews had many a pitched battle with the narrow-gauge Burlington & Western, which was constructing a road between Winfield and Oskaloosa. Both roads met in Brighton, and it is said that it took nearly a half year to build through that community. The two lines were to cross west of town, but hardly were the frogs spiked into position when they were pulled up. At night Burlington & Western crews hooked a long chain to a doubletree, and three teams of horses made short work of the standard-gauge track. Finally, after a series of fist-fights and a succession of injunctions, a truce was signed and the crossing allowed to stand.

By the end of 1882 the Oskaloosa-to-the-river portion of the Central Iowa was in operation. A short time prior to that the Chicago, Burlington and Pacific had completed a line from New Sharon to Newton.

Meanwhile, developments on the Illinois side of the river were shaping up to make a through route from Peoria to central Iowa. On March 27, 1869, a company was formed which called itself the Peoria and Farmington Railway. Its principal object was to transport coal from the mines in the vicinity of Farmington to the growing industrial city of Peoria. Part of the road was built along the old grade established by the State of Illinois in the thirties. The state had attempted to construct a railroad from Peoria to a point on the Mississippi in Warren County, but the project was later abandoned.

Another old roadbed embodied in the Peoria and Farmington was that of the Burlington, Monmouth and Illinois River Railroad, a narrow-gauge line chartered on November 30, 1875. From the remains of the state grade and the uncompleted right-of-way of the narrow gauge the Peoria and Farmington connected the two towns in its name and pushed westward toward Monmouth and the Mississippi. During this period Iowa interests became active in the management of the road, and on December 7,

1882, they changed its name to the Central Iowa Rail way Company (of Illinois).

By 1883, there was a through route from central Iowa to Peoria. The only obstacle was the Mississippi, and this obstacle was overcome by the use of ferries. Some of the veteran railroaders still recall seeing the *William Osborn* steaming across the river with its maximum load of four freight cars. Afterward, they assert, came the *Golden Eagle* with two tracks and double the capacity of the *Osborn*. During the winter, however, passengers and parcels were taken across the frozen Mississippi on sleighs. But there was one year at least when a temporary wooden trestle was constructed after navigation had closed for the winter. To the casual observer the structure looked as if the tracks were laid on ice, for the bridge was scarcely above water level. As soon as the river was opened to traffic in the spring the trestle was removed and the car-ferries again brought into play.

The saga of building and financing the first permanent bridge is a story in itself. On December 19, 1881, the Mercer County Bridge Company was formed to span the river. Four years later the name was changed to the Keithsburg Bridge Company, and that firm existed, separate and distinct from the railroad, until it was finally purchased by the Iowa Central in 1901. The $600,000 structure consisted of eight spans and a 362-foot swing-draw, all of through-truss design. Eleven stone piers, many of which are still standing, supported seven 205-foot spans and one 255-footer.

When the bridge was finished in 1886, the Central Iowa became a unified road, physically as well as corporately, and it made a strong bid for through traffic. Since the Central Iowa was not authorized by charter to build branches, its feeders were constructed by other companies. The Grinnell and Montezuma, which Josiah Grinnell built and headed, was a typical example. It linked the county seat of Montezuma with the main line of the Central Iowa. The road was later sold to the Keithsburg, Grinnell & Dakota Railway, connecting State Center with Newburg; and the latter company was, in turn, deeded to the Central Iowa in 1882.

To trace in detail all the mergers and reorganizations of the Central Iowa and its antecedent companies would tax the mind of a Philadelphia lawyer. The Hawkeye State was full of construction companies and interrelated railroads, of which the Central Iowa controlled more than its share. The mutations of, for example, the high-sounding Iowa Pacific, would make a thumping long chapter in itself. That company was incorporated in 1870 for the purpose of becoming an important trunk line. Considerable grading was done on the section from Dubuque to Belmond and from Mason City to Fort Dodge. Its unfinished right-of-way, however, was soon parceled out after the inevitable sheriff's sale. Some parts of the weed-grown grades were subsequently used by the old Fort Dodge and Fort Ridgeley, the predecessor of the Minneapolis & St. Louis, and the Iowa Central and Northwestern. The latter road used the grade for its Hampton-Belmond line. The Iowa Central and Northwestern Railway, which also operated a route from Minerva Junction to Story City, came under the wing of the Central Iowa on March 1, 1882.

As related earlier in this chapter, Isaac M. Cate succeeded Gilman as president, and Cate remained in office for a dozen years. Then came Alfred Sully, and in quick succession, Elijah Smith and A. B. Stickney. In the meantime, another foreclosure had taken place, and the buffeted-about road emerged as the Iowa Central Railway on August 1, 1888. On that date the Central Iowa Railway (of Illinois) was also knocked down to the Iowa Central. Finally, to complete the picture, the Keithsburg and Eastern Railroad, which owned some land but no railroad, came into the fold in 1890.

Enough of tangled corporate history; now a word about the road itself. Having no important terminals, it was essentially an intermediate carrier and to a very large extent dependent on its connections. Whichever connecting line had influence on its management, that road called the cards. For a time the Milwaukee was the favored link from Mason City to the Twin Cities. Between St. Paul and St. Louis the timetable of 1885 shows through Pullmans running from Mason City to Albia over the Central Iowa, and on the Wabash the remainder of the way. But the next year A. B. Stickney headed the Iowa road, and there were many and far-reaching changes.

Stickney was a man of vision and imagination. He was also president of the Minnesota & North-western, which was later to become the nucleus of the Chicago Great Western. Naturally, he shunted the Iowa road's traffic to and from the Twin Cities over his Minnesota & North-western, which had a line from Mason City to St. Paul.

At the lower end of the Central Iowa, Stickney switched the Wabash connection from Albia to Ottumwa. Between Ottumwa and Givin the Iowa road went over what is now the Rock Island.

The 1886 timecards show Stickney not only fostered the St. Paul-St. Louis through service but he also added St. Paul-Kansas City cars in conjunction with the Wabash at Ottumwa. Iowans woke up to the fact that the local road was becoming an artery of travel undreamed of a few years previous.

Long before Robert R. Young, today's stormy petrel of the Chesapeake & Ohio, was even born the ebullient Stickney questioned the need of making Chicago or St. Louis the terminals of sleeping car routes between the East and Midwest. If a car of freight can go through Peoria, why not a sleeper? Going on this assumption, President Stickney put a "Woodruff Drawing Room and Sleeper Car" in service between the capital of Minnesota and the capital of Ohio. The car ran over the Minnesota & North-western-Central Iowa route to Peoria, thence over the Indiana, Bloomington & Western (now the Big Four) through Bloomington, Danville, Indianapolis, and Springfield to Columbus.

Equally bizarre was the Marshalltown-Chicago through service, likewise indicated in the 1886 schedules. A Pullman left Marshalltown for Keithsburg, where it was shunted from Central Iowa rails to the Burlington's Aledo Branch to Galva, thence along the "Q's" main line to the Windy City. Some of these strange through-car routings were short lived, yet they show the aggressiveness of the management in doing all it could to get its share of long-distance travel.

By 1890 Russell Sage, the New York financier, had replaced Stickney as president, and more changes were in order. Sage, variously termed the "wealthiest straphanger," "king of the money lenders," and "the meanest man in the world," was indeed a character. No stranger to the company—he had been vice president for about a decade—this man of millions was associated with a score of railroads, but the Iowa Central was one of the few roads of which he ever held the presidency.

Sage, along with Alfred Sully and others, played a prominent role in many of the construction companies which built the Iowa Central. Marshalltown, to say nothing of the rest of Iowa, seldom saw the tall, plainly dressed financier whose parsimonious habits were legend. On the other hand, all the employees and most of the youngsters along the line knew *Russell Sage,* the locomotive. Engine No. 10 with its gold eagle on top of the sandbox and the name Russell Sage printed on the cab could easily be identified by sight or sound. The little locomotive, outshopped by Manchester in 1880 and (according to ex-Master Mechanic C. B. Rogers) originally named *J. M. Cate,* had a chime whistle very pleasing to the ear. To railroaders the dulcet chimes were most welcome because No. 10 generally pulled the pay car when not at the head of a directors' special.

Soon after Sage took office, the agreement with Stickney's Minnesota & North-western was abrogated, and the Iowa Central switched back to the Milwaukee. About the same time, trackage rights were arranged over the Milwaukee from Hedrick to Ottumwa, and the crack Twin City - St. Louis trains used this route instead of going through Eddyville. The shifting of traffic connections and wheelage rights under the varied and sundry managements is a study in itself.

Added to this are the other properties closely allied with the Iowa Central. Around the middle of the eighties, Sage, who was always alert to pick up a railroad going under the hammer, acquired control of the Centreville [sic], Moravia & Albia at a receiver's sale. This line, built

115

by General Francis M. Drake, one-time governor of Iowa, connected Albia with Centerville. The Iowa Central then operated the road from approximately the end of the eighties until 1910.

The independent operation of the Centerville line came about when new owners decided to manage the property. Since the annual deficit was met by the Iowa Central it was felt that the bigger road would not relinquish control without being amply compensated. The Centerville officials then decided to take the line by force. Eight a.m., November 26, 1910, was the time secretly agreed upon to take over. They borrowed an engine, a coach, and crewmen from the Burlington and, after disconnecting the telegraph wire, followed the regular Iowa Central train out of Centerville wthout the IC's knowledge and without a train order or any rights whatsoever. On the way to Albia they stopped whenever they came upon an employee and discharged him as a representative of the old company and then immediately rehired him to work for the newly reorganized road. The Iowa Central, however, learned of the coup and planned to block the track behind the train when it reached the Albia depot. But the Centerville crewmen had anticipated the move and never left their own rails.

The Sage regime, while not outstanding, was marked by a competent operating staff which did what it could with mediocre equipment and a limited budget. Indeed, the Hook and Eye was a training school for many an executive who learned to "railroad" the hard way. During part of the Sage tenure, C. H. Ackert was the general manager and C. W. Huntington general superintendent. In later years Ackert went to the Southern as its chief executive, and Huntington ended up as president of the Virginian, a road as rich as the Iowa Central was poor.

When Russell Sage in the annual report of 1890 referred to the company as "being managed with a view to strict economy and the best net results," he was not speaking in parables. Some money was spent for urgently needed improvements, but as a whole the Sage administration was marked by a very conservative budget. Moreover, he was always eager to increase his own fortune and often sank to skulduggery and sharp practices to achieve this end. The following story is an illustration.

To comply with Illinois statutes requiring that at least one of the directors of the company incorporated in that state be an Illinois resident, Sage appointed as a director Henry A. Gardner, whose law firm in Chicago looked after the company's legal matters arising in that vicinity. The by-laws of the Iowa Central stipulated that a ten-dollar fee should be paid to each member attending a directors' meeting. Gardner, along with the other directors, received his ten-dollar gold piece at the close of each board meeting.

Russell Sage, however, awaited his opportunity; he buttonholed Gardner in a quiet corner and politely but firmly informed him that he was only a director at his (Sage's) beck and call and not entitled to the gold piece. Thereupon the ten dollars reluctantly went from the pocket of Gardner to the greedy palm of Sage. The Illinois lawyer, probably to keep in good graces with the railroad president and to continue having the Iowa Central as a client, condoned this petty larceny. Perhaps there is some comfort in knowing that almost all of Sage's fortune, estimated at 100 million dollars at the time of his death, was left to his widow, Margaret Olivia Sage, who used the bulk of the moneys to set up the Russell Sage Foundation, which sponsors many humanitarian endeavors. It is quite possible that some of the ten-dollar gold pieces which were pilfered from Gardner have been spent to keep a roof over the head of some needy family.

Sage relinquished the presidency in 1897 and was followed by Horace J. Morse, who a year later was succeeded by Robert J. Kimball. The much tossed-about railroad went on its stormy course until the coming of Edwin Hawley. When Hawley took office in 1900, he had bought control and operated the property in conjunction with the Minneapolis and St. Louis. The changes Hawley made—and they were many—have remained from 1900 to the present day. The Iowa road, however, was not formally purchased by the M&StL until 1912.

The original plan to make Albert Lea the gateway for Iowa Central traffic had, until the end of the nineteenth century, failed to materialize. The northern end of the line from Manly Junction to Northwood had regressed to the status of an unimportant branch. It had long since been leased to the Burlington, Cedar Rapids & Northern, now the Rock Island.

One of Hawley's first moves was to make a new contract with the Burlington, Cedar Rapids & Northern for joint use of the line from Manly Junction to Albert Lea. The constant bickering for connections was over; the historic gateway turned out to be the practical, permanent gateway that it is today.

The Iowa Central is awash with memories of by-gone industries, half-forgotten railroads, and homespun ways of living. The numerous shaft mines in southern Iowa and western Illinois, which contributed much to its revenue, are now a thing of the past. One looks in vain on the

118

map for the village of Muchakinock, but there was a day when it was on the busy mile-and-a-half line from Givin, serving extensive coal fields. The collieries no longer provide employment for hundreds of men. The mine spur was abandoned around the turn of the century.

There was a time, too, when coal by the trainload went from the Excelsior mines, a few miles south of Oskaloosa, to Capron on the State Center branch. At Capron it was turned over to the Milwaukee to provide fuel for its engines. The Iowa Central itself acquired the Hocking Coal Company on the outskirts of Albia in 1902, and for many years its mines were a fruitful source of income.

A familiar sight thirty or more years ago were the miners' trains or "crummy runs," made up of improvised boxcars fitted with wooden benches and stoves. Such equipment was used to take the miners from Albia to the Hocking coal field, as well as between Peoria and Maxwell, in the Kickapoo district. This specialized service was also provided for the extensive mining operations dotting the countryside from Farmington to Middle Grove. The latter "crummies" took men to the once-famous collieries such as the Silver Creek, Alden 8, Maplewood, Black Hawk, Jerkwater, and Pond Lilly.

Peoria, being the largest city served by the Iowa Central, was also a busy terminal for many travelers on their way east. Trains first ran uptown over the Burlington until about 1882 and later over the Rock Island or the Peoria & Pekin Union, depending on the year in question. It was a common sight on weekends to see throngs of passengers on the open-ended wooden coaches going to town to shop or visit. The small, eight-wheel engines could not pull many coaches, but they did speed along at a good rate. Past crude, unlighted switch-stands and

119

over stub-switches the short trains reeled. (To this day a lone stub-switch is still in use just west of the depot at Story City, Iowa.) Notwithstanding sharp curves and roller-coaster grades, light rails, and earth ballast, the Hook and Eye ran on a schedule which, all things considered, was little short of remarkable.

The "boomers' last chance," as the road came to be known, paid less-than-standard wages in its earlier years, and consequently had a large labor turnover. Times were indeed poor when a man could not hire out on "The Hook." If a railroader was out of work, he would first go to the larger roads such as the Burlington, the Great Northern, or the Milwaukee. Failing to get on the payroll of the "big boys," he'd try the "Red Stack," as they called the Chicago Great Western; then the "Skally," which was the St. Paul-Duluth line of the Northern Pacific; and finally, the "Louie," or the Minneapolis and St. Louis. When all these failed, the boomer went where all boomers ended up—on the Hook and Eye. It was a common saying on the Iowa Central that they "never had the same crew twice." Still quite a few of the men who sought temporary work stuck with the road and later made able executives. But by far the bulk of the officials were Iowa lads who had come from towns along the line and had made good on their home road.

A part of the road's tradition were the specialized movements of specialized groups peculiar to the state. The Quakers had a particular fondness for the Iowa Central because they could depend on it to bring folks from all over the state to attend their annual gatherings at Oskaloosa. Special trains from Centerville, from Marshalltown, from Newton, and even from Monmouth, Illinois, deposited Friends by the thousands at the old Quaker Camp Grounds on the north side of town. One may be sure that Elmer Johnstone, the roadmaster, was down there building a temporary platform and that Ross Brown, the passenger agent, was on hand to see that everything went smoothly. Going to Yearly Meetings is to Friends what the pilgrimage to Mecca is to Mohammedans. That annual movement, along with the periodic Sunday School picnics, the baseball outings, and the lodge junkets, was very much a part of the road's duties. The Iowa Central was more than a railroad; it was an institution.

The fact is now definitely known that when the extension was ordered to the Missouri river it was the intention of the backers of the road to go to the coast.

Minneapolis *Journal*, August 4, 1907.

10

"... & Pacific"

Beyond Watertown, South Dakota, around the turn of the century was *the West*. One could conceive of that community as being part of the Midwest, like the Twin Cities or Des Moines. Between that point and the growing cities along the Pacific coastline, however, settlements were few and far between. Going into this frontier-like land was like taking an ocean voyage. One either stayed near port, taking a short cruise, or made a long trip to the distant shores of Europe or Asia. So it was with the railroads; they ran short feeders into the Dakotas *or* they went to the Pacific shore. It was one or the other. The Minneapolis and St. Louis, apparently, had only the means for a short cruise, though it dreamed of a trans-oceanic voyage.

The building of the M&StL to the Missouri River was part of the road's expansion program during the early years of the twentieth century, and yet it was so different from the rest of the system as to warrant separate treatment. Like the broad-brimmed hats, the high-heeled boots, and the leather chaps of the cowboys, the westward extension had little in common with the company's conservative growth in Minnesota, Iowa, and Illinois. Building west meant a break in policy—a daring, unpredictable sortie into a new and untried field.

To construct the new road, a company was formed on December 18, 1905, entitled the Minnesota, Dakota & Pacific Railway. As its immediate objectives it had two prairie terminals, one at LeBeau on the Missouri River, and the other at Leola, seat of McPherson County. The distance from Watertown, where it connected with the M&StL, to the Missouri River was 172 miles. The branch to Leola, which connected with the LeBeau line at Conde, measured 57 miles. With the exception of Aberdeen on the Leola route and, of course, Watertown, there were few towns which did not owe their existence to the new railroad.

From the start, the Minnesota, Dakota & Pacific was financed, controlled, and operated by the Minneapolis and St. Louis interests, and it may be referred to as an M&StL project. The actual building was done by the Dakota Construction Company, and the colonization was taken care of by Thomas A. Way, townsite agent for the M&StL and president of the Dakota Town Lot Company. Way had a bright red open automobile which was a familiar sight on the crude dirt highways along the new railroad. Besides attracting the attention of homesteaders and settlers, the touring car also aroused the ire of cattle grazing in the fields. On one occasion, it is said, an outraged bull charged into the automobile, and both car and bull came out of the encounter considerably battered.

On December 20, 1906, the McPherson County *Herald* announced: "Red Letter Day For Leola; M. & St. L. Construction Train Enters Town at Noon Today." Because of inclement weather and frozen ground, regular service was not begun until the land thawed in the following year. By the end of 1907, trains were also running on the LeBeau line all the way to the Missouri River.

124

Of the many communities on the West End none had more frontier flavor than the wide-open cattle town Le-Beau. A county seat at one time and for three eventful years one of the largest cattle-shipping points in the nation, it had a turbulent history. The old town, about a mile up Swan Creek from the later LeBeau, was settled by Antoine LeBeau, a Frenchman from St. Louis, in 1875. In 1883 the town of LeBeau was laid out, and by the end of the year it had a population of about two hundred with stages running to Aberdeen, Blunt, and Bismark. The Northern Pacific planned to cross the river at that point and surveyed a line from Breckenridge, Minnesota, to the banks of the "Big Muddy," as the Missouri was called. The NP, however, never built into South Dakota, and the fortunes of LeBeau languished. When the M&StL reached the river, a new town of LeBeau came into being, a little south of the original village, and old LeBeau was soon forsaken.

The new LeBeau had a spectacular growth, because the railroad made possible the opening up of the grasslands west of the river and the exploiting of them to the full. Trainloads of white-faced Herefords from Texas and beefs from New Mexico, Colorado, and other southwestern points came to feed on the buffalo grass across the Big Muddy. They went to Murdo MacKenzie's Matador Land & Cattle Company pastures, to Mossman and Gates' Turkey Track, and to the Diamond A ranch...names to reckon with in the heyday of LeBeau. The fattened cattle would then be sent back across the river on the paddlewheeler, *Scotty Phillip,* to be loaded on stock cars for South St. Paul and Chicago.

"Fifteen hundred head of fat cattle from the Turkey Track pastures west of the river are enroute for LeBeau

125

for shipment over the M. & St. L. road," reported the LeBeau *Phenix* for September 10, 1908. "A trainload of 30 cars will go out Saturday and a similar train Monday." On November 19, the same paper stated that a "round million" dollars worth of cattle and horses went out of LeBeau during that season. The town weekly estimated approximately 12,000 beefs were shipped in 1,000 cattle cars.

By the end of the year the unofficial census of the town was 3,000. Tom Way glowingly extolled the virtues of the community in a back-cover advertisement of the November, 1908, *Dacotah Magazine*.

> LeBeau Has:
> Natural Gas, Artesian Water, Brick and Potters Clay, the Western Terminous and Rail Road Division Point of the Minneapolis & St. Louis Railroad on the Missouri River. It is the natural point of debarkation for Homesteaders and the Front Door of the Cheyenne, Standing Rock and Butte County Homestead Lands. EIGHTY ACRES of Main Tracks, Sidings and Station Grounds. Yards and shipping facilities to handle 100,000 head of cattle annually.

On June 10, 1909, the *Phenix* noted a new high in stock arrivals—a weekly movement of fourteen trainloads of cattle, of twenty-five cars each. LeBeau was in its glory! But while Texas longhorns were coming in to be fattened and departing after their fill of buffalo grass to command high prices in the big city markets, the town's decline was imminent. The Government was preparing to open the Cheyenne and Standing Rock reservations to the public. Its untoward effect on the community, however, was not at first apparent. Upon learning of President Taft's proclamation making LeBeau a registration point, the

126

August 26 issue of the *Phenix* cried out: "Visitors [will] Step from Train and View the Promised Land 20 Minutes Later." With sublime egotism the weekly observed: "The great majority of all applicants will register at LeBeau." Actually, 3,023 land-seekers did come to the town, although some 55,364 piled into Aberdeen and thousands more to the other registration points at Mobridge, Lemmon, Pierre, and Bismark.

Now for a look at LeBeau at the crest of its glory. It had two banks, a couple of general stores, and a like number of hotels. Saloons, gambling establishments, and bawdy houses were plentiful. On Saturday night when cowboys flocked in from the range, all bars were crowded and everyone had a riproaring time. In the back of Phil DuFran's saloon roulette wheels were a-whirl and faro banks were wide open. Phil dispensed the drinks and Ed Trice managed the gambling, a formidable twosome anytime and doubly so on the weekend. It is reputed that the DuFran-Trice combination took in more money on Saturday than the local bank received in a week. On one of the busier days the house is said to have made a "haul" of over $3,500; and that, older trainmen maintain, was a conservative estimate.

LeBeau was the railhead, the terminal, the beginning and the end of everything. Main Street extended from the city limits at the top of the hill, down to Railway Street and the depot. It was a railroad town as well as cattle headquarters, and whatever happened on the M&StL was top-drawer news in the papers. Conversely, whatever occurred in town filtered down to the depot and the employees on the West End. There was nothing, perhaps, which was more talked about in the engine house, at the depot, or around the stove of a caboose than the killing of "Dode"

127

MacKenzie, manager of the Matador ranch and one of the railroad's biggest shippers. "Done in cold blood," some people said. "An act in self-defense," others positively asserted. Here is the story:

On a chilly Saturday morning in December, 1909, David G. "Dode" MacKenzie strolled into Phil DuFran's saloon for a friendly glass. Crouched behind the bar was Bud Stephens, a discharged employee of the Matador ranch, and an arch-enemy of Dode. Apparently there had been a feud of long standing between the two men, and both were anxious to settle the score. When Dode walked into the bar, Bud was first on the draw and plugged him with his 45-caliber Colt. The son of Murdo MacKenzie, the well-known cattle man with holdings in both Americas, died almost at once. "Premeditated," the *Phenix* said, for was not the Colt an old style six-shooter which had to be cocked before each firing? Three months later Bud Stephens was acquitted.

That was LeBeau where firearms were constantly advertised in the newspaper, and where hardly an issue came off the press without Winchester reminding its readers to "Look for the Big Red W." But with a show of respectability, Hotel LeBeau stated pointblank: "No dogs allowed in Rooms." The town was coming of age. It was not uncommon, however, to see snakes on railroad property, and a nine-button rattler was actually killed in the depot.

A cold-blooded murder, the opening up of a 2,600,000-acre reservation, or the laying of concrete sidewalks was important news some of the time; but the barest squib on the M&StL was news all of the time. The slightest rumor on the road would sometimes be expanded into a two-column story. Hon. A. B. Funk, a visitor from Spirit Lake, Iowa, was quoted in the *Phenix* for December 17,

1908: "At LeBeau the iron horse impatiently awaits orders to cross the muddy stream and plunge into the wilderness beyond..." Everyone looked for the day when the "... & Pacific" in the road's name would mean just what it said, thereby assuring LeBeau of a permanent future.

Time and again the *Phenix* had "positive assurance" that the Big Muddy would be bridged. On May 20, 1909, the sheet told how the M&StL surveyors were making from "8 to 10 miles a day," and on July 22, the weekly stated that the engineers had reached Flint Rock Creek about one hundred miles west of LeBeau. September saw two steam piledrivers on the river bank. The bridge would soon become a reality.

After that came only rumors. For one thing, the river bottom was found to be unsuitable for piers, but more significant and ominous was the news that the Milwaukee Road was pushing westward. A branch line of that rival company was being built from Moreau Junction to Faith, cutting directly into the territory staked out by the M&StL. Moreover, the Milwaukee, with the Rockefeller and Standard Oil millions behind it, had extended its main stem to the West Coast.

Fate was against LeBeau, the cattlemen, and the M&StL. With a branch line west of the river there would be no need for the picturesque *Scotty Phillip* to ferry cattle across the Big Muddy to the railhead at LeBeau. Again, the farm was crowding out the ranch; and the stolid toiling husbandman came to supersede the dashing, riotous cowboy. Furthermore, it was highly impractical to build a fourth "transcontinental" from the Twin Cities to the West Coast. Many people were of the opinion that the Great Northern and the Northern Pacific were sufficient to serve the northwestern routes to the Pacific; and with

129

the building of the Milwaukee, what chance would there be for the M&StL?

The plight of LeBeau became apparent during the summer of 1910 when the Chicago, Milwaukee & Puget Sound Railway ran full-page "ads" in the *Phenix* announcing the sale of town lots in Faith, South Dakota. Then came the fire which swept away part of the ill-fated town. In 1911 a second conflagration made short work of the remaining structures. The hopes and aspirations of LeBeau were cremated there and then.

LeBeau has been dwelt on at length because it symbolized the dream of westward expansion. But if the M&StL was thwarted at the Missouri River, it did not give up hope of building extensions elsewhere in South Dakota. Around the eighties a road was projected and partially graded from Aberdeen to Pierre. Styled the Duluth, Pierre & Black Hills, this company never operated a train, and for many years its charter lay dormant. In 1909 the directors' minutes of the Minneapolis and St. Louis showed the company had purchased a substantial interest in the defunct Black Hills road. It was planned to extend the LeBeau line from a point at Cresbard, where the unfinished grade crossed the M&StL, to Pierre over the abandoned right-of-way. Despite encouraging newspaper reports, the extension to South Dakota's capital was never undertaken.

Similarly, plans were afoot to push the M&StL from Leola to Ashley, North Dakota, over the unused Soo grade in that area. The *Phenix* for March 11, 1909, even states that through trains were anticipated from Chicago to the west coast of Canada over the Illinois Central, M&StL, Soo Line, and Canadian Pacific. Indeed, on November 24, 1911, the Minneapolis *Journal* went even farther and said that the M&StL rails would soon reach Canada. None of these ambitious plans, however, worked out.

Anticipating considerably expanded facilities on the West End, an entire floor of a new building in Watertown was leased in 1909. It became the western headquarters of the railroad. For a time, the uptown office had a superintendent, chief dispatcher, roadmaster, traveling engineer, freight traffic manager, trainmaster, and a staff of clerks. Later the office was given up, and most of the officials and clerical workers were sent to other parts of the system.

During this period the M&StL, and Tom Way, in particular, did much to foster Yahota, a summer resort on Lake Kempeska, six miles west of Watertown. Sunday excursions were run from Watertown at a nominal fee of 25 cents for a round trip. The railroad, up until the widespread use of the motor car, took thousands of week-enders boating, fishing, and bathing on one of the biggest and most beautiful lakes in South Dakota. Because of frequent and inexpensive train service, many cottages were built along the shore line, and it became a popular watering place for perspiring Dakotans.

It has been seen that with few exceptions the communities along the West End were small. The people living there now are as hardworking, thrifty, and neighborly as one can find anywhere. Of predominantly Russian-German stock, with a sprinkling of other nationalities, they came to Dakota seeking freedom, independence, and the right to worship in their own way. Some have old-country mannerisms and quaint religious customs, but practically all have a genuine friendliness and an open-handed hospitality, rare in this machine age. There are, for example, Dukhobors in Wetonka, who hailed from Canada to try

131

their hand at farming in the States. The custom of putting vinegar in their tea may set them apart; yet, they make admirable farmers and God-fearing neighbors. Again, the Hutterites, a sect akin to the Mennonites, who came up the James River Valley and settled along the M&StL in Spink County, are known for their skill in raising excellent wheat.

Probably the most impressive sight on the way to LeBeau is St. Anthony's Church at Hoven. The lofty spires of that structure, which is one of the largest houses of worship in the state, can be seen ten miles away. Catholic folk from the village and the surrounding countryside had put their savings together to complete this structure, seating a thousand people in a community of half that number. The church was started in 1912 through the efforts of Father A. C. Helmbrecht, who in 1949 was still the pastor.

The spirit of the prairie and the nature of its people are well brought out by the following incident. On Christmas day a few years after the road had been opened the train for LeBeau was flagged down at Northville. It was one of those white Christmases which the Dakotans do not sing about, and the roads were blocked with snow. It would be late in the evening before the crew could return to the division point at Conde, and they would miss their Christmas dinners. The engineer "wiped the clock," as an emergency stop is called, when he saw a red petticoat waving down the track. There on the right-of-way was Mrs. Hughie Luke, locally known as "Mother" Luke because of the maternal interest she took in helping others. She apologized for not being able to get to the station to meet the train on account of the drifts. Would the crew like to have a hot meal which she had prepared for them?

132

No need to wait for an answer. A hired man lifted an array of victuals, dishes, and silverware up to the train.

Christmas to "Mother" Luke was unthinkable without turkey and all the "fixings." She told the grateful railroaders they could return the dishes on the way back; and then, after wishing them all a Merry Christmas, departed. The train, according to the story told by the baggageman of that run, made a longer than usual stop at the next station. Here the crew feasted on generous helpings of turkey and dressing, potatoes and gravy, several vegetables, along with coffee, cookies, and desert. "Mother" Luke, a New Englander, had Old England's knack of cooking delicious meals, and the holidays always called for her best efforts.

Before concluding this chapter, let's have one last look at LeBeau as it is today. After the fire destroyed most of the town, train service dwindled until only an occasional trip was made, if and when there was any freight. The road petitioned to abandon the twelve-mile segment from the river to Akaska in 1924. The receiver's report shows that the cost of operation on that section of track for the preceding year was $7,939.87 and the income from all sources was $467, of which $2 was from passengers. The petition stated: "There are at present but two families in the town of LeBeau, while the surrounding country is sparsely settled. It is cut off entirely on the west by the Missouri River, over which there is no bridge at that point. Business in and around LeBeau has practically ceased; the soil has proved to be unproductive; there are no local industries, and the general situation precludes any reasonable expectation that this portion of the road will become self-sustaining in the future." Apparently, a member of each family made one round trip into Akaska a year, which would just about account for the revenue from "Passengers forwarded."

Probably there was no clearer case for abandonment in the nation. At any rate, the Interstate Commerce Commission gave its stamp of approval to junk the line serving what was once termed the "Coming City of [A] New Empire."

It was the author's privilege to view what was left of LeBeau, in company of Dave Huber, proprietor of the drug store in Akaska. We rode out to the wind-swept hills on a bleak October day. Coming to the bottomlands of the Missouri River, we stopped at the Boehmer ranch, the only habitable building left in LeBeau. Here Charlie Franceau, a grey-bearded rancher, joined us. Despite his advanced age he is alert with memories of other years. With Charlie acting as senior guide, we toured old and new LeBeau. We pushed the bushes aside to look at the two pits where the enginehouse had stood; we bumped across a field to get the car as near as possible to an embankment, which ended abruptly—that was as far west as the ". . . & Pacific" ever went. We drove to the depot site and walked up to the rusted pipe of the artesian well on the crumbling remains of the platform where passengers used to board the trains.

From the station Dave put the auto in low gear, and the car jounced up Main Street hill to the center of town. The road was hardly visible, but the two concrete sidewalks, each 10 feet wide, from the top of the hill down to the "railroad" were intact. Along the weed-rimmed thoroughfare were gaping basements and, occasionally, cement steps, one of which had the inscription HOTEL LEBEAU and another, L. E. PIERCE. BUFFET.

"There," pointed Charlie to a cellar full of rubble,

134

"was Phil DuFran's saloon where Dode MacKenzie was shot!"

Further up the hill we saw the stark brick walls of the First State Bank, a desolate picture indeed, with its roof caved in and its doorway permanently open. The bank is the only uptown building still standing, a mute reminder of the flourishing, heady era when LeBeau was in its glory.

Leaving the "new" town, we rocked across the fields, and then over a bridge spanning Swan Creek to old Le-Beau. Here nothing was discernable except the old railroad grade to the east. "Over yonder was the public school," Charlie indicated with a sweep of his hand, "and further on the bluff was the center of the old town." Having seen both LeBeaus, we drove the veteran rancher back to his home on the prairie.

On the return trip to Akaska Dave Huber suggested we "try and follow the railroad," which we did. Meanwhile, the setting sun had cast a glow of light on the distant Missouri and the rolling hills. The auto lurched on, down in a gully one minute, up on a summit the next. We blazed our own trail, frequently stopping to open and close cattle gates, and occasionally pausing to trace the contour of the derelict line. For the last few miles we drove along the old right-of-way, as the sun went down on a Ghost Road to a Ghost Town.

*Regulation 5. Spittoons. Each smoking car shall
be provided with at least twelve (12) spittoons.*
Northwestern Sanitation Association, December 5, 1912.

11

High Back Seats and Electric Lights

It was a grand and glorious era when the *Cannon Ball Express* sped over the rails of the Minneapolis and St. Louis, the old Burlington, Cedar Rapids & Northern, and the Rock Island from the Twin Cities to Chicago. No less colorful was its successor, the *North Star Limited,* traveling between the same terminals on an accelerated schedule with a little spit and polish. The *North Star* chuffed over Minnesota's own St. Louis Road, south to the state line, thence over Illinois Central tracks to the Windy City in thirteen and a half hours flat. That was fast timing from St. Paul to Chicago in 1902. And the equipment? To quote the yellowing timetable:

"Trains Nos. 5 and 6—North Star Limited—Run through solid, are Broad Vestibuled throughout and consist of Compartment and Standard Sleepers, Free Chair Cars, Coaches...Buffet Library and Dining Cars, all just from the Pullman shops. The latest and most expensive equipment attainable."

To this day, if one mentions Nos. 5 and 6 to any M&StL trainman whose hair is gray and whose face shows lines of long service, he will get a story. A few polite questions will bring a flood of reminiscences, a match, and more than likely a smoke. What legends of Lake Minnetonka are to oldsters out Excelsior way, stories of Nos. 5 and 6

A handbill advertising excursions to the Twin Cities, June, 1914.

(railroaders refer to trains by number, not by name) are to old-timers on the Minneapolis & St. Louis. Indeed, the importance of the role Minnesota's local road played in carrying trainloads of passengers to the East, the South, and the West was almost incredible for a line of its size.

It is difficult to determine the exact date when the M&StL first ran through cars to Chicago or St. Louis. One of the earliest mentions of such service is featured in a full-page advertisement appearing in a *History of the Upper Mississippi Valley* of 1881. It stresses through equip-

138

ment from Minneapolis to St. Louis over the "new Chicago line." By the end of the 1880's Nos. 5 and 6 were crack trains to Chicago, with the *St. Louis Specials,* Nos. 3 and 4, taking care of passengers to St. Louis. All M&StL service to the Twin Cities, by the way, used Northern Pacific tracks between St. Paul and Minneapolis. These limiteds operated over routes popular with Minnesotans for a score of years before 1902, when the Rock Island built its own line into St. Paul.

The Albert Lea Route, as the M&StL was known, became synonymous with speed and comfort; it was the best line south, and a favorite to the East. The *Cannon Ball,* as mentioned before, operated over the M&StL, the Burlington, Cedar Rapids & Northern, and the Rock Island, switching from one road to another at Albert Lea, Minnesota, and West Liberty, south of the Iowa boundary. In past years, Albert Lea was a passenger gateway of considerable importance, with a hotel and a station all in one and extensive dining facilities to boot.

The *St. Louis Specials* also used the Albert Lea Route, but they ran over the Burlington, Cedar Rapids & Northern to Burlington and thence on the St. Louis, Keokuk & North-western to the southern destination. Incidentally, the route south of Albert Lea is the same as that over which the *Zephyr Rockets* travel today.

Before the century ended, fast-stepping limiteds of the M&StL, pulled by high-wheeled "Standards"—locomotives with four pilot wheels and four large drivers—were heralded all over Minnesota. Drummers found the smoking cars much to their liking, tourists noted that the Albert Lea Route made connections in all directions, and excursionists eagerly looked for the road's cut-rate specials. Much of the road's popularity was due to good service,

139

and not a little was traceable to aggressive publicity. In the 1890's there were no stringent regulations governing the issuance of passes, and mileage books or free transportation were given in exchange for advertisements.

Newspapers on and off the line, many published a long way from M&StL rails, carried notices of the road's service. The company's advertisements may have been naïve, but they were uninhibited and "pulling." Here is a typical example, culled from the Excelsior *Cottager* for January 3, 1896:

> The Minneapolis & St. Louis R. R. Company.
> A New Train to Omaha and Des Moines.
> It is a Hummer!
> Look out for it!
> Through Cars,
> Pullmans & Coaches.
> Great!

The new train consisted of through cars to Fort Dodge, where it split, one section going to Omaha via the Illinois Central, and the other continuing south on theM&StL to Angus, and thence running over the historic Des Moines and Fort Dodge Railroad to the Iowa capital. Another advertising technique frequently used was the question-and-answer method. In the *Cottager* for January 17, 1896, under the title of "Going to California?" queries were volleyed at the reader: "What line will get you there seven hours quicker than any other?"; "What line operates Phillips Celebrated Tourist Car Excursions?"; etc. The answer was, of course, the M&StL.

During the Republican national convention at St. Louis in 1896 the road's advertising leaflet caricatured the five presidential candidates—McKinley, Reed, Davis, Harri-

son, and Allison—all sketched by the inimitable Charles
L. Bartholomew. Beneath likenesses of the nominees,
"Bart" depicted a crowd of people boarding a train. "Po-
liticians are Divided as to the Candidates," said the cap-
tion, "But are Agreed on the M. & St. L. Road."

The through trains with vestibules, gas lights, and "re-
clining chair cars (seats free)" were indeed "modern"
around the turn of the century. Not so the coaches on the
locals. Yet, what they lacked in refinements they made up
in hospitality. Fifty-seven-foot cars, with red plush, low-
back seats, coal stoves at each end, and kerosene lamps giving a dim, flickering light—that was standard equipment.
The "combine"—a half express, half passenger unit—with
its cuspidors, tobacco juice stains, and informal good fel-
lowship throughout, was as much a part of the accommo-
dation train as the tall fluted stacks of the engines.

Happy and carefree were the throngs in the wooden,
open-platform coaches, off for a day at Waterville, Waconia, or Excelsior. The M&StL was handy for the folks in
Minnesota. In many instances it took picnickers and fishermen right to the banks of the lakes. Waterville had a
half-mile spur to Tetonka Lake; Waconia, an extension
to Clearwater Lake; and Excelsior, the popular Tonka
Bay branch, which almost reached the piazza of Lake
Park Hotel and the waters of Minnetonka. One car or
eighteen, it made no difference; the M&StL would take
members of a Sunday School group, a lodge, or a club,
safely, if not swiftly, on a ride which gave everybody a lot
of fun.

When the Rock Island constructed its line to St. Paul
in 1902, the M&StL routed its Chicago trains over the
Illinois Central south of Albert Lea. To celebrate the occasion a new train fittingly called the *North Star Limited*

replaced the then somewhat shabby *Cannon Ball*. But railroad men still referred to Nos. 5 and 6. According to the late A. B. Cutts, who was the road's passenger agent at the time, a contest was conducted and a prize of twenty-five dollars was offered for the best name. Vice President L. F. Day and Cutts selected "North Star Limited" out of approximately a thousand entries. The train split into two sections south of Albert Lea, one going to Chicago, the other over the Iowa Central to Albia, and thence on the Wabash to St. Louis.

The "North Star Limited"

A NEW TRAIN
BETWEEN

St. Paul - Minneapolis

AND

St. Louis

ELECTRIC LIGHTED SLEEPERS AND CHAIR CARS.
DINING CAR SERVICE

ST. PAUL
MINNEAPOLIS
Chaska
Waterville
Waseca
ALBERT LEA
Mason City
Sheffield
Hampton
Marshalltown
Pickering
Grinnell
Oskaloosa
ALBIA
Moulton
Glenwood
Kirksville
Macon
MOBERLY
Mexico
Gilmore
ST. LOUIS

For a quarter of a century the M&StL-Iowa Central-Wabash route from the Twin Cities to St. Louis was well-nigh invincible. It was "the short and direct line," it offered the fastest service, and it was the only line that could boast of dining service. Through trains to Chicago were cut out about the time of the first World War, but the *North Star* to St. Louis continued operating until 1935.

In an era before the widespread use of the automobile,

142

a through-car route would appear without much provocation. For a time the road had Pullmans from the Twin Cities to Aberdeen, South Dakota; to Peoria, Illinois, in conjunction with the Iowa Central; and to Kansas City via Omaha over the Illinois Central and the Missouri Pacific. A through sleeper was even routed to Hot Springs, Arkansas, by way of St. Louis during part of the year. From that city it was shunted to the "Iron Mountain" (now the Missouri Pacific) for the Springs.

But the road's crowning achievement took the form of through tourist-sleepers to California. They had, to quote the advertisements, "carpets in the aisles, upholstered seats, clean linen and blankets for berths, cooking ranges in separate compartments, gentlemanly conductors and careful porters." Such service had long been an institution on the M&StL. By December, 1900, the popular Phillips tour had a car leaving the Twin Cities every Tuesday morning for the West Coast. The route? The M&StL to Fort Dodge, the Illinois Central to Omaha, the Kansas City, St. Joseph & Council Bluffs (now the Burlington) to Kansas City, and the Santa Fe to Los Angeles and San Diego. Three and a half days en route and then sunny California. Or if a traveler preferred the "Scenic Route," he could leave Thursday evening and, barring snow in the Rockies, arrive in Los Angeles the following Tuesday shortly after noontime. The car went over the above-mentioned route to Omaha, where the Rock Island picked it up for Pueblo; the Rio Grande, for Ogden; and finally, the Southern Pacific, for romantic San Francisco and balmy Los Angeles.

The M&StL meant many things to many people. To James F. Waite, who "commuted on the Louie from Excelsior from August 18, 1898, to May 5, 1935" (what a

143

memory that man has!) it stood for local color. He recalled Conductor Alex Campbell, a Sioux Indian; Billy
Watson and his dog up in the cab of engine No. 7; and
the roomy, sixty-passenger suburban coaches that greeted
commuters one memorable morning. Others remember the
era when the road proudly advertised "high-back seats
and electric lights" on its limited trains.

Anyone who rode on the West End shortly after the
turn of the century will remember "Smitty," the news
butcher. No one apparently recalls his full name—it was
just Smitty. Had Smitty been in his prime when the radio appeared, Charlie McCarthy might have had stiff
competition. Smitty was a ventriloquist, clever, resourceful, mischievous. A favorite trick of his was to open the
ventilators to the roof of an old wooden coach and shout,
"Hey, what are you fellows doing up there?" Immediately
all eyes would be focused on the ceiling. Then a retort
would come back: "It's none of your damn business!" The
parrying would continue until the train stopped at a station and Smitty alighted to chase the "free riders" from
the top of the smoker. A cluster of people usually gathered, with everyone peering up to the roof; alas, no one
was there.

The stories about Smitty are legion. Veteran trainmen
still chuckle over an incident involving the late Governor
Theodore Christianson of Minnesota, who was traveling
in the chair car of the *Watertown Express* when Smitty
started an altercation, seemingly between the conductor
and a lady whose child had been left at a station.

"But madam," the conductor said, "we can't stop this
train for your little girl."

"My child, I must get off and get my child!" the lady
cried distractedly.

"I'm sorry, madam," replied the conductor firmly, "we'll stop at the next station and not before."

"I must get off, I..."

With that, Christianson, so the story goes, leaped up and shouted: "Mr. Conductor, you *will* stop this train!"

It took quite a while for Christianson to regain his composure and his temper, when neither the distraught lady nor the conductor could be found.

Sometimes a student brakeman would rush to the lavatory in response to a voice shouting, "Lemme out of here, I'm locked in; lemme out, I say," or a new agent would come running to break up a cat and dog fight which he thought he had heard in the waiting room. Nearby stood Smitty, serious as a parson. So clever was the amateur ventriloquist, he sometimes fooled the older trainmen who thought they knew all his tricks. Nobody liked the newsboy's foul-smelling stogies with bands taken from imported cigars and offered from boxes that once held expensive smokes, but everyone liked Smitty. As Arthur Kingsbury, a former baggageman on Nos. 1 and 2, put it: "Smitty enjoyed life to the full; he was just as much a tradition on the Louie as was Sammy Dunn in the company's ad."

Sammy Dunn and the company ad!

All Minnesota and a good part of the Midwest knew of the "little man" on "The Road that Runs." It was a classic, as popular in the Midwest around 1908 as "Chessie," the Chesapeake & Ohio's kitten, is today in the East. Folks who had traveled with Samuel Dunn when he was a brakeman on the M&StL, and then looked at Charles L. Bartholomew's clever caricature depicting a little man on the run saw the resemblance at once. Actually the resourceful Cutts suggested the idea for the advertisement to "Bart" and the artist carried it out. Since Bartholomew commuted on the train on which Sammy worked, the similarity between "Bart's" man and the brakeman may or may not have been coincidental. For several years that caricature was the informal symbol of the M&StL. Sometimes the little fellow carried a suitcase; on other occasions his arms and legs protruded from a big circle, having "Minneapolis & St. Louis Railroad Co." near its periphery and the "Albert Lea Route" in the center. On calendars, in newspapers, and on timetables the little man of "The Road that Runs" popularized the M&StL passenger serv-

146

ice in a way which was quite unlike that of any other railroad in America.

There was something very human and appealing about the St. Louis Road; a warmth and friendliness which pervaded its operation. Most of the division points and many of the terminals had lunch counters, where everyone from the engineer to Aunt Mary stepped off the local for a cup of strong coffee, a sandwich, and a generous cut of pie. Albia, Oskaloosa, Marshalltown, Albert Lea, Waterville, Fort Dodge, Winthrop, Morton, Conde, and Aberdeen were, and some still are, depots where passengers could "pick up a bite" between trains or during a lunch stop. No matter what train one took on the Louie, one could bank on the funny little mark or a suggestive "e" on the timecard. On close inspection one found that it stood for meals or, as the youngsters said, "eats." M&StL trains have been known to pass up coal and water, but to skip a lunchstop—never!

Sometimes when it was time to eat, a train pulled into a town which had no restaurant in the station. Such was the case of No. 2, *The St. Louis & Kansas City Mail,* on its arrival at Grinnell, Iowa. There was an "e" on the timetable, however, and long before that college town was reached a brakeman would come through the cars very solicitously inquiring how many wanted supper. Then, upon ascertaining the number, he would wire ahead to the station agent, who thereupon contacted Hotel Monroe on the west side of the tracks. When No. 2 pulled into Grinnell, the passengers walked across the street to the inn and to a hot meal. The brakeman, for his bit of salesmanship, was given dinner on the house.

But, it may be asked, suppose there were no hotel or

restaurant near the railroad? This contingency, too, was provided for at such stops as Livermore and Hampton, Iowa, and St. James, Minnesota. Trainmen merely wired ahead, and when the coaches came to a grinding halt at the respective communities, there would be a townsman with plate dinners, all prepared and packed in market baskets. The meal might consist of roast beef, pork, or fried country chicken, vegetables, a salad, rolls, and hot bottled coffee. Price: fifty cents.

The first World War, however, brought changes, and the late Henry Ford still more. During the fiscal year of 1915 the Minneapolis and St. Louis Railroad carried a little over two and a half million passengers. After that date improved roads and Model T's made an alarming dent in the road's coach and Pullman traffic. Then came the concrete highway, the six-cylindered automobile, and the motor bus. Passenger revenue melted like a snowbank under a hot sun. The era of short-haul passenger traffic was ending; the day of heavy time-freights on express-train schedules had begun.

Hawley Interests Planning Through "To Gulf" Road.
Minneapolis *Tribune,* November 19, 1911.

12

The Clover Leaf and the Alton

While the colorful expansion to the West was taking place there were even stranger things developing in the East. The news of reaching the Missouri River in 1907 made headlines but not nearly so many as Hawley's other plans did a few years later. Although 1908 went by quietly enough, the following year marked the issuance of the First and Refunding 4 per cent Bonds to take care of matured notes on the so-called Iowa Extension from Albert Lea to Fort Dodge. To be sure, traffic was interrupted by the switchmen's strike in the Twin Cities, which lasted from December 1, 1909, to April 12, 1910. But things went along smoothly, as a whole, until the latter part of 1910, and then...

Imagine, if you will, a local passenger picking up an M&StL timetable during that period and in a perfunctory manner turning to the map. By this time he was accustomed to the extension almost straight west to LeBeau, and the curved route of the Iowa Central on the south and east to Peoria. But what's this? Perhaps he would blink his eyes and try to remember what happened last night, for, sure enough, they had the Louie going to Kansas City, St. Louis, Chicago, and Toledo. There was no mistake about it, the thick lines with countless town names were of uniform size all the way from the Missouri

River to Lake Erie. Upon closer inspection he'd read the inscription: MAP OF THE TOLEDO, ST. LOUIS & WESTERN; CHICAGO & ALTON; MINNEAPOLIS & ST. LOUIS; IOWA CENTRAL AND CONNECTIONS. Confusing? Indeed it was, both to the patrons and the employees.

Investors in the road also received a jolt when they looked over the annual report for the year ending June 30, 1910. Hawley had been elevated to the chairmanship of the board and T. P. Shonts had come in as president. Three new names appeared as vice presidents: George H. Ross, W. L. Ross, and C. H. Ackert, all of Chicago. The Rosses were strangers to the Louie, but many recalled Ackert as having been general manager of the Iowa Central in the last century. The comptroller, E. S. Benson, likewise made his headquarters in the Windy City. With the exception of S. G. Lutz, the key traffic men were newcomers, and all, including Lutz, conducted their business at the foot of Lake Michigan. The M&StL was run from New York, where Hawley and Shonts made their headquarters; from Chicago, where most of the other ranking executives held office; and from Bloomington, Illinois, where P. Maher, superintendent of motive power, held sway.

To the man on the street the four-company system looked like a hodge-podge of lines running every which way, having little organization or pattern. The Toledo, St. Louis & Western, familiarly known as the Clover Leaf, cut a diagonal route across Ohio, Indiana, and Illinois from Toledo to St. Louis. The Alton, likewise, ran cater-cornered from Chicago to St. Louis, with an additional line westward to Kansas City. But, it may be asked, where was the tie-in with the Iowa Central or the M&StL? The answer was, by an indirect *north-and-south* branch of the Alton to Peoria.

This unification of control was an attempt to tighten the rather loosely-knit lines of the four Hawley companies. It was never an outright consolidation—only a centralization of authority and a merging of traffic representatives. To the M&StL it meant sending reams of paper-work to the general office at Chicago.

The titular head of the "merged" roads was, as we have seen, Theodore Perry Shonts, an executive well known to the public. He came into the limelight when Theodore Roosevelt appointed him chairman of the second Isthmian Canal Commission in 1905. Teddy Roosevelt, after considerable search for his "hundred-thousand-dollar-man" to be czar of the huge Panama undertaking, selected Shonts. Prior to his isthmian appointment, T. P. Shonts headed the Toledo, St. Louis & Western. The rail president stayed with the canal until 1907, when he resigned to become chief executive of the Interborough Rapid Transit and there to untangle New York's chaotic electric railway situation.

Shonts, being a "Hawley man," was familiar with the M&StL and even more so with the Iowa Central. When he was a boy his parents had moved from Pennsylvania to Appanoose County, Iowa, and his early railroad experience had begun in that state. Shortly after graduating from Monmouth College (Illinois) he became interested in railroads and was subsequently employed by the Iowa Construction Company to build one hundred miles of line within ninety days. The job was completed on time despite fifty-one days of rain, and the roadway was taken over by the Central Iowa Railway, predecessor company of the Iowa Central.

153

The period in which Shonts headed the M&StL and the other three roads marked the peak of Edwin Hawley's vast railroad interests. Hardly a week went by without some mention of mergers, traffic agreements, or proposed extensions to properties controlled by the House of Hawley. Just as authors since the days of Washington Irving have been wanting to write the Great American Novel, so railroad tycoons have tried to control a coast-to-coast line within the United States. The Great American Railroad has perhaps come much nearer to fruition than the Great American Novel. Hill and Harriman began the task, George Gould tried and almost succeeded, and the brothers Van Sweringen came within an ace of reaching the goal. Edwin Hawley tried, too; and if death had not overtaken him, he might have reached his objective.

It has been said that Hawley intended to extend the M&StL westward, with visions of reaching the Pacific. Nothing can be found in writing, however, to prove or disprove this conjecture. In regard to Hawley's later plan to control a southwestern route to the Pacific, there is tangible evidence. Immediately there come to mind the coastal ports of Los Angeles and San Diego. Edwin Hawley could not very easily gain entry to these harbors, for they were already pre-empted by well-established "transcontinental" lines. He would settle for an almost unheard-of port called Topolobampo on the Mexican coast.

Of all the strange dreams for a transcontinental route this, perhaps, was the strangest. It called for a company with a far-reaching name, every bit as intriguing as that of its proposed western terminous. They called it the Kansas City, Mexico & Orient. Hawley was captivated by its possibilities and so was Shonts. The outcome was that they both bought into "the Orient" and were soon made directors.

"I have designed a railroad 1,600 miles long," said Arthur E. Stillwell, the originator, builder, and president of the Orient, in his *Saturday Evening Post* article of February 4, 1928, "which will bring the Pacific Ocean 400 miles nearer to Kansas City than any other present route. Not only that," averred Stillwell, who relied on hunches in planning all his major moves, "but it will be 1,600 miles nearer to Central and South America than San Francisco."

The Orient was to run from Kansas City to Topolobampo, and at the time Hawley was elected to the board, it had only about seven hundred miles to be completed. The road was, of course, only a link in the chain of his cross-country dream. With the Hawley-controlled properties, like the Chicago & Alton and the Chesapeake & Ohio, which he had also acquired, Edwin Hawley would have a system extending from ocean to ocean.

Meanwhile, the M&StL had plans for widespread extensions; and Newman Erb, who succeeded Shonts as president in 1911, predicted early construction of a line from Albia to St. Louis. The newspapers of that day were filled with rumors, statements from Erb, and editorial prognostications as to what the Minneapolis and St. Louis intended to do in the near future. Erb and the papers liked to elaborate on the Louie running from Canada to St. Louis and at the latter point making connections over the Hawley-controlled Missouri-Kansas-Texas to Galveston on the Gulf. When the press learned of Hawley's election to the board of the Kansas City, Mexico & Orient and later received the statements of Newman Erb as to the M&StL-Iowa Central expansion program, its imagination went wild. Would the M&StL become part of a vast network in the Hawley dynasty of railroads, an empire spanning America from the Gulf of Mexico to Canada and from the shores of the Atlantic to the calm waters of the Pacific?

Unfortunately, or perhaps fortunately, all of the grandiose extensions never materialized. Indeed, the "consolidated" M&StL-Iowa Central-Clover Leaf-Alton system soon broke up into separate units, independently managed and operated. The Minneapolis and St. Louis-Iowa Central combination was both logical and practical. Of all the talk and planning, it alone survived and emerged into a *bona-fide* consolidation. First the M&StL leased the Iowa Central as a brief prelude to direct ownership. On January 1, 1912, the Louie purchased the Hawkeye road, lock, stock, and barrel. One month later Edwin Hawley died.

Mr. Erb was best known as a dealer in railroads.
           Railway Age, March 28, 1925.

13

Retrenchment and Reorganization

When Hawley died, the Minneapolis and St. Louis was at sixes and sevens. Whatever else may be said about the Hawley regime, it was generally conceded that there was solidarity and unity during most of his administration. The Alton and Clover Leaf episode, during the brief Shonts administration, did not bespeak so well of Hawley's later years; but, generally considered, the Hawley and L F. Day overlordship was one of accord and stability.

Newman Erb, the new president who followed Shonts, inherited his predecessor's enthusiasm for expansion—with a few ideas of his own. It took quite a while for the new chief to realize that he could not readily get money and backing to push the M&StL up to Canada on the one hand and down to St. Louis on the other. Westward the picture was very bleak. In 1912, when Erb was managing the road, there was an almost complete crop failure in South Dakota and a greatly curtailed farm output in western Minnesota and northwestern Iowa. The time for retrenchment was very much in season.

The year 1912 emphasized the need to build up certain underdeveloped services of the road to balance overexpansion. Many expected to see the road revitalized by westward construction; and in so doing, they overlooked the definite advantages at hand, principally the Peoria Gateway. Hitherto, the Oskaloosa-Peoria line had been little more than a branch of the Iowa Central, which was operated in close conjunction with the M&StL shortly after the turn of the century. Its strategic importance was realized but never very adequately exploited. The traffic through that gateway was to become a nest-egg in periods of depression—and a kind of bonus during prosperous times.

In contrast, the lines to the West were a great disappointment. They represented unfulfilled hopes and dreams, cut short by dearth of funds and pre-emption of areas by other railroads. Perhaps some day the picture would change. Meanwhile, there were bills to be paid and interest to be met. It was idle to talk of fanciful plans embodying hundreds of miles of track until the property was in a sound financial condition.

With this in mind, the directors authorized the Oskaloosa-Peoria line to be gravel ballasted and its light, worn-out steel to be replaced by 85-pound rails. To lessen the difficulties caused by the grade at Kickapoo hill, immediately west of Peoria, a terminal was created at Maxwell, near the summit. An enginehouse was built at this new location, and a $15,000 pumping plant provided on Kickapoo Creek to force water up to the crest of the hill. Road-engine runs then terminated at Maxwell, and cuts of cars were taken down into Peoria by switchers.

A dozen Consolidation-type locomotives were purchased to expedite freight movement, and an effort was made to secure a greater diversity of tonnage. The M&StL was a "granger" road, largely dependent on crops; and it suffered from seasonal business fluctuations associated with agricultural products. The $667,041 deficit for the fiscal year of 1911-1912 drove home the urgent necessity of having variegated tonnage, likewise the need for bridge traffic in conjunction with connecting carriers. Times were good in the last year of Taft's administration in the White House. If the road could not make money in prosperous days, it stood little chance of making both ends meet in times of recession. Already the fixed charges were piling up at an appalling rate.

Newman Erb was a bundle of energy, flitting hither and yon to oversee the various properties he headed. Minneapolitans remember him as a slightly stooped executive, carrying a cane and always hurrying from one appointment to another. Being president of the Ann Arbor, chairman of the executive committee of the Pere Marquette, and head of the Denver & Salt Lake, he was constantly on the go.

Erb started his railroad career as attorney for the Kansas City, Fort Scott & Gulf (now part of the Frisco), and he subsequently held executive positions, varying from general manager to president and receiver, for several short lines and traction companies. For a time he headed the Wisconsin Central and was instrumental in selling that property to the Soo.

If the Twin Cities did not become well acquainted with President Erb, they did with his chief of staff, William G. Bierd. As vice president and general manager, Bierd had much to do with the stewardship of the M&StL. He was a likeable, unassuming person, having a southern drawl stemming back to his boyhood in Baltimore, Maryland. Although he started railroading as a bridge-crew laborer for the North Western, his training was country wide. From yardmaster on the Union Pacific to trainmaster on the Norfolk & Western, from operating positions on the compact Lehigh Valley to the sprawled-out Rock Island, and from managerial duties down on the Panama Railroad to superintendency up on the New Haven, Bierd indeed was a man of parts.

On the M&StL he was known as "Baraboo" Bill, for he loved to dwell on his experiences in train service on the North Western out of the Wisconsin community of Baraboo. Like many other good men, he enjoyed talking and was given to making lengthy reports. Once, to an important meeting which he could not attend, Bierd sent a long report, which he intended to be read. A presiding officer at the meeting looked over the sheaves of paper and then inquired who had written the epistle. "Mr. Bierd," was the reply. "Then just read the first and last paragraphs," was the blunt decision. Bierd had a way of putting all of the essential material at the beginning and end of his reports.

Bill Bierd, however, only remained on the M&StL for about four years, when he was called to head the Alton. When the popular executive bade the employees goodbye, he commended their fine spirit, adding in effect that "when a family is poor they all stick together." Whatever compensations poverty has, the employees did stick together with commendable fortitude. The Louie was, indeed, hard up. All during the Erb regime the road was constantly borrowing money on short-term notes to meet the heavy fixed charges.

From the traffic standpoint, however, the road was making a better showing. In the year which ended June 30, 1915, passenger traffic swelled to 2,574,797 riders, the greatest the company ever had. The next year gross revenue and freight tonnage reached all-time highs. On August 9, 1915, the M&StL purchased the Des Moines and Fort

Dodge Railroad, which had hitherto been leased, thereby creating a short, direct route from Minneapolis to the capital of Iowa. That road also had a line from Tara to Ruthven, with trackage rights over the Milwaukee to Spencer.

In spite of the increasing traffic, the road was in dire need of cash to take care of its obligations in connection with the South Dakota lines west of Watertown. Newman Erb and his associates finally evolved a plan to consolidate the thirty-six-mile Iowa Central and Western, extending from Belmond to Algona, with the M&StL. The short line, incorporated October 29, 1898, was formerly leased to the Louie. To effect the consolidation, the M&StL retired $23,811,000 of common and preferred stocks and issued $25,792,600 worth of shares in its place. Of these new securities, $9,000 of capital stock was issued in exchange for Iowa Central and Western, and $25,783,600 in exchange for Minneapolis and St. Louis Railroad (of Minnesota and Iowa), the old company. Stockholders were in effect assessed $20 a share, thereby bringing in $4,500,000 of much-needed capital. Apart from changing the "and" in the company's name to the ampersand and acquiring thirty-six miles of additional line, the M&StL remained unchanged.

To succeed Bierd, C. W. Huntington was brought from the Jersey Central in an effort to rehabilitate the Louie. Previous to his eastern appointment, Huntington had been general superintendent of the Iowa Central; and he knew the meaning of economy. During this period, the M&StL moved from the historic Metropolitan Life to the Transportation Building, across the street. For over two decades the general offices were to remain in the more modern structure.

Huntington soon moved to greener pastures and late in 1916 was appointed chairman of the board of the Virginian, a wealthy coal road. Newman Erb also resigned the same year and was succeeded by Edward L. Brown, formerly vice president of the Denver & Rio Grande. Brown's tenure was slightly over four months, for he was obliged to retire on account of ill health. Notwithstanding the constant changing of executives, the financial picture improved. The war in Europe and a fair yield of crops helped the nation's economy and stimulated buying. The M&StL, which was chronically short of rolling stock, put into service 1,000 box cars and 500 gondolas during 1917. The hire of equipment, which accounted for an outgo of $392,683 in 1915, was turned to a credit balance of $7,409 two years later. By 1916 a score of superheated Mikado-type locomotives had appeared on the company's roster.

The M&StL had constant changes in its executive staff, but the turnover out on the line was far greater. Boomers, many of whom were good for only a couple of pay checks, swarmed over the line. There was a ditty to the effect that:

> When I was young and in my prime,
> I worked for the I C Line.
> Now that I'm old and shot to hell,
> I have to work on the M&StL!

The road, like some of the employees who worked on it, had seen better days. On the other hand, the loyalty of some of the men was remarkable. Many had grown up on the Louie, and had stuck with it. To a majority of railroaders, the M&StL was regarded as a family road. It was too large to be called small and too small to be called large. There was a great deal of personal contact between

164

the employees and their bosses, and many of the officials called the men by their first names.

The history of the M&StL is filled with stories of rank and file workers doing good jobs even in the humblest capacities. Take, as an illustration, the scarcely known incident of how Tony, a little Italian roundhouse helper, saved the day at Marshalltown.

The year was 1916; the occasion the opening of a 90-foot through-plate-girder turntable at Marshalltown. "The first operation of this table was regarded locally as analogous to the launching of a new ship," reflects Hugh McCarthy, a trainmaster at that time. The day of the "launching" the men were rounding up their work on the turntable, hoping to be finished by 11:00, the time the officials were to appear. Everything was to be in perfect condition for those who had authorized such a princely expenditure. Included in the inspection party were to be the president, the general counsel, and the chief engineer. At about 9:00 a. m. the bridge and building crew put the table on its base and breathed a sigh of relief. Then, alas, it was discovered the table would not move. There were four projecting steel flanges on the side girders about three feet long and a half-inch thick which rubbed against the retaining walls. The workmen looked at each another with a "my god" expression. The "B and B" foreman was almost hysterical. He shouted for men and chisels and began to enlarge the diameter of the circle by chipping away at the wall. That would have taken days!

About that time Tony came along and, sensing that something was amiss, inquired as to the nature of the trouble. When the workers pointed to the projecting flanges, he just stood there a moment, watching sympathetically. Soon, however, his face lit up and he blurted out: "Tell ya what ta do, get a da torch and burna da damn thing off!" "Oh boy," commented McCarthy in recalling the incident. "How that lifted the morale of the group!" In twenty minutes the blue acetylene gas flame was making molten metal of the offending projections.

Soon the turntable, with a locomotive aboard, was functioning perfectly. When the officials arrived, everything was in order, although the table was discreetly angled to hide the chisel marks. Superintendent J. P. Houston took Tony aside and secretly handed him a five dollar bill. At that time the cutting torch was new at Marshalltown. The shop men were familiar with it, while the bridge and building crews were not. But Tony "learn't" them in a way they would not easily forget.

The ingenuity of the old-time railroader is legend. Around the same time the new turntable was installed, the road's fast freight, No. 95, was derailed at Mason City Junction. The big Mikado pulling the train jumped the rails at a switch and remained upright. It was not a bad accident, just enough to tie things up until the wrecking crew came from Marshalltown. Frank "Windy" Snyder was the conductor—a man who had worked on the section gang as well as in train and engine service. Windy sized up the mishap and then snapped out a string of orders.

He called the train crew, the section and the yard men. He called for claw bars, lining bars, and spike mauls. Then, while the "big hook" was on the way Windy built a "shoo-fly" around the derailment, thereby keeping the line open. By extending a side track beyond the crippled engine and connecting it with the main line, he by-passed the accident. Hours later the locomotive was rerailed, but

166

the important thing—keeping the trains moving—had been uppermost in Windy's mind. With Windy, first things came first.

Windy Snyder had a keen mind; and with his wide range of experience in train, track and yard work, was conscious of his more-than-ordinary ability. Moreover, he hated delays, whatever the cause. Once a trainmaster flagged down his time freight for a reason Windy thought quite unnecessary. Finally, after getting underway again, he clenched his fist and shouted back to his superior, "If you weren't you, I'd turn you in!'

Probably the most talked-of incident during the Erb administration, as far as trainmen were concerned, had to do with the strange disappearance of a race horse from an Iowa Central box car. Not long before this chapter was written, February, 1949, newspapers were filled with stories about "Grady," a cow in Yukon, Oklahoma, which jumped through a silo opening 17 by 25 inches. But Grady's escapade had nothing on a horse's trick of escaping through an end-door of an Iowa Central car back in 1913. The story runs as follows:

An Albert Lea to Fort Dodge stock pickup, known as "the Bull Run," was rolling along in the late dusk between Albert Lea and the Iowa state line. A short way south of where the Rock Island bridges the M&StL, are a series of knolls. While the train was steaming through this hilly countryside, the "air" was suddenly applied, and the freight ground to an unscheduled stop. Upon learning that no emergency application of brakes had been made by the engineer, the crewmen went back over the train to find out what was wrong. Presently, they came to a coupling between an Iowa Central box car and a low-sided gondola filled with coal. They were surprised to find the angle

167

cock on the air hose turned and no one anywhere near the train. When they looked through the end-door of the box car, the race horse was not inside. Both Conductor Ed Carter and Brakeman Billy Rabens maintained that the animal was in the car at Albert Lea. They had seen its nose sticking out of the end-door. Moreover, the seals on the side doors were intact.

Upon closer inspection, horsehairs were seen lining the end-door and blood on the coal in the gondola opposite the box car. The two cars were sidetracked, and at the first available telegraph office the trainmen relayed their fantastic story. The crew finally concluded that when the slack ran together in one of the dips the horse was pitched out of the small end-door. Apparently, the animal, in its hasty exit, had kicked the angle cock, thereby stopping the train. To expect headquarters to believe this incredible tale was even more fantastic. One thing they could expect—and that was an investigation in which everyone concerned would be called on the carpet. In this they were not disappointed.

Meanwhile, another incident occurred which seemed to prove that the animal had escaped on its own. A horse was reported killed by No. 3, the *Capital Limited,* at about 3:45 a. m. that same night near the spot where the emergency stop had taken place. But this did not exonerate the crew from having "taken part" in letting the valuable animal escape.

The investigation was a spirited affair, according to A. T. "Bat" Nelson, a former trainmaster, who aided in the cross-examination, and Billy Rabens, one of the crewmen. Superintendents, claim agents, railroad detectives, and lawyers took part in the inquiry. A Simplex angle cock was brought into the hearing. It seemed preposterous then, as it does today, that a horse could have been thrown through such a narrow opening. (The *Equipment Register* for July, 1913, gives the largest end-door of Iowa Central box cars as being 2 feet by 2 feet 7 inches.) All the testimony presented, however, confirmed the crew's assertion that the animal had escaped in the manner indicated and that it had been killed by No. 3.

Unfortunately, the legal record of the case went up in flames during the Western Avenue (Minneapolis) roundhouse fire of 1929. All the essential data of the incident have been corroborated by men who participated in the investigation. Rabens puts the date of the accident at approximately June, 1913, "Because it was just after I was taken off the local freight and promoted to the highball job."

Here, then, are some highlights in the history of the M&StL up to the time America entered the first World War. The Albert Lea Route, as the road was called, played an invaluable role in the movement of passengers as well as of war freight. Albert Lea symbolized a busy terminal, through which limiteds and locals funnelled many a traveler to widely scattered midwestern destinations. It brings back memories of the "drummer," as the salesman in the pre-automobile era was called. It recalls to mind the days when the drummers had their own house organ, called *The Crescent and Grip; A Journal for Commercial Travelers,* published in St. Paul. That publication tried to help the traveling man secure better train service and adequate hotel accommodations. To be sure, the M&StL carried advertisements in its pages, for the "commercial" passenger represented a tidy sum at any ticket counter. Drummers even rode the mixed trains and depended on the engineer to give two blasts of the whistle ten minutes before the switching of cars was completed. In a more leisurely era salesmen liked the mixed run, because it gave them an opportunity to "work" a town and then take the same train to the next community.

In following chapters it will be seen how during World War I the Albert Lea Route gave way to the Peoria Gateway Line. Freight and the gateway of Peoria! They were destined to loom large in the M&StL of the future. The first world struggle was to give the road a new slogan and a new role.

*The President of the United States has aptly said
that there should be more business in government and less government in business and of all
lines of business there is none in which the hand
of government is felt more than in railroad
management and operation.*

William H. Bremner in the *Annual Report* for 1921.

14

Bremner Takes Hold

William Hepburn Bremner came to head the M&StL the month America entered the first World War. For seventeen years he was to guide the destiny of the road, with varying titles including those of president, federal manager, and receiver. From the traffic peaks in the hectic war years to the nation's worst depression, Billy Bremner's lot was not a happy one. Probably no industry suffers more severely than the railroads when times are bad, and few industries pick up faster when business is good. Bremner had the misfortune of heading the company during a few brief years of prosperity but also during a long era of adverse conditions due to drought and depression.

While the M&StL served practically no defense industries, it, in common with most of the nation's railroads, was stimulated by the war boom. The conflict also brought the Peoria Gateway to the fore as a means of lessening delays incident to the over-crowded yards in Chicago. Frank B. Townsend, the road's traffic manager, foresaw that the future of the company was in freight and that the value of the M&StL as a bridge line could hardly be overestimated. He coined the phrase "The Peoria Gateway Line" to replace "The Albert Lea Route" as the road's slogan. The new name soon won favor, and it became permanent.

When the Government took over the roads on December 28, 1917, William G. McAdoo was appointed director general of railroads. On tickets, timetables, and stationery, United States Railroad Administration appeared with Mc-Adoo's name more prominently in the public's eye than that of Woodrow Wilson. As Arthur Guiterman put it:

> His name appears on Scrip and Tissue,
> On bonds of each succeeding issue,
> On coupons bright and posters rare,
> And every Pullman Bill of Fare.

The M&StL came within the area of which R. H. Aishton, formerly head of the Chicago & North Western, was regional director. Bremner was made federal manager of the road on July 1, 1918; and having a government office, he was obliged to resign from the presidency. Townsend left the road to go with Aishton's staff of the USRA in Chicago. Much of the road's personality was lost under the Government's stewardship. In the larger cities all of the downtown ticket offices were consolidated under one roof.

The most memorable happening just before America entered the war, however, was an act of God and not of man. It was a Dakota blizzard that bottled things up for the best part of a month. When storms whip across the bleak, frozen plains, the folk out Dakota way do just what New Englanders did in Whittier's *Snowbound*. They sit by the hearth, play games, read, and relax. Not so the railroads.

On the morning of January 28, 1917, snow was in the

174

air, and by nightfall the storm had developed into the start of a three-day blizzard. For some forty-eight hours not one M&StL train ran west of Minneapolis. Two days after the storm had subsided a wedge plow from Cedar Lake opened the line to Watertown, South Dakota. Beyond the latter point, however, the battle had just begun.

The first equipment to start west from Watertown consisted of a wedge plow, pushed by a powerful Consolidation. About twenty miles out the plow stripped its wings, bucking the drifts in a deep cut. The crew, under the guidance of Assistant Superintendent Robert E. Ryan, managed to get the train back to Florence, the nearest town, where they tied up for the evening. Another blizzard came up during the night, and on the following day the wind-tossed snow was so blinding one could not see the towering grain elevator from the station platform a few feet away. Indeed, the fires in the engines had to be drawn, because it was impossible for the men to remain outside to shovel snow from the drifts into the tender of the locomotive for water. When the wind let up a day or so later, Ryan walked to Watertown to begin the fight anew.

While Ryan and his men were tackling the snow westward, Roadmaster Jim Murphy started out of Conde to open the line east to Watertown with two small Moguls and a wedge plow. But the high drifts at Crocker, less than twenty miles from Conde, proved to be his undoing. In hitting the tightly packed snow, the plow broke in two, derailing both engines. Every inch a railroader, Murphy had the "B and B" men bring jacks and blocks from Conde on a farm wagon with runners. After several days he and his men had the engines on the rails and the plow-car clear of the main track. If Murphy could not open the line, he at least worked hard to prevent blocking it!

It was not until February 7, that Ryan could again leave Watertown, to renew the struggle with a rotary commandeered from the New Ulm-Estherville line. That evening he reached Wallace, the next station beyond Florence. Drifts had piled up 18 and 20 feet high. It took a week to cover the next eight miles to Bradley, and another week to get through the snow a similar distance to Crocker. Between Wallace and Crocker, twenty boxes of dynamite a day were used to blast the snow and ice and dirt which had packed in the drifts above the rails like concrete. Again the plow broke down and had to be replaced by another rotary, borrowed from the Great Northern. Up to this time the men had worked day and night to open this difficult part of the line. Beyond Crocker the cuts were not so deep, and more rapid progress was made. On the last day of February the train plowed its way into Conde. Fifty-seven miles of line opened in three weeks, with 115 miles to go before reaching LeBeau. And still things went amiss.

After several days of fighting the snow west of Conde, they expected to take water at Chelsea. Events turned out differently, for the section foreman had emptied the tank. The late arrival meant a grueling night of shoveling snow into the tender. At Hoven the borrowed rotary broke down, and there was a delay while the men waited for another plow to arrive from Cedar Lake. On March 7, after a weary month of snow fighting, the engines finally panted into LeBeau.

A Dakota blizzard was—and is—something to reckon with. To this day one can see rails excoriated by drivers slipping as the locomotives buck the drifts and then back up for new onslaughts. Snow has since blocked the West End many times, but no winter has ever equaled the one just before Uncle Sam entered World War I.

As Yankees poured into France and Germany more men were drafted and the Des Moines line became of greater importance. This route served Perry, Iowa, where trainloads of coaches and many cars of freight went over the Inter-Urban Railway to Camp Dodge, eighteen miles distant. During the first year of the war, coal traffic showed a large increase. Building materials, on the contrary, slumped, due to the Government's restriction of open cars for only those products most essential to the war effort. Grain later provided a substantial amount of tonnage, as market conditions became more favorable. Passenger revenues likewise stood up well, on account of troop movements and higher fares. All in all, however, the war-time picture was not as rosy as it seemed.

Charles Hayden, chairman of the board, who took the place of Bremner in the corporate organization, lamented the extravagance of the Railroad Administration. He stated that the M&StL had been allocated 300 box cars during Federal control at an average price of $2,919; whereas, two years previously the road had purchased similar rolling stock costing only $947.61 apiece.

Another bone of contention was the "standard compensation" during the period of Government operation and six months thereafter. Uncle Sam had arrived at one figure and the railroad at another. The roads were returned to their owners on March 1, 1920. The matter of remuneration was not settled on the M&StL, however, until several years thereafter. The Transportation Act of

177

1920 provided that the compensation should be equivalent to the average net railway operating income of the road in question during the three years ending June 30, 1917.

The Government's figure for the M&StL and the Railway Transfer was $2,745,005, but the road contended it did not take into consideration some $2,000,000 for 1,500 freight cars put into service just after the test period. Nor did it allow for $4,500,000 provided under the readjustment plan of January 31, 1916, in which stockholders contributed $20 a share on their stock. Again, the road pointed out, the Director General did not provide funds for necessary additions and improvements. Finally, the Government agreed to pay an additional sum of $67,000, which the road accepted.

During the period of Federal control the task of protecting the M&StL interests fell heavily on the shoulders of L. C. Fritch, corporate vice president and William C. Knoble, corporate auditor. Fritch also held a similar position on the Rock Island, and he later severed his connection with the M&StL. Knoble, on the other hand, remained with the Louie and subsequently became its treasurer. At this writing he is the oldest employee in years of service in the higher official brackets, having rounded out nearly a half century of service "all on the Saint L."

After World War I, William Bremner returned to the presidency and piloted the company's course for the remainder of his life. Born in Marshalltown, October 24, 1869, he was graduated from the state university at Iowa City with an engineering degree, and later received an LL. B. His first rail job was that of baggage clerk for the Central Iowa in 1886. Before turning to law for a livelihood, he worked with an engineering party on the Burlington, locating parts of the road. Later he hung up his shingle in Des Moines and in a comparatively short time was elected city solicitor. Bremner came to the M&StL as general attorney in 1909, and rose to general counsel prior to becoming president.

Frank Townsend, whose uncanny memory enabled him to cite rate cases the way a station agent calls trains, came back to the Louie as vice president of traffic. Other veteran M&StL men holding key positions were genial Dexter (Deck) M. Denison, freight traffic manager, and resourceful A. B. Cutts, passenger traffic manager. One of the few newcomers was Elliott E. Nash, who had come from the Chicago & North Western to be the general manager. He was later to be remembered for his "Booster Clubs," which flourished in the twenties and brought the officials and men together on many enjoyable picnics.

The post-war years for the M&StL were trying, and the financial condition of the road was precarious. The drubbing that the rolling stock and track took in the Federal control period meant millions would have to be spent to put the road in first class condition. Meanwhile, prices soared and wages kept going up, as inflation swept the nation. Although freight rates increased and interstate coach rates jumped from 2 to 3.6 cents a mile, revenue declined. Crop failures were frequent. The truck and the private automobile and later the motor bus made deep inroads into the railroad's business.

The shopmen's strike, which began on July 1, 1922, was long and drawn out, seriously impairing the motive power. The company's position in the labor dispute is summed up in the annual report of that year:

179

Your shop employes went out on this strike not because of any grievance which they had against this railroad but in common with the mechanical forces of the other roads, as a protest against an order of the United States Railroad Labor Board reducing their rates of pay. The strike, therefore, should properly be considered as against the United States Government inasmuch as the Labor Board was established by Congress for the purpose of settling disputes between railroads and their employes with respect to rates of pay and rules of working conditions. In view of the character of the strike it was felt by your Management that it would not be proper to make any settlement which ignored or modified in any degree the order of the Labor Board, although for some considerable time after the strike started the Management was ready and willing to take back practically all of the striking employes, provided they would return to work at the rates of pay fixed by the Labor Board. This the men refused to do...

The road advertised for men at the current wage of 75 cents an hour for machinists, boilermaker inspectors, and welders, 70 cents for blacksmiths, boilermakers, and passenger carmen. Freight carmen received 63 cents an hour, and all classes of helpers, 47 cents. There was practically no violence or destruction of property, but traffic was considerably slowed down on account of inexperienced shop help. The strike finally died out, with the wage scale unaltered.

The deficit, which was $1,836,222 in 1921, remained a little over the million mark the following year. Clearly the road could not go on at that rate. The ax fell on July 26, 1923, when the company was plunged into receivership. William H. Bremner was appointed receiver by the court, and in that new capacity he continued to head the road. The company kept plugging along, laying new rail whenever the slender finances permitted, and patching up equipment and soliciting traffic. Bremner's cheery smile brought confidence, and Nash's flair for organizing the Booster Clubs and forming some really good ballteams helped the employees morale. For all its poverty, the M&StL had a fine spirit and a will to serve. Plans to reorganize the road were bruited about, but the stock market crash of October, 1929, brought on a new round of troubles.

During Bremner's receivership, costs were cut whenever possible and branch lines that had outlived their usefulness were torn up. The first abandonment, as already mentioned, occurred when the Akaska-LeBeau line was scrapped in 1924. Two years afterward the little-used Van Cleve-State Center portion of the branch that veered off the main line at Newburg, Iowa, met a similar fate. In the latter part of 1929 a couple of Electro-Motive gas-electric units left the St. Louis Car Company's plant for service on the M&StL. The two units, named *Peoria* and *New Ulm*, with facilities for handling passengers, baggage, and mail, were the forerunners of a fleet of eleven motor cars. Steam trains, the company found, were costing 68 cents a mile to operate. The self-propelled units were to cut the outlay to 40 cents.

Whether the road purchased a locomotive or built a tool house, the matter was duly recorded in the ponderous receivership records. Starting out with "Comes now W. H. Bremner," the records indicate how all moneys were spent, since every expenditure had to be approved by the court. The entire receivership papers fill twenty-four volumes, of which fourteen concern Bremner. In painstaking detail they show the troubles that beset the road.

The financial plight of the company was mirrored in the physical condition of its rolling stock and track. Out along the line, particularly in Iowa, folks had a bountiful supply of M&StL jokes, patterned after the old Ford anecdotes. Townsmen jested about its service and equipment. But let an outsider poke fun at the road and the natives would immediately take umbrage. They regarded the outlander as not of their kind, with the intimation, perhaps, that he drank too much or chased after women. Despite its faults and shortcomings, the rural people quite generally liked the Emmy, or the Louie, or the St. Louis (each section on the sprawled-out system had its own localism) and treated it like a respected, if impecunious, friend. The folk who often had the most yarns about the road were frequently the first to rally to its defense in times of trouble.

Even the employees polished up some of the old stories and embellished the anecdotes with gusto. For years the Monmouth freight office had a copy of the late Stewart Brown's long "poem" on the wall. The homely stanzas of the elderly gentleman who lived in London Mills, on the eastern division of the road, are part of the warp and woof of Illinois folklore. The verse, as trainmen recall it, starts something like this:

> The M&StL is a bum old road
> With an unpaid debt of long ago.

In warming up to his subject, Brown depicted the track as being held together by tenpenny nails. The philosophic

LUCIAN CHARLES SPRAGUE — Under Mr. Sprague's stewardship (1935-   ) the M&StL was transformed from a weak, poorly-equipped and unprofitable railroad into a modern, highly-efficient and prosperous carrier. He is the eleventh president of the railway.

Top: Veteran Consolidation outshopped by Baldwin in 1909 and originally used on the Iowa Central. *Center:* Looking east at St. Louis Park, Minn., showing untreated ties and cinder ballast. *Bottom:* Old gondolas with wooden bodies, composite underframes and arch-bar trucks. Many "gons" of this type were in service in the early thirties.

Top: Rebuilt Mikados largely supplanted Consolidations, and the Mikes in turn were superseded by Diesels. *Center:* Same spot at St. Louis Park after rehabilitation with rock ballast and No. 5 treated ties. *Bottom:* A fleet of all-steel box cars. Eighty-two per cent of all freight-train cars now in service have been acquired new since 1936.

Semi-streamlined Mikado wheeling Minneapolis-bound freight on a bleak spring day at the crest of the grade in Eden Prairie, Minn. Until the coming of road Diesels, the modernized Mikes were the pride of the M&StL.

Through the lush green countryside south of Merriam, Minn., this three-unit Diesel is on the last lap of its 476-mile run from Peoria to Minneapolis. The "distant signal" on the left is for the Omaha Road's crossing 4,500 feet ahead.

The M&StL crosses the Rock Island's double-track main stem in front of Grinnell's picturesque old-fashioned depot. North of the station, the Peoria Gateway Line runs through the center of the Grinnell College campus.

Robert Milner

Down by the station early in the morning is No. 7, the Albia-Albert Lea motor-train. On the second floor of the building are the Eastern Division headquarters. Note initials of the Iowa Central, original owner of the station.

Right — Snowbound and off the track with the plow-car jammed in the drifts, this locomotive was marooned for weeks during the blizzard early in 1936. The setting is north of Sioux Rapids, Iowa, on the now-abandoned Spencer-Storm Lake branch.

Below—Keithsburg bridge as seen from the Iowa side of the Mississippi. The 2,304-foot structure across the main body of the river was completed in 1910 replacing a bridge on almost the same site. In the background, near the Illinois shore, is the lift-span.

Railway Transfer yard showing Minneapolis milling district in background. The Railway Transfer Company is an 11-mile subsidiary of the M&StL, serving nationally-famous flour mills near the Falls of St. Anthony.

Middle Yard in downtown Minneapolis. Beyond the first bridge and adjacent to the cold storage plant is the freight station. The twelve tracks on the right belong to the M&StL; the remainder to the Great Northern.

Cedar Lake: left to right are the roundhouse, machine shop, blacksmith shop, car shop and Diesel shop. Great Northern yard in foreground.

Engine 545 "displaying white" eases 'round a curve running south through Helena, Minn. This extra freight has just left the Minnesota River Valley and is in the rugged terrain of southern Scott County.

Backing off the diamond, local freight No. 70 is getting ready to spot cars at the pretty town of Chaska, Minn. This community, near the foot of long Chaska Hill, is also served by the Farmington-Cologne Branch of the Milwaukee Road, whose tracks cross the M&StL.

Working steam with a clear board at Hopkins, Minn., the 611 speeds a solid train of sugar beets for the refinery at Chaska. Beyond the station, the Western Division joins the main line, which is double-tracked from Hopkins to Minneapolis. Hopkins is also the home of BeBe Shopp, Miss America of 1948.

No. 20, the flagship of the M&StL's fleet of time freights, rumbling through Rockwell, Iowa, about 45 m.p.h. The dispatcher put up a meet with No. 7, the passenger train, which stands on the siding in the background.

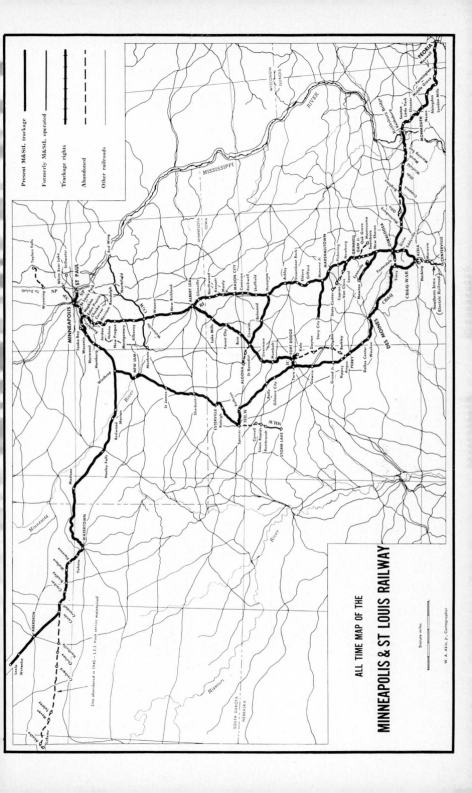

ALL TIME MAP OF THE

MINNEAPOLIS & ST LOUIS RAILWAY

W. A. Akin, Jr., Cartographer

Statute miles

Present M&StL trackage
Formerly M&StL operated
Trackage rights
Abandoned
Other railroads

Line abandoned in 1940 — L.C.L. truck service maintained

Redwood, Minn., where Richard W. Sears sold tickets — and watches. At this station in 1886 Agent Sears started the mail order business known the world over as Sears, Roebuck & Co. The depot has remained substantially unaltered except for the shed on the left and a change in the bay window.

New "bric-block" station at Madison, Minn., with Agent J. F. Ess and his son Donald out front. Nearly a dozen bric-block buildings at various points on the system have replaced the familiar Kelly-green wooden depots.

An extra of mixed freight heading south through the tablelands near New Prague, Minn. Until the coming of Diesels, the revamped Mikado-type engines were the most popular and versatile locomotives on the road.

Coming into "Osky" with No. 19 from Peoria. The trestle in the southeast side of Oskaloosa has since been replaced by a fill.

Robert Milner

At Olds, Iowa, the old and the new. Bob Milner snapped this study in contrasts from the cab of a two-unit Diesel. The coal chute and water tank are to be razed.

Monmouth-Peoria way freight rounding the bend at Allen's Curve near the bottom of Kickapoo Hill. A few minutes later the train was clicking over the switches in Peoria's Bartlett Yard.

Once the pride of the road and a favorite of President Sprague, the 502 is now scrapped in favor of the Diesel. The trim Pacific, however, took part in the pageant at the Chicago Railroad Fair in 1949, as the fitting climax of a distinguished career.

Center — Three-unit, 4050 h.p. Diesel. This is one of the three which pull the crack time freights, Nos. 19 and 20, between Minneapolis and Peoria. Bottom — One of the latest 3000 h.p. two-unit Diesels. Six of these efficient road engines are in fast freight service on the M&StL.

Above and below — Interior and exterior views of lightweight, stainless steel passenger coach. Cars of this type are standard equipment on all passenger trains.

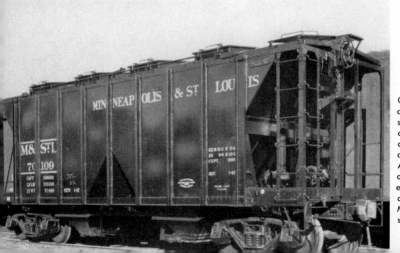

One of the 71 covered, all-steel hopper cars used principally in handling cement. A wide variety of specialized equipment characterizes M&StL freight service.

One-thousand h.p. road-switcher. Thirty-three Diesel engines of this horsepower rating were in road or yard operation in 1950. There are also three 380-; one 660-; two 600- and two 900-h.p. Diesels in switching service.

Above and below — Outside and inside views of new Diesel shop at Cedar Lake in Minneapolis. The building is scientifically designed for repairing and servicing of internal combusion locomotives.

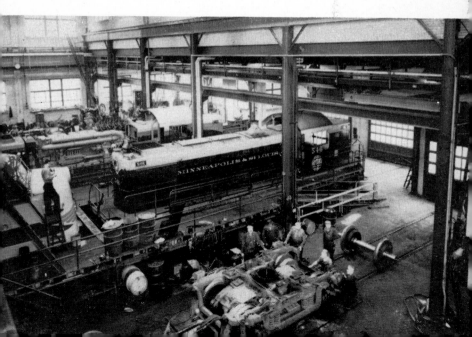

For a dozen years the M&StL had its headquarters in the Northwestern Bank Building, the largest office structure in Minneapolis. The road occupies nearly two upper floors with additional space on the street level.

New Home of the M&StL as it will look when completed early in 1951. Of concrete construction, faced with red Minnesota granite around the base of the walls and cream-colored brick above, the million-dollar building will be modern in every detail. The structure fronts on Franklin Avenue between Stevens and First Avenues South.

sage ended his homespun verse by adding, "You never can tell what will or won't happen on the M&StL."

Regardless of the financial quagmire it was in, the Peoria Gateway Line fought a good fight. It had long pioneered in interline package cars, and in the twenties launched a through route between New York and Minneapolis. An L.C.L. car left the Lackawanna's freight station in Hoboken for a fast run to Buffalo, then over the Nickel Plate-Clover Leaf Route to Peoria, where the M&StL dispatched the shipment to the Twin Cities area. Four days en route! The department stores and manufacturing firms liked this service. Here was one road which did not treat the less-than-carload business like an unwanted stepchild.

The will to serve! Even if the track was a bit below par and the equipment left much to be desired, shippers knew the men and management would exert every effort to "get the stuff through." On occasion the Louie went far beyond reasonable efforts to aid a friend. Take the case of the Ford plant which, at the time of this incident, was in Minneapolis. Someone had blundered in ordering parts, and the large factory would have to shut down unless the necessary materials were promptly secured. "Time" freights were much too slow to meet the deadline. Detroit, where the material originated, was a long way off.

In desperation, a Ford executive contacted the M&StL. What would they do; what could they do? The traffic and operating departments went into a huddle. Word went along the wires to "high-tail" the urgently needed material on No. 95, the road's fastest freight, from the Peoria connection to Marshalltown. From the latter town the company would dispatch a special to Minneapolis, stop-

183

ping only for coal and water. Near midnight an engine, with white flags fluttering in the breeze, puffed into Cedar Lake, pulling fourteen cars and a caboose. The Ford Special! It had slashed a dozen hours from the fastest "time" schedule, and the next day hundreds of employees went to work as usual assembling automobiles.

Due to the efforts of Bremner and Nash the company was instrumental in getting the Middle Grove mine in operation, which added greatly to the revenues from the Illinois section of the road. To transport the parts for the mine's electric shovel alone required nearly a trainload of cars. At the time, the huge shovel was said to be the largest of its kind in the world.

Until the early thirties there were homeseekers excursions to South Dakota from M&StL points in other states. With a "free side trip" and a fifteen-day return limit, the cheap fares attracted many prospective settlers and inquisitive tourists. A ten-dollar bill took one from almost any station in Minnesota and Iowa, and fifteen dollars covered the round trip from any Illinois station on the road.

Toward the end of Bremner's administration traffic fell off to such an extent that all passenger trains except Nos. 5 and 6 were motorized. The *North Star Limited*, on the contrary, continued with steam—a proud symbol of a passing era. It usually had a light Pacific, mail car, baggage car, coach, and the sleeper *Circumnavigators Club* or *Propeller Club*. The cafe-lounges *Mason City* and *Marshalltown* were also part of the consists up until the last few years of operation. To help check the rapid decline in passenger traffic, radios were installed in the lounges and wholesome Midwestern fare advertised in the

184

timetables. As late as 1932 the road featured "Unsurpassed meals, table d'hôte and à la carte service." A typical $1.50 dinner menu read as follows:

Purée of Tomato Soup   Chicken Broth with Rice

Choice of
Chicken à la King

Broiled Steak   Fried Chicken

Grilled Lamp Chops on Toast

Loin Pork Chops Sauté with Fried Apple

Omelet with Bacon or Chopped Ham

Ham or Bacon with Eggs

Baked Potato

Garden Peas   or   Stewed Corn

Head Lettuce with Dressing

Assorted Bread with Butter

Lemon Cream Pie, Apple Pie or Ice Cream

Coffee   Tea   Milk

(Fish or Eggs substituted if desired)

Such was the Peoria Gateway Line during the last years of William Bremner's regime. On December 12, 1934, after a brief sickness, the veteran head of the M&StL passed away.

F. R. KING

Out of the longest railroad receivership in history has come a booming carrier. Thank Lucian C. Sprague.

"Rescued: One Railroad," *Forbes,* December 15, 1942.

15

Doctor of Sick Railroads

They called it the "Misery and Short Life" or the "Maimed and Still Limping" when Lucian Charles Sprague first came to the Minneapolis & St. Louis. Folks looked upon the ills of the road as organic, and its plight as chronic. But "Dr." Sprague pronounced the condition functional and, figuratively putting away the stethescope, started to administer treatment. In less than a decade he had the 1,400-mile road in tip-top condition, earning a good living, a credit to it owners, employees, and the communities it served.

Who is this Lou Sprague? Ask that of any of the road's twenty-nine hundred employees and they will tell you about their president. The enginemen will explain how he started railroading on the "Q" and ran a locomotive just as they did. Shopmen will point out the beautiful streamlined Mikados, the rebuilding of which Sprague supervised, greatly increasing the tractive power. Freight solicitors will tell you their best "traffic man" is the chief executive of the road.

"Made one trip with Mr. Sprague years ago," a train-man told the author over his wheel reports in a speeding caboose, "and do you know when I saw him the other day that man remembered me by name." It has been said that whether Lucian Sprague walks along Hennepin Avenue, Minneapolis; Broadway, New York; or Main Street in a South Dakota hamlet he'll greet someone he knows *by name.*

"Doctor of Sick Railroads," we have called this stalwart dynamic white-haired executive, and yet his internship began on one of the soundest of roads, the Chicago, Burlington & Quincy. Young Sprague, a native of Illinois, saw Burlington trains puffing by Serena, the town where he was born September 29, 1885. That was enough; a locomotive is a machine, and next to people there is nothing he likes better than machinery. At the age of fourteen, Sprague hired out on that road as callboy, learning railroading the hard way. Promotion came fast; a spell as machinist helper, a few years firing a locomotive, and then the right-hand side of the cab.

From the Burlington, Sprague went into engineering and to the Great Northern as superintendent of air brakes over the entire system, then into sales work in connection with railway equipment. He also held responsible positions in the mechanical departments of the B&O and the Great Northern, and later did consulting work for the Denver & Rio Grande Western, becoming familiar with operating features on both eastern and western roads. The real test of his mechanical ingenuity, however, came when he was appointed vice president and general manager of the Uintah Railway in 1923. This was only a three-foot-gauge, sixty-eight-mile line, but it had everything in the books in the way of tough operating problems. Crooked as a billy-goat's trail, with 66-degree curves and grades up to 7½ per cent, the Utah ore road was a challenge to any brass hat.

General Manager Sprague took one look at the worn-out geared locomotives and decided the No. 1 need of the road was modern motive power. His prescription: articulated Mallet-type engines strong enough to pull twice the tonnage of the played-out geared jobs. "Can't be done," mused some of the old timers, "not on a narrow zig-zag line like the Uintah." But Sprague and representatives of Baldwin Locomotive Works put their heads together, and the order was filled as requested. Incidentally, the Mallet articulateds—engines hinged in the center—which he designed, are reputed to be the heaviest locomotives ever to polish the rails of a three-foot line in North America.

"Can't be done," retorted the self-styled rail experts in 1935, when Sprague came as receiver to rehabilitate the Minneapolis & St. Louis. The road had been in the hands of the courts ever since Aunt Mary's Day, and practically everyone regarded it as a "dead duck."

Lucian Sprague examined the ailing road and then, in his quick, intuitive way, prescribed treatment. There was nothing inherently wrong with the property that up-to-date motive power, increased traffic, and loyal co-operation of the M&StL family couldn't cure.

He got all three, and got them abundantly. But it was hard pulling and slow going; a bit of inspiration and a lot of perspiration on the part of everyone concerned. Many and frequent were his trips to the Cedar Lake shops. He redesigned the road's "Mikes," making them vastly more efficient engines.

When Sprague came to the M&StL as a co-receiver he had a theory that the best way to get traffic was to help the shipper sell his product. He kept hammering away at this theme, and in the end it brought results. Close co-operation between the road and the shippers, each mindful of the other's problems, is now a *must* along the road.

Lucian Sprague is about as American as the Midwest

in which he was born. It goes without saying he is fond of baseball. It is a poorly-informed railroader who does not know of the M&StL ball parties in which thousands of tickets were given to employees to see the Minneapolis Millers in action. Sprague, moreover, is a follower of Izaak Walton and knocks off occasionally to try his luck with rod and reel. In the last few years he has helped his friend James Melton, the opera singer, collect old automobiles, and Sprague is now the proud possessor of a 1909 Stanley Steamer. "Runs as good as the day it was built!" he says.

Enthusiasts of the turf, however, think of Lucian Sprague as a horseman, and well they may. He is a lover of standard bred trotting horses, from a long way back, and owned five world champions, four of which he drove to victory himself. Then there are the Iron Horses of which Sprague has photographs hung up in his office along with illustrations of the four-footed flesh-and-blood variety. Although the M&StL's passenger service is motorized, Sprague has until recently preserved the 502, a handsome Pacific, to do miscellaneous chores on the railroad. Once, according to roundhouse gossip, he climbed into the cab, pulled open the throttle, and gave the board of directors a run which they still remember.

In contrast to Sprague's dramatic and spectacular career the events which led to his stewardship of the M&StL were grim and discouraging. It is said of Henry Ford that he did not care what color they painted his automobiles as long as they were black; so it may be said of the M&StL

bondholders they did not care what kind of aid the company received as long as it was money. Cash was the vitamin "B" which the road urgently needed and which it had singular difficulty in obtaining.

Sprague's oft-demonstrated ability to resuscitate moribund railroads and then operate them with the sort of efficiency that makes money was the prime factor that led to his selection for the big M&StL job. Here is how it came about.

During the early 1930's, a number of appeals for the financial help that seemed necessary to keep the M&StL going were made to the Reconstruction Finance Corporation, depression-born loaning agency of the United States Government. F. J. Lisman, of New York, the chairman of seven different groups of M&StL bondholders, applied first for a loan of $7,500,000; then for one of $5,000,000.

Both of these pleas were rejected by Jesse Jones, RFC chairman. Reluctantly concluding that the situation had became hopeless, Lisman resigned as chairman of the bondholders' groups. Philip J. Roosevelt, another New York investment banker, was elected as temporary successor to Lisman.

Roosevelt wanted no part of the bondholders' chairmanship as a permanent job. What he sought was opportunity to influence the selection of the one man who, he thought, could lead the bankrupt railroad out of the financial morass into which it was sinking deeper and deeper. Specifically, he wanted to help pick the sort of practical, aggressive railroad man needed to run the M&StL right, once its pressing money problems were solved, and restore it to its rightful status as a useful and eventually prosperous freight carrier.

Roosevelt urged the bondholders' committees to elect, as

their permanent chairman, one of the most distinguished figures in the annals of railway reorganizations: Walter W. Colpitts, member of the famed railroad engineering firm of Coverdale & Colpitts, with offices at 120 Wall Street in the New York financial district.

Colpitts agreed to take the job but tied a string to his acceptance—just one string, but an important one. The bondholders must agree to let him select a man to run the M&StL. Colpitts said he was sure he could pick one who would do it well.

"Where will you find such a man?"

"Not far," replied Colpitts. "In fact, I have him waiting in the next room."

Lucian Charles Sprague was brought in, and that marked the beginning of a new chapter in the history of the M&StL; a new chapter and an inspiring one, filled with the drama of hard-won success and progress.

Introduced to the roomful of creditors, Sprague was questioned at length as to himself and his railroad career and as to what he thought he could do with the M&StL if placed in command. Sprague convinced his listeners that his experience qualified him to run almost any sort of a railroad, even one beset with financial and physical problems.

The bondholders, however, were dubious as to whether Sprague—or anyone else—could secure the volume of freight traffic which the M&StL obviously needed to be rehabilitated and transformed into a moneymaker. Sprague, with the vigorous support of Colpitts, convinced the creditors that he could do that. For one thing, they pointed out that Sprague's record as assistant to the president of the Missouri-Kansas-Texas, or "Katy," had demonstrated his ability to get business.

192

The conference finally ended and the bondholders voted unanimously authorizing Chairman Colpitts to recommend to Judge Wilbur F. Booth, of the U. S. District Court in Minneapolis, that Lucian C. Sprague be appointed receiver of the M&StL as successor to the late W. H. Bremner.

This was done and Sprague arrived in Minneapolis January 1, 1935. The weather, stormy and bitter cold, made the outlook for the task of rebuilding a broken-down railroad seem even bleaker. As an added complication, the plan for the dismemberment of the M&StL was just starting to boil. For the next three years this plan kept the Midwest in an uproar.

At the start, Sprague was not the only boss of the M&StL job. Judge Booth appointed co-receivers. The other was John Junell, a prominent Minneapolis lawyer. This arrangement of divided authority did not last. In fact, it could not, if rehabilitation was to be a complete success. After about two years, Junell resigned.

Sprague plunged into his work of securing traffic for the road, while getting a start on the huge task of rebuilding its physical properties.

"The day I took the receiver's job," he recalls, "$524,000 in unpaid vouchers for current bills were dumped on my desk with the warning, 'You'll never get another dollar's worth of material'!"

It was well and good to talk of increasing traffic and other long-range programs, but the road could not pay the men today out of tomorrow's earnings. Sprague realized something had to be done—and quickly! The opinion expressed by many that the property was "of little worth as a railroad but of considerable junk value," was in a sense heeded. The first thing Sprague did was to sell

193

for scrap a thousand obsolete freight cars to help meet the payroll. He asked Judge Booth for a court order to approve of the sale after showing him photographs of the old cars along with a certified check for $60,000 in part payment by the wrecking company. He received the court's approval and continued to dispose of worn-out rolling stock, which had not turned a wheel in years, at high salvage value. All in all, some 75 rusty locomotives and 2,887 superannuated cars brought in much-needed payroll dollars and cash to help pay debts.

A man, a plan, and wholehearted support from the rank and file of the railroad made progress a reality. It was a case of the workers uniting shoulder to shoulder under inspiring leadership for a common cause: to help their railroad, to safeguard their jobs, and to raise the road's standard of service.

Unlike many roads in which a change of management takes place, there was virtually no change in the personnel. With the exception of Herbert W. Ward, who came from the Omaha Railway to be traffic manager and later vice president of traffic, and William L. Trout, who was brought in as mechanical superintendent, the executive staff remained unchanged. The secretary to the former receiver, Merle E. Eaton was retained, and today he is assistant to President Sprague and regarded by his boss as the "best executive assistant on any railroad in the United States." The same policy of keeping the staff intact holds true for the men out on the line.

In every sense realistic, the new management took a practical viewpoint of the M&StL's place in the economy of the Midwest. The short-haul passenger service was very much a thing of the past. Many of the road's local trains were operated at heavy loss, seriously draining the

finances of the system. Moreover, competition of stream-
lined trains between the Twin Cities and Chicago tended
to draw an increasingly large share of riders from the
once-famous *North Star Limited*. It was often faster and
more convenient to go through the Chicago gateway between the Twin Cities and St. Louis than to use the
M&StL-Wabash route. With considerable regret sleeping
cars were taken off the *North Star* on May 30, 1935. From
that time on no Pullman has been in regular service on
the M&StL.

Henceforth the road would do one job and do it well.
That was to expedite freight, giving the best possible service to on-line and off-line shippers. For the first time in
the company's history the manifold advantages of shipping
by the Peoria Gateway were *fully* brought out. To ac-
quaint the nation's shippers with the role of the M&StL
as a strategic bridge route, new off-line agencies were established. During the thirties, when depression reigned
throughout the land, it was said that "the other roads
knew there was no business and they didn't go after it,
but the M&StL didn't know any better and went out and
got it." The road spent money to make money, expanding in time of depression when other carriers were pulling
in their belts. But the policy brought results. Similarly,
the company speeded up service as fast as improved tracks
would permit and strove to run its freight trains on time.

To do this the motive power was overhauled and redesigned by Sprague. The standard type of locomotive on
the M&StL was the Mikado, which before modernization
fell far short of standard performance. Consequently, they
took the wheezy, leaky hogs and rejuvenated them with
syphons, stokers, feedwater heaters, improved superheater
units, and other improvements, stepping up the tractive

effort from 46,000 to 61,300 pounds. Then, with a liberal use of paint and some external revamping, the old steamers were given a semi-streamlined appearance.

Things were slowly but surely on the up-grade on the M&StL. The Sprague salesmanship, which trickled down to the youngest employee, was reflected in increased earnings. For example, gross revenues, which had fallen to $7,514,180 in 1934, were raised by about $100,000 in 1935, the first year of the new administration. In 1936 the gross swelled to $8,955,364, something like a million and a half more than the two preceding years.

Conductors began carrying their lanterns a little more jauntily, enginemen began to have more interest in their duties, and clerks took greater pride in their work when black ink began replacing red. Perhaps they were going to make a real railroad out of the Louie yet!

It was beginning to look as if the management and the men would lick the problems besetting the road. More freight was moving with greater economy and dispatch. Men were at work on the track and in the shops rebuilding the old M&StL. The results were not conclusive but...

Then came a series of events which jeopardized the independent management of the road, to say nothing of the jobs of thousands of employees and the continued operation of a third of the M&StL's mileage.

Like sharks around a swimmer spent,
  Who in the ocean fell;
Our foes now seek dismemberment
  Of the M. & St. L.

C. R. Fehr, in the Minneapolis *Journal*,
April 27, 1936.

16

"Oh No, Day Kan't Do Dat!"

In one of the M&StL offices in downtown Minneapolis an employee was looking dejectedly at the glaring newspaper headlines on his desk. He had his hands propped up against his cheeks and was staring at the paper as if in a trance. This man was one of the many faithful employees who had stood by the "road" in good times and bad. Finally, he straightened up and, slowly shaking his head, murmured: "Oh no, dey kan't do dat!" Being of Polish background, he sometimes lapsed into broken English in moments of excitement or crisis. Here, indeed, was a crisis.

Can't do what? How did the headlines affect him? He had a steady job and was well thought of by his boss. All through the long depression he had been on the payroll. Railroad work was permanent—or was it?

According to the headlines, his job and some two-thousand others' wouldn't be worth a snap of the fingers. According to the headlines, there would be no more M&StL. According to . . .

The news, in short, was that an outside company had been formed to dismember the road, scrap a third of its mileage, and parcel out what was left among eight competing trunk lines. Two-thirds of the employees would lose their jobs, and a large proportion of those out of

199

work would come from the road's shops at Cedar Lake and Marshalltown and from the general offices at Minneapolis. Since the M&StL would be split up like a jigsaw puzzle to form branch lines of the bigger roads, there would be no need for large repair centers and good-sized headquarters. Moreover, the paper stated, if the plan went through, twenty-one villages would be left without rail service.

Of all the crises in the road's existence this was the most serious. Heretofore there had been headlines, and *big* headlines, too, in the local papers about the financial aspects of the Louie, but now news of the road was making national periodicals. Farmers and merchants formerly not greatly concerned about their railroad now began to read sadly about planned wholesale abandonments and large-scale partitioning. What if the plan did go through, the individual wondered. How would it affect my farm, my business, my freight routing? The answer was: adversely. From Akaska to Peoria, from the Twin Cities to Des Moines, sentiment was rapidly crystallizing against dismemberment; and the much-publicized Associated Railways Company was becoming the *bête noire* of virtually every M&StL town.

Associated Railways Company!

This was the newly chartered corporation which would take over the poor old M&StL. The Associated was formed on the premise that the Peoria Gateway Line, as it existed, could never operate at a profit, that a large portion of its mileage should immediately be abandoned, and that the rest of the system could be more economically operated by eight neighboring Class I carriers. In other words, the roads would form a kind of pool whereby Associated would purchase the M&StL and take title. The carriers participating in this surgery were to be the Burlington, Rock Island, Milwaukee, Great Northern, North Western, Illinois Central, Great Western, and Soo. Later, the fifteen hundred-mile Chicago Great Western (about the size of the M&StL at that time) withdrew from the pool, and so did the Great Northern.

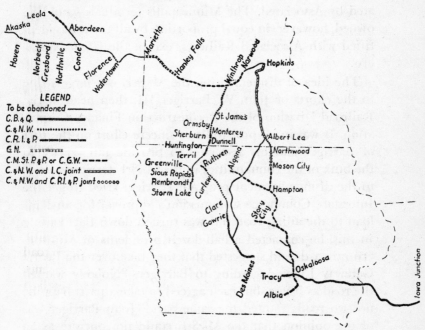

Map showing Dispositions Proposed for M. & St. L. Lines

As soon as details of the new company were made public, the local populace raised a howl that was heard clear to Washington. The M&StL employees and labor in general took up the fight; and the newspapers, particularly those in the Twin Cities, kept the people informed as to day-by-day events. For a long time the M&StL was front-page news in Minnesota's biggest city.

201

Associated Railways Company proposed to buy the bankrupt carrier for $7,200,000 and sell or convey various parts of it to the roads in the pool. The terminal facilities in the Minneapolis area, extending from Hopkins to the downtown milling district, including the valuable property of the Railway Transfer Company, would be operated by Associated. The Minneapolis terminals would be owned, however, in equal proportion by all the roads identified with Associated Railways, except the Great Northern.

The idea of dismembering the M&StL was largely due to the efforts of John W. Barriger III, then head of the Railroad Division of the Reconstruction Finance Corporation. It was in all probability a sincere effort on the part of Barriger and his associates to provide rail service to the bulk of the communities in the M&StL territory. Prior to the dismemberment proposal Barriger tried to get the Interstate Commerce Commission's approval for an RFC loan to the ailing road but was turned down flat. Failing in this, he contacted a half-dozen presidents of Midwestern railroads and suggested that they take over the Peoria Gateway Line. According to Barriger, "Nobody wanted the road as it was, but each agreed to take a part; happily, no two roads wanted the same part." John Barriger was of the opinion that the M&StL could not operate as an independent unit very much longer and the only alternative was to parcel out the company among the neighboring carriers.

While the plan had some merit, the people, the shippers, and practically all the communities along the road felt it was no solution to their transportation problems. The overwhelming majority were of the opinion that it

202

would have a harmful effect for all of them. Take the matter of leaving twenty-one towns without rail service. If the plan went through, the 103-mile direct line between Albert Lea and Fort Dodge was slated to be junked. Other smaller segments on many parts of the system would be abandoned.

The prospect of turning two thousand workers out of jobs, many of them veteran employees too old to get positions elsewhere, was another gloomy feature of the dismemberment program. The provisions proposed by Associated to take care of the unemployed were considered inadequate, and it was felt there was no real justification for removing so many men from the payroll.

A third factor which tended to discredit the new plan was that it would curtail competition rather than foster it. At first glance this may not seem very significant, but in the last analysis it would have had a tremendous effect on the economy and industrial well-being of communities along the M&StL. The advantages of the Peoria Gateway would be nullified. Established channels of commerce would be closed. "Time" freight service to many communities would be eliminated.

With one fell swoop, Associated would obliterate the Minneapolis-Peoria route as a main line and deal it out among several roads. The Illinois Central and the North Western would jointly own the track between Hopkins and Albert Lea. The Rock Island, as pointed out elsewhere in this book, owned the trackage from Albert Lea to Northwood, Iowa; and under the new set-up it would take over the M&StL from the latter point to Mason City. Between Mason City and Albia, a 169-mile stretch, Associated planned to put the road in the lap of the

Milwaukee. On the other hand, the east-and-west part of the M&StL in Iowa and Illinois, linking Tracy and Peoria via Oskaloosa, would go to the Burlington.

It was asserted by the proponents of the dismemberment program that several of the applicant roads already had service between the Twin Cities and Peoria, as justification for closing the M&StL gateway. The selfsame roads, the opponents countered, also had service to Chicago. Naturally, a road would utilize established routes and terminals and there would be no incentive for shunting traffic over a branch line to Peoria.

In addition there would be no direct route from Minneapolis to Fort Dodge. The M&StL had the shortest line between these points. The Winthrop-Spencer-Gowrie route would be butchered in such a way as to junk six parts of it and dole out what was left to the North Western, the Milwaukee, and the Rock Island. Time-freight service from Minneapolis to Morton, Minnesota, would be eliminated. In fact, the Milwaukee would take over the route from Norwood to Hanley Falls and the Great Northern, from the Falls to the western state line. Almost half of the mileage in South Dakota was slated for abandonment, and the remaining portions were to be divided between the Milwaukee and the North Western.

With all this shuffling about, there was still no guarantee that more wholesale abandonments would not take place a little later. As the ICC put it, "Under the proposed plan the only lines that are assured of continued operation are the Minneapolis-Albia line, the Gowrie-Des Moines segment, and that part of the Tracy-Peoria line between Middle Grove and Peoria." This totalled 408 miles, or a little less than one-third of the M&StL at that time.

Probably the most cogent reason why Associated's plan failed to enlist much support was that it just wasn't necessary. With the new management, the M&StL was making a good showing; and given a little more time, it would carve its own destiny very nicely. By 1936 the road was showing a net income of $687,192 and an operating ratio (the total cost of operation as compared with the total of all operating income) of 79.44 per cent, a modest figure. The farmers and merchants may not have known Shakespeare, but they firmly believed in Hamlet's soliloquy that it is better to "bear those ills we have than fly to others that we know not of." The road had been sick; now it was merely recuperating; tomorrow it would be entirely well—that was the prognosis of folks along the line.

But the M&StL was still in receivership; and as its executives were instruments of the court, they could not foster their own ideas for rehabilitation, those of Associated, or any other program for putting the road on its feet. If anyone was going to champion the cause, it had to be the employees, the shippers, the communities along the line, and public-spirited statesmen. As a matter of fact, it was all four; and they responded with a will.

How the employees rallied to preserve the road! They came from retirement; they came from engine cab and caboose, from head-end cars and coaches; they came from yards and roundhouses, from country depots and general offices. Men who had left the road five, ten, even fifteen and twenty years before reappeared to testify against dismemberment.

To unify the efforts of objectors to dismemberment, the railroaders, local businessmen, and community officials formed the M. & St. L. Executive Defense Committee.

Fred K. Gage, a Fairfax, Minnesota, lawyer, was appointed chairman and Herbert F. Horner, representing the Minneapolis Grain Exchange, was made secretary-treasurer. The other executives included William F. Lewis, an M&StL locomotive engineer; S. W. W. Carr, secretary of the Aberdeen (S. D.) Chamber of Commerce; E. T. O'Connor, corporate counsel for Peoria; L. M. O'Leary, traffic representative for the Fort Dodge Chamber of Commerce; and D. C. Noonan, Watertown businessman and at one time general superintendent of the M&StL·

Also associated with the Defense Committee were the general chairmen of the railway brotherhoods, including the engineers, firemen, conductors, trainmen, telegraphers, train dispatchers, maintenance of way employees, clerks, and shop craft workers. In many cases these representatives worked on the road; and after putting in a full day's labor, they would convene at night to formulate ways and means of saving their company. Quite a few of the employees donated small parts of their pay to help defray expenses of the Defense Committee. Bill Lewis left his engine cab to go to Washington, along with Albert L. Gardner, a former M&StL station agent at Eldora, to testify against Associated's plan to split up the road. Railroad labor as a whole was very ably represented by E. L. Oliver, research director of the Brotherhood of Railway & Steamship Clerks.

In the Senate, before the Interstate Commerce Commission in Washington, and also at commission hearings at various points along the line, strong opposition arose to any and all plans for dismemberment. While Senator Henrik Shipstead of Minnesota was conducting hearings on Resolution 287, authorizing an investigation of the dismemberment proposal, Fred Gage was barnstorming the rural areas for money and support to keep the M&StL intact. In Minneapolis Adolph Karlsson, an engineman, and Carl Boehme, a clerk in the general offices and chairman of the Clerks' Adjustment Board, spent most of their free time soliciting funds and arousing sentiment to aid the Louie. As chairman and secretary, respectively, of the local Defense Committee, they enlisted much support in the road's home town.

Out of nowhere, it seemed, ex-M&StL men came to defend their old road. Congressman Fred H. Hildebrandt, of South Dakota, a former conductor, was active in the movement, as was Frank B. Townsend, director of the Minneapolis Traffic Association. Townsend, at one time vice president of the road, is said to have been almost in tears at the hearings. Men like these, plus the shippers, state regulatory commissions, and humble folk who were reared on the Louie, defeated Associated Railways hands down. A few outsiders got in the habit of regarding the M&StL as a corpse; but, as one defense lawyer put it, "the corpse got up and drove them off."

The offense had not reckoned on such public sentiment, which amounted almost to a crusade. Nor did Associated Railways fully comprehend the progress Receiver Sprague was making in rehabilitating the road and getting additional traffic. But the Senate, the ICC, and the state railroad commissions did! Comptroller George A. Anderson and his associates saw to that. For months he and his staff had been marshalling figures. Cold, impersonal, telling figures showing unequivocal improvement. And in the end it was the Associated Railways which died and not the M&StL.

When the ICC quashed Associated's plan in 1938 the employees and friends of the road planned a three-day celebration. The long and bitter struggle to remain solvent and independent was aptly told in an informal story by Harold E. Bloom, a clerk in the general office. Titled, "Come to the M. & St. L. Party," Bloom, in his own droll way, recounted the troubles of "M. N. Saintell."

Once upon a time there was a railroad whose name was M. N. Saintell. He lived many years in the States, where he was born. He was a peace-loving railroad, always minding his own business and never trying to get anyone else's.

Mr. Saintell was very generous, giving of his income to those who worked for him. In fact, he even went so far as to go through the length and breadth of the land to borrow to keep himself going. This made him very poor. The tracks he ran on could no longer carry the weight of his box cars. His buildings were falling apart. He looked at his locomotives and said, "Everything looks black."

One beautiful morning Saintell awoke and had his usual look in the morning paper. He glanced at the blazing headlines and fainted. A passerby threw cold water on him and said, "That will make your locomotive tender." M. N., however, was used to having cold water thrown on him, so that didn't phase him. They tried every known means of resuscitation, but to no avail. Finally, someone gave him a carload of business. The shock was effective.

Asked to explain, he exclaimed, "See the headlines—my seven enemies want to tear me to pieces! What shall I do?"

Poor Saintell! He was at the end of his line. Everything looked dark. He put his head in a coal bin, hiding for shame, but everything looked darker still. He was sick and despondent. No one held any hope for him. Hadn't he been sick with receivership twelve years? Also, he was suffering with poor publicity. No one cared.

To Saintell, however, it meant his life. He looked at his little hungry box cars and saw red. He said, "I'll fight!" He raised up on a branch, when suddenly he was yanked to his feet.

Who could that be? A new management was coming into

his life, headed by L. C. Sprague. Help was coming. The
Defense Committee gave him a number of transfusions,
donating part of their pay. More help was on the way.
Senators, Congressmen, Governors, newspapers, municipal-
ities, and warehouse commissions came to the rescue.

Gradually, Saintell became stronger. This made the seven
enemies more determined than ever to cut him in pieces.
Maybe Saintell would get another carload of business. But
the enemies were honest—they would do their crooked
work legally. They went before the Interstate Commerce
Commission with their petition to take Saintell off the map.

"You must have hearings," said I.C.C.

"There's nothing wrong with my hearing," said Saintell,
"I feel fine."

"We'll have hearings anyway and find out," replied I.C.C.

The hearings were held. Doctors, experts, and specialists
were called in. Consultations were held. Even engineers
were called to look over Saintell's system.

Meanwhile, M. N. was growing stronger under the new
management. He learned to run straight and faster. He
stopped at better buildings. He had money in his pocket.
The people working for him were happier.

When the doctors were through with their examinations,
consultations etc., the I.C.C. gathered the evidence and from
Washington announced that M. N. Saintell was in good
condition physically and would not be turned over to the
seven hungry anemic enemies.

"Am I glad," exclaimed Saintell, "I'm going to celebrate!
I'll rent the Minneapolis Auditorium three days, July 21st,
22nd and 23rd and I want all my friends to celebrate
with me."

The Victory Jubilee in 1938, a three-day affair, was a
celebration the like of which Minneapolis had never witnessed before. The opening feature was a mayors' handcar race along Third Street from Third Avenue South to
Nicollet. Trolleys were rerouted and streets closed as
crowds lined the sidewalks to see the Mayor's Cup Sweep-

stakes Handcar Derby. The rules were rigid; the partici-
pants couldn't get out and push; they had to have a
"physical" before entering the race and weigh in before
the event. Any mayor "who had professional experience
as a handcar operator" would be immediately disqualified.

About noontime, Mayor George Leach, of Minneapolis,
fired a gun at "Third and Third," and they were off!
Five mayors on each vehicle, four pumping as if their
life depended on the outcome and one shouting directions.
The car captained by Mayor Edgar L. Hayek, of Albert
Lea, got off to a good start, leaving Mayor Albert D.
Flor, of New Ulm, a few rail-lengths behind. Their Hon-
ors huffed and puffed, sweated and strained in the hot
July sun. Second Avenue went by as first one car clicked
over the crossing and then the other. Al Flor's team was
catching up. Marquette Avenue sped by as *both* handcars
thumped over the crossing frogs. It was nip and tuck as
the mayors from along the M&StL strove for the goal.
Perspiration rolled down from their brows—it was the
toughest assignment they had ever had. The crowd was
cheering. The KSTP radio announcer was yelling into
his portable "mike." It was going to be close; it *was* close.
Ed's crew valiantly tried to maintain their lead but Al's
was inching ahead. When they hit the tape at Nicollet
Al won by a fishplate. His Honor, Mayor Albert D. Flor,
of New Ulm—the *winnah*!

After that came the mayors' luncheon at the Radisson
Hotel, with speeches by prominent citizens, including
George K. Belden, chairman of the Jubilee Committee.
Nightfall found the mayors at the Municipal Auditorium
harmonizing to "I've Been Working On the Railroad"
and participating in a spirited waltzing contest. Thou-

210

sands of people joined them in singing, dancing, and playing games.

The next two days of the Jubilee celebration featured more fun and frolic. Some twenty-two bands from communities along the M&StL took part in parades. Girls from Montgomery clad in brightly colored Bohemian dresses sold kolacky buns, a delicacy of dried fruit baked in a roll, for which that community is famous. A double header at Nicollet Ballpark gave thousands a rousing good time. Indeed, the booming of drums and the singing and dancing lasted until the crowning of Queen Loella Braun in the auditorium the third and last day of the fête. The Jubilee took on the characteristics of an old-time railroad celebration marking the opening of a new line about the middle of the last century. Instead of the *building* of a new road, this celebration marked the *salvation* of an old one, which many people in four Midwestern states considered fully as important.

Within five years after facing dismemberment and complete destruction of its entity as an individual railway, the Minneapolis & St. Louis has emerged triumphantly from a 19-year receivership.

Railway Age, September 19, 1942.

17

Sale and Salvation

There are two dates in the history of the M&StL which should be remembered: the one is May 26, 1870, when the road was born; and the other July 24, 1942, when it was reborn. The sale of the company on the latter date and the subsequent termination of receivership marked a new era in the road. Unfortunately, Howard S. Abbott, who conducted the first auction in 1934 and forty-one other attempts to dispose of the road, was not present when the sale was consummated. Due to illness, the veteran Special Master could not attend the forty-third time the company was put on the block. His place was taken by H. D. Irwin, who knocked down the property for $2,010,100, the minimum price fixed by the court. The bidder was Coverdale & Colpitts, reorganization manager of the road.

Reorganizing a railroad which had remained in receivership for over twenty years, however, was no child's play. When the road had gone bankrupt, claims totalling over 5 million dollars had been filed against the company. Considerable litigation had ensued as to the priority of creditors, all of which had to be thrashed out before the receivership could be lifted. Too much credit cannot be given to C.W. Wright, counsel for the receiver and for the reorganization manager, who with infinite patience made

213

the reorganization an accomplished fact. He and his staff frequently worked nights, week-ends, and holidays, laboring long and hard to see the thing through. Finally, on December 1, 1943, the road was turned back to its owners.

Two companies were formed to take over the reorganized road. One was called The Minneapolis & St. Louis *Railway Company* and the other, The Minneapolis & St. Louis *Railroad Corporation*. Both were incorporated March 9, 1939. The former operated about nine hundred miles of road east and south of Minneapolis; whereas, the latter took over the lines west of the city and the Winthrop-Fort Dodge branch, approximately five hundred and fifty miles. Under this arrangement the more prosperous eastern and southern section, known as the *Company,* issued stock and bonds; while the lighter traffic areas of the west, forming the *Corporation,* issued only non-par stock. All of the latter stock was held by the *Company,* leaving the less-prosperous parts of the system with no funded or short-term debt.

Under the reorganization plan effective December 1, 1943, 150,000 shares of common stock were issued in exchange for defaulted bonds totaling $44,286,000. About $25,000,000 in capital stock was wiped out. In addition $2,015,000 of 4 per cent bonds were issued, but six months later they were paid off in cash. This left the M&StL in an enviable position with no bonded indebtedness. Even more noteworthy is the fact that the road was reorganized *without* one dollar of borrowed money, but *entirely* out of earnings from increased overhead and local traffic. A good portion of this augmented traffic may be attributed to many new industries which the company was successful in locating at points along its line. Incidentally

214

the two-company setup proved unnecessary, and in December 1, 1944, the *Railway Company* absorbed the *Railroad Corporation* and the latter went out of existence.

Almost a decade of planned modernization, however, made the M&StL virtually a new railroad. Under the leadership of L. C. Sprague, all departments worked together to rebuild the road physically, as well as financially, improving morale as well as tracks, and increasing the tractive power as traffic mounted.

The first requisite of a good railroad is adequate track. New rails, ties, and ballast brought the main line and important branches up to that of any well-kept property. Battered and poorly aligned 70-pound rail gave way to 90- and 100-pound; and track which in many sections had no ballast at all was securely anchored in washed gravel and crushed rock. Rotted and scored ties were replaced with oak on the main line and cedar on the branches, all purchased from on-line producers, thereby saving freight charges entailed by the former practice of buying from lumber dealers on foreign lines. Even the lowly switch lamps came under the scrutiny of the management; and, as a result, have been superseded by oilless reflectors, saving $18,000 a year.

Next came motive power and rolling stock. It has been related how the road's Mikados were improved, making two locomotives in some cases do the work formerly performed by three. Economical round-the-clock operation of Diesel switchers took the place of steam in many yards, and the company was looking forward to the time when the internal combustion engine would be extensively used in road service. Modern steel box, flat, gondola, and hopper cars superseded the older wooden equipment. Now for the first time in many a year there were sufficient cars and ample motive power to meet the needs of current traffic.

The old slogan, "Between East and West, Peoria Gateway Best," coined by Robert Golden in the twenties, came into its own in the forties. The off-line freight solicitors, in 1934 numbering twenty-nine, were increased to over seventy a half-dozen years later. New agencies in Winston-Salem, North Carolina, in Portland, Oregon, and in Boston, Philadelphia, Dallas, and Omaha meant more business over the Peoria Gateway Line from points in New England, the East, South, Midwest, and Far West.

Another factor in speeding up service on the Peoria line was the switching over from the old M&StL route between Martinsburg and Coppock, Iowa, to that of the Chicago, Burlington & Quincy. This twenty-two mile segment of the "Q" had been purchased prior to 1935, but no work had been done in making the road available for use. When Sprague came into control, he ordered the ex-Burlington branch rebuilt with better ballast and new ties and rails so that it would conform to main line standards on the M&StL. A 350-foot bridge gave way to a long fill with two 120-inch culverts. The new line eliminated thirty-seven bridges and many sharp curves and steep grades.

To attract new factories, an industrial traffic department was formed under an experienced manager. Due largely to the efforts of this department, hundreds of new industries, including oil and storage units, coal and lumber yards, and varied manufacturing plants, were located along the M&StL.

Meanwhile, the company's finances showed results of a similar overhauling. Instead of having a constant stream

216

of creditors seeking payments, the road made a practice
of paying all bills promptly when due. In the case of all
equipment obligations, payment was made systematically
and with scrupulous fidelity. Probably the most remarkable thing about the rehabilitation was that almost all
improvements were made out of earnings.

Along with the improvement program came a gradual
pruning of branches which had outlived their usefulness.
Most of the lines subsequently abandoned were on improved highways, and many served communities also
touched by other railroads. One of the first segments to
go was the old Mud Line, the original M&StL route linking Fort Dodge and Angus, Iowa. This paralleled, most
of the way, the Des Moines and Fort Dodge, which was
purchased by the M&StL in 1915. The bulk of the forty-
eight-mile Mud Line was abandoned in 1936, and the
short remaining segment in the vicinity of Angus and
south of Kalo Junction was scrapped a year or so later.

The Montezuma branch, serving the seat of Poweshiek
County, was lopped off in 1936. The somewhat longer
Spencer-Storm Lake line, also in Iowa, quit the same
year. The latter road is remembered for its many spindling trestles, maintenance of which was all out of proportion to the slender revenue derived from its operation.
A thirteen-mile stretch, however, between Rembrandt and
Storm Lake was purchased by the Milwaukee Road. Short
sections of branches to the Hawkeye towns of Van Cleve
and Algona were likewise discontinued.

It was a coincidence that while the southernmost track
on the original M&StL line to Angus was being pulled
up, the most western point on the system was slated to
undergo a similar fate. The 103-mile Conde-Akaska extension in South Dakota, which at one time went on to

217

the Missouri River at LeBeau, rarely if ever paid its own way. The heavy losses it incurred in the thirties seriously affected the financial status of the entire railroad. Permission to abandon the line was granted by the Interstate Commerce Commission in 1940, and the line was accordingly scrapped.

Before the M&StL took off train service, however, a provision was made to have a joint rail-truck tariff published for the handling of wheat from the prosperous grain areas along the route. Although trucks now haul grain from Akaska and intermediate points to the M&StL cars at Aberdeen, the rate is the same as was the all-rail charges. This is one of the earliest truck-and-rail tariffs ever to go in effect in the United States. The M&StL also inaugurated less-than-truckload operation daily except Sunday to serve the towns along the former rail route. At the same time, truck service was also established between Aberdeen and Leola to supplement train operation.

The company pioneered in inaugurating highway transportation for delivery of less-than-carload freight to many points on the railroad. In 1941-42 big trucks with the M&StL herald were running between Minneapolis and Mason City, Albert Lea and Des Moines, Monmouth and Peoria, and Fort Dodge and Estherville. Late at night or early in the morning large tractor-trailers left the downtown Minneapolis freight station for points along the railroad. Goods received one day were assured following morning delivery to many localities in Minnesota and Iowa. By this coordinated road and rail service, the truck and the train each served the shipper where it was best fitted.

While most of the local L.C.L. freight is better adapted

for carriage by the road's motor trucks, an increasingly large share of interline package freight goes by train. Again, the M&StL pioneered in providing through cars for many off-line cities, probably more so than any road of comparable size in the Middlewest. By the eve of the second World War, L.C.L. service was being provided from Minneapolis to Kansas City in the Southwest, to St. Louis in the South, and to such distant eastern points as Indianapolis, Cincinnati, and Buffalo. The Minneapolis freight depot, with its cars and trucks containing parcels destined to hundreds of localities in the Midwest, is a busy place.

Just before World War II, the road staged the heaviest short-haul passenger movement in its history. It all came about when the M&StL co-starred with Cedric Adams, a Minneapolis newspaperman, in winning the hearts of youngsters. The railroad and the columnist worked together to give the kids a day at Excelsior. The idea originated in the summer of 1938 when Adams' column *In This Corner,* of the *Star,* suggested a picnic for orphans and settlement house youngsters in the Twin Cities area. The M&StL was willing. It would provide the crews and motive power free of charge if the other roads would furnish all-steel coaches. They did. What was to be a load of fifteen hundred children turned out to be over two thousand. Even at that, to quote Cedric Adams' column (August 9, 1938) , "The dear old M. & St. L. came through in grand style."

The second season, the railroad prepared for a moderate increase in the number of young excursionists; instead it received a deluge. Kids came by droves and packed the coaches. Two trains totaling twenty-eight cars were

219

put to the task of moving the youthful regiment. On they poured, two to a seat, then three, then four. They crowded the aisles and jammed the platforms. They packed the baggage cars. When all the tykes had squeezed into the cars, the harried trainmen estimated a total of forty-five hundred. A few straggling left-overs went by auto, but apparently they all came back to Minneapolis by train. Some five thousand moppets now, eating popcorn, yelling, and squirming. Never in the heyday of Minnetonka had there ever been a mass movement like this. When it was all over, the only mishap was a mashed thumb—and that was of a lady reporter. The next year, the excursion was called off; Uncle Sam needed all the available equipment for the nation's defense.

At the time of Pearl Harbor, the M&StL was in good physical condition. Although the road was then still in the court's hands, it was just a question of time—and legal red tape—until the company would be restored to private management. No better picture of efficiency can be had than in comparing operations during World War I with those of the second global conflict.

The rigmarole of government inspectors, government supervisors, and government orders was totally lacking during the late conflict. Inefficiency and terminal congestion, run-down equipment and an under-maintained plant were factors which the Peoria Gateway Line was spared, from Pearl Harbor to the cessation of hostilities on V-J Day, September 2, 1945.

While there were few war industries along the M&StL, it hauled considerable defense material and many trainloads of troops. The Peoria Gateway, as in World War I, proved to be an important factor in by-passing the overcrowded Chicago terminal area. The road's fastest

220

freights, Nos. 96 and 97, linking Minneapolis and Peoria, often ran in sections or were operated as extras.

The busiest section of the system, however, was on the historic main line between Minneapolis and Albert Lea. Instead of ten through-trains between these communities, the number was doubled, tripled, and on occasions went even higher. In addition the Omaha Railway, which has trackage rights from Minneapolis to Merriam, operated its own squadron of extras. Along with greatly increased tonnage came many troop trains. The majority of these special passenger movements were from the Twin Cities to Albert Lea, with Albia next, and Fort Dodge and Des Moines also in the running. Practically all troop runs went through the Twin Cities gateway. The car service department shows that some 946 extra passenger movements went over M&StL rails in the period of national emergency.

A comparison of the results of operation during the two world wars may be in order. War was declared on Germany April 6, 1917, and on December 28, the Government took over the railroads. In 1917 the M&StL handled 1,119,920,904 ton-miles of revenue freight and showed an operating ratio of 71.51 per cent and a net income of $651,050. The following year, during Government operation, the ton-miles slipped to 1,021,838,170, but the operating ratio rose to 94.73 and the combined corporate and federal annual report showed a net *deficit* of $1,878,578.

How different was the road's picture during World War II! The ton-miles increased only slightly over World War I, the figure starting at 1,323,286,817 in 1942 with a constant rise to 1,517,806,108 in 1945. The average operating ratio (operating expenses divided by operating revenues) for the four-year period was 74.46 and the average net income slightly over two and a half million. From every viewpoint, this is vastly better railroading than that of World War I.

When peace returned in 1945, there was no appalling neglect of maintenance or car repair. All during the war the roadbed was kept up, and as steel was made available new rails took the place of the old on the main line. With shortages of manpower and materials, the company could not always continue improvements as in peacetime, but the road was far from rundown. Indeed, during the latter part of the war era two powerful three-unit Diesels added a new look to the fastest freights.

There were some things, however, which money could not replace. Loss in war service of employees who would never railroad again left heavy hearts in the rank and file. The postwar M&StL with all its optimism and hope for the future had also a tinge of sadness.

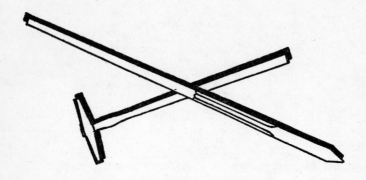

Your Railroad is better equipped today than ever before to provide the quality and type of freight service necessary in the highly competitive field of rail transportation.

Annual Report, 1948.

18

Peace and Prosperity

Receivership, war, and then peace. Normal times with *competent* local ownership and management. A dream fulfilled! The St. Louis Road, as Minneapolitans liked to call the M&StL in bygone years, had at last come into its own. After nearly every conceivable type of operation, including domination by other roads, management from New York, a stint of Federal control, and a long period in the hands of the courts, the Louie had finally made good as a home enterprise.

The war's increased traffic aided in the road's financial comeback although the physical rehabilitation was well under way at the time of Pearl Harbor. But when the conflict ended, the management made an even better showing. By 1948 the company's net income had risen to over 2 million dollars, the highest in its history. The peak in ton-miles of revenue freight had passed, but new highs in operating efficiency were just beginning. Along with practical, hard-headed railroading came an enthusiasm, fostered by Lucian C. Sprague, which simmered through the rank and file.

In the 1920's and early 1930's the road practically ceased to advertise, and few people heard of the M&StL other than those who lived along its route. The picture is different today. Some of the agents in the smaller stations are so proud of the calendars which the new management first brought out in 1937 that they have almost every issue hung on the walls. One can still see pot-bellied stoves (occasionally with the name Iowa Central on them) in a few of the smaller depots and, in the background, a calendar showing a three-unit Diesel!

The road makes it a policy to participate in local events, whether it be the Minnesota State Fair, with a model train exhibition; the Minneapolis Aquatennial, to which it contributes parade floats; or civic, business, and social gatherings, before which the company might show its movie, *Fast Freight*. To publicize its service nationally, the pages of *Business Week, U. S. News, Newsweek,* and other well-known magazines carry the Peoria Gateway Line's advertisements. Vigorous trade and specialized publications like *Railway Age, Traffic World,* and *Trains* are also included in its advertising budget. Of great importance, too, is the local press. In many on-line newspapers and smaller regional magazines the M&StL herald is frequently seen. The road has a story to tell and a service to render. As a bridge line its customers embrace all America, and as a local carrier it originates traffic destined for many parts of the nation.

The backbone of the M&StL is the Minneapolis-Peoria line—something to remember. During the war a large share of the improvements were concentrated on the main stem between the two cities. Up on the seventh floor of the Northwestern Bank Building and down at the Cedar Lake shops in Minneapolis conferences were held and plans discussed. Tests were made on the two giant three-unit Diesels, one arriving in April and the other in May of 1945. In June the news broke. Two fast freights would be put on between Minneapolis and Peoria, clipping over eight hours off the swiftest eastbound run and better than nine hours off its western counterpart. The new hotshots, Nos. 19 and 20, were to "hightail" right through, pausing only to change crews and to set out or pick up cars at Oskaloosa. They would replace Nos. 94 and 97, formerly the best "time" freights on the line, south of Albert Lea.

To the old engineers it seemed incredible. Fueling once at Cedar Lake and then batting through to Bartlett Yard in Peoria, 475 miles away! Railroading was not as it used to be—even on the M&StL.

The operation of Nos. 19 and 20 soon became an institution. People began to judge the time of day by observing these crack trains rumbling by their farms or through their communities. With the onrush of long "time" freights pulled by shiny Diesels, the once-popular M&StL jokes and anecdotes were a thing of the past. There are still some old-fashioned, wooden, green stations, those quaint structures with the bay windows fronting on the tracks and the order-boards overhead. Some have given way to smart "bric-block" buildings, but it will be years before all the aged depots are replaced. Many of the veteran agents and trainmen who have seen the Louie in its worst days are still making out waybills and punching tickets. Likewise, the conductors' caps continue to carry the familiar M&StL insignia with "The Peoria Gateway" on the two-color rectangle encompassed by a circle. The personalized service remains much the same—one can scarcely add to that. But the physical plant is tailored for today's business, from the track up.

The postwar period is essentially a continuation of the improvement program, partly curtailed by the war. Enlarged sidings, spring switches with signal protection, automatic interlocking devices installed at additional railroad crossings, and block signals safeguarding movement on the four-mile Kickapoo Hill out of Peoria are some of the many current improvements. Up and down the line caterpiller tractors are busy "daylighting the cuts," as widening the right-of-way through summits is termed. When this is done snow is less likely to pile up on the tracks. Where many wooden trestles once stood, there are now fills with small culverts to take care of the drainage. Getting rid of the troublesome and expensive timber bridges is a vital part of modern railway engineering. When a bridge is necessary, wood is replaced by stout deck-girders placed on solid concrete piers and abutments.

Traffic-wise, peacetime expansion took the form of opening new off-line agencies at Houston, Texas, and Great Falls, Montana. It has witnessed the inauguration of tele-type to nearly all agencies, far from M&StL rails. On the Louie, promptness in tracing a car is second only to promptness in delivering it. Nothing irritates a shipper more than inability to get specific information concerning the whereabouts of his freight. Unlike the proverbial rail-roader who closes up like an oyster every time a passenger seeks to get an inkling as to why his train is delayed, the M&StL gives a junction-to-junction follow-up on each car. Shipments are sometimes delayed on the best of rail-roads, and the M&StL is no exception. But there is no hedging from M&StL men; a detailed check is yours for the asking. The car service department has highly-trained sleuths, specialists in tracking down shipments and bringing wayward cars to book.

Sometimes the traffic department is called upon to render a service on which the very fate of a community depends. Take the case of Dallas Center, Iowa. This is an attractive community, with the most homelike station on

228

the M&StL. Thanks to Charles F. Beard, the agent, the depot has Venetian blinds, easy chairs, current magazines, and a beautiful flower garden. A few years ago in a contest conducted by the Dallas Center *Times,* smiling Charlie Beard was acclaimed the friendliest person in the county. The town, like its genial agent, is even-going and self-sufficient—normally, that is. But the summer of 1949 was not normal in one vital respect: there was no water. The town's wells had run dry. The lofty tank supplying the citizens with water was empty. Insurance rates were to be increased because there was no fire protection. To build a pipe line about five miles to the nearest river would take several months. A temporary alternative had to be found.

At this juncture the town fathers called upon the M&StL. Water could be had for a nominal fee from Des Moines. Could the road provide tank cars in this crisis?

The company replied it would do all it could to aid the stricken town. A car could be ordered from the General American Transportation Corporation; the road would clean it to the satisfaction of the Board of Health; the roundhouse-spout in Des Moines could be used to fill the tanker; arrangements would be made to unload the car near the storage tank in Dallas Center. The town council drew up a contract to rent the specialized rolling stock, made arrangements with Des Moines to buy water, and cleared with the health authorities in regard to inspection. All this took time. But on the afternoon of May 20, 1949, GATX 1286 came rolling into Des Moines on extra freight No. 895 from Oskaloosa. The car was promptly filled with water, and Dallas Center once more went on its serene course.

The post-war years saw readjustments in service to meet

changing conditions. Six streamlined coaches, the finest that money could buy, were put on passenger runs from Minneapolis to Des Moines, Minneapolis to Watertown, and Albert Lea to Albia. The remainder of the system is about equally divided between mixed service and exclusive freight operation.

A few minor abandonments have taken place; the seven-mile branch between St. Benedict and Corwith, Iowa, and a five-mile segment between Fosterdale and Tracy, which was part of the freight route between Oskaloosa and Des Moines. When the Des Moines River went on a rampage a few years ago and washed out part of the latter line, it was never restored. Today, M&StL freights linking Oskaloosa and the Iowa capital go south to Albia and then over the joint Burlington-Wabash line to Des Moines.

The so-called Tracy branch is remembered in one unusual respect. It had a bridge over the Des Moines River of a unique metallurgical composition called "Hay" steel made under the supervision of Abram Tuston Hay. Since the Oskaloosa-Tracy line was purchased from the Chicago, Burlington & Quincy in 1934, the history of the bridge goes back to that road. The through trusses of the span were originally used on the Burlington's line crossing the Missouri River at Plattsmouth, Nebraska, in 1880. Later, a bigger structure was constructed over the Missouri, and the old 400-foot spans were utilized on the "Q's" Oskaloosa-Tracy road to carry its tracks over the Des Moines River.

No further thought was given to the historic span until near the end of the second World War. At that time tests were being conducted on the various types of steel, and the old, transplanted Plattsmouth girders were remembered. Ralph Budd, then president of the Burlington, requested that a sample of the unique metal be cut out of the bridge for analysis by the United States Steel Corporation. This was done. Whether the findings will contribute to the scientific advancement of mankind is problematical. Metallurgically, however, it remained the only bridge of its kind in America. Moreover, the lofty trusses in the Tracy structure were from the second oldest steel railroad bridge in the nation.

In 1950, the M&StL is passing another mighty significant milestone in its progress up the long grade of financial and physical rehabilitation. Early the next year the Minneapolis headquarters of the railway will be located in its own building, for the first time since the early days nearly three-quarters of a century ago.

Climaxing the first fifteen years of the improvement program, begun when the present management headed by Lucian Sprague took charge, the M&StL will erect a new million-dollar general office building about a mile from the downtown business district, on Franklin between Stevens and First Avenues South. This is to be a modern but strictly utilitarian structure, designed and built for exclusive use of the railway and the 400 men and women who work in its many departmental offices. Ground was broken early in 1950 and the building is scheduled to be completed in about twelve months.

The first modest headquarters of the M&StL were in its own small station in the Minneapolis milling district, near the Falls of St. Anthony. A few years later, the general offices were moved to the Boston Block and since then have been located in rented quarters. Next, the railway moved to the Metropolitan Life Building and then to the Transportation Building. About ten years ago, an-

231

other move was made, to the Northwestern Bank Building, largest office structure in Minneapolis, where the M&StL now occupies nearly two floors.

The transformation of this Midwestern prairie road from a weakling to one of solid strength having been dwelt upon, a word about the men who shape its policies is now in order. First on any railroad is the president. "Lou" Sprague brought foresight, business acumen, and enthusiasm to the road when urgently needed. But Sprague is aided by five vice presidents with specific major responsibilities. Without the constant teamwork of such lieutenants no railroad can achieve a measure of success. It is pointless to establish a hierarchy, for each of the presidential advisers, as it were, is master of a very specialized function. A good place to start is with operation— the most dramatic phase of railroading.

Vice President and General Manager John W. Devins is boss over operations embracing maintenance of way and structures, maintenance of equipment, together with train movement, car service, engineering, and purchasing. Starting with the M&StL in 1912 as an accountant, he later turned to yard and road service, becoming successively switchman, yardmaster, general yardmaster, trainmaster, and superintendent. By 1935 he was made general manager and in 1943 vice president and general manager.

A quick thinker and close observer, he carefully weighs problems before deciding on a course of action. He is thorough in giving instructions and careful to see that they are readily understood. While exacting in his requirements, John Devins is also considerate of the problems of others. His sense of humor and appreciation of the human side of life are frequently evinced in the expression of his eyes and by his pithy remarks.

Getting freight is fully as important as moving it; hence Arthur C. Leake, vice president, in charge of traffic, is also a key man on the M&StL. A newcomer to Minneapolis but a veteran on the road, Leake assumed his present office in 1948 when his predecessor, Herbert W. Ward, left to head the Illinois Terminal Railroad. Smiling, approachable, and sincere, Art Leake has done much to win friends for the Peoria Gateway Line. He came to the M&StL from the Frisco as traveling agent in 1929, and was soon heading the company's off-line agencies in Birmingham and St. Louis. Then Arthur Leake was summoned to Minneapolis. Actually, however, he is the M&StL's ambassador-at-large to all the United States. Big shippers and small greet him warmly on his constant trips over his territory, a territory spanning the nation.

Much of the credit for rescuing the company from receivership should be given to C. W. Wright, vice president and general counsel. Wright came to the road as general attorney in 1922, just before it lapsed into the court's hands. He has seen claims pile up and creditors line the company's office in appalling numbers. For over five years he worked to reorganize the road. Wright was selected by W. W. Colpitts and L. C. Sprague as attorney for the reorganization manager because of his knowledge of the property, the legal details, and his skill as a diplomat. The long pull back would have been much longer without the sound judgement and tireless effort of the general counsel.

Newest of the vice presidents and one of the older employees in service among the higher executives is George

A. Anderson, vice president and comptroller in charge of the accounting and treasury departments. Starting with the accounting department at the age of seventeen, Anderson has never left the road or the department. Every ticket, every waybill, all the vouchers, and all payrolls must pass through his office. Indeed the graphs, charts, and annual reports which emanate from the comptroller's office are a barometer of the road's health, and his advice in matters of finance is of vital significance.

Finally, there is John J. O'Brien, vice president and secretary, who came with the road to expedite its reorganization. As reorganization committee secretary, much of the detail in launching the new company fell into his lap. Associated with Coverdale & Colpitts, consulting engineers, he has an admirable background in railroad finance and engineering. Experience in revitalizing other major railways helped him tackle the problems besetting the M&StL. As secretary of the company, details of directors' and shareholders' meetings and other corporate matters are left in his capable hands. O'Brien proposed the pension plan now in effect on the M&StL, and it was largely through his efforts that the plan was carried out. He also serves as New York representative for the road and is in close touch with banking houses, the Big Board, and eastern stockholders.

Here, then, are the five vice presidents, the men who form the president's cabinet. To them is intrusted the job of working with Lucian Sprague to make the M&StL a finer and more efficient railroad. On the Peoria Gateway Line one is not an executive or an employee of *the* railroad—it is always *our* railroad. The spirit of the employees, no less than that of the officials, has made the road what it is today.

*There is perhaps no railroad in the Middle West
that has a more loyal staff of employees.*
228 I.C.C. 277
(concerning the proposed dismemberment
of the M&StL)

19

Men of M. & St. L.

A railroad is ninety-five per cent men—and five per cent iron. Without the whole-hearted teamwork of the rank and file, no railroad can give good service, regardless of the state of its equipment or the condition of its track. Basic to all forms of unified endeavor is loyalty. Moreover, it is cumulative. On the M&StL, loyalty is a byword; it has been that way ever since the road began, and it is that way today. The fortunes of the road have varied, but it has always had more than its share of executives who have been exceedingly human and considerate, leaders who have given their best for the company and the men. The employees, in turn, have shown an admirable spirit, noticeable all over the system.

The Louie is not the longest railroad in the country, nor the wealthiest, nor does it haul the heaviest traffic. It is, however, as often heard up and down the line, "one of the best roads to work for." The day of the boomer is past. Once a man hires out on the M&StL, the chances are that he'll remain on the road all his life. The chances are not remote, either, that his sons may work for the road—and even his grandsons.

Even the Railway Transfer Company, wholly-owned subsidiary of the M&StL, has its own way of rewarding long and faithful service. It takes a capable man to run this little railroad, for it is an exceedingly busy terminal property in the downtown mill district. From the time it was formed in 1883 until 1928, a man with the good County Cork name of Jerry A. Moynihan "worked" the Transfer. Switchman, yard foreman, then superintendent, Jerry knew railroading and he knew men.

Take the case of how Jerry handled a particularly trying situation just after World War I. Many of the switchmen were new and inexperienced, and the yard did not run as smoothly as in normal times. The superintendent of a gas works served by the Transfer, a Scotchman by the name of MacArthur, was in high dudgeon about the inefficiency of the switchmen, and told his troubles to Jerry. The railroader listened for a few minutes and then said, "Mac, are you better than God?" MacArthur did not get the meaning of the question but replied he was not better than the Almighty. Jerry then said, "Well, Mac, God made those men that you have been so critical of. Do you think you could have done a better job?"

When Jerry retired, the company presented him with a cloth-bound book entitled *One of the Moynihans.* It recounts the story of this veteran executive, who, along with three brothers, came from Ireland to learn railroading in America. And the Moynihans are still working at the Transfer. Jerry is now dead, but his son, Frank, carries on as yardmaster. Two of Frank's sons are, in turn, following in their dad's and grandad's footsteps by working at the Transfer; Frank, Jr., as a switchman and Jerry as a clerk.

On the M&StL proper the record of James Teyro, a veteran roadmaster, is much like Moynihan's. In 1931 Jim Teyro took his long-earned rest after completing fifty-one years of service on the Louie. That, too, called for a celebration. In his home town of Hopkins, Minnesota, the high school auditorium was hired for the occasion, and Jim's many friends came on special trains to congratulate him. From the receiver to the laborer on the extra gang, the old man was acclaimed. Jim's career is briefly told in a booklet called *After 51 Years*, published by the company in his honor. Coming to this country from Bohemia in 1880, he hired out on the St. Louis Road as a laborer at $1.25 a day. Jim Teyro knew no English when he came to America, but he was just as adept in learning the new tongue as he was in catching on to trackwork. He started on the payroll when 40-pound rails were being replaced by 56-pound rails; and when he retired, 85-pounders were giving way to 100's. The short tribute to the faithful road-master ends as simply as it begins, with a homely farewell: "Goodbye, Jim, take keer yerself." Jim has passed on, but his son, George, carries the Teyro banner as general road-master for the entire system.

In the general office only one or two of the older employees remember Joseph Gaskell, an Englishman, who was secretary of the company from 1894 to 1907. Gaskell looked like a character out of Dickens—one of Dickens' better characters—having side whiskers and a very stately bearing. His methodical, painstaking records are a contrast to the slipshod methods that were so prevalent in nineteenth-century railroading. Gaskell was, indeed, part of the M&StL tradition. So, too, was John B. Kelly, a tall, lanky roadmaster, who could easily have doubled for Abraham Lincoln. Like Abe, Kelly was plain, honest, and forthright; a familiar figure, slowly walking the tracks, ever on his guard for defects and irregularities on the right-of-way. His long, measured step, solemn countenance, and kindly manner, to say nothing of his dry, Irish wit, made "J. B." a character whose memory lingers on.

Some of the veteran employees who worked for the road in the last century are still living. In Marshalltown that grand old "B and B" man, Swan Johnson, recalls building bridges on the old "Cannon Valley" when the M&StL operated that line. Never was there a more devoted and faithful man than this quiet, mild-mannered bridge and building supervisor... In Estherville, Gustav M. Dallman, a retired section foreman, lives in the eve of life. Gus started railroading in 1895, and helped to build the New Ulm-Estherville line around the turn of the century. His three sons, Hugo, John, and Paul, carry on the tradition of their father, working in the same capacity on the same road... In Minneapolis resides John Steinhagen, another former sectionman with a long, admirable record. Among a lengthy list of awards for excellency in trackwork, dated November 21, 1885, is found his name, having won the "Third Premium" of $5 for his section of road on the Pacific Division. The next year, his well-kept roadway at Hamburg, Minnesota, won the "Second Premium" of $10. Today, the Steinhagen's home is just as neat and tidy as was his track in the eighties.

In the operating department no executive on the M&StL was better liked than James P. Houston. Houston worked up from the ranks to become general manager and he knew railroad operation like a book. Rough and unpolished, he was genuine and sincere, a top-of-the-rail executive beloved by all. Many a time he could be heard all over the building disciplining an employee for an infraction of the rules. But Houston was not a man to hold a grudge. After the punishment had been meted out, it was not uncommon for the erring railroader to come out of the general manager's office smoking one of the "old man's" cigars. If an employee had been injured, he would seek advice first from "J. P." A fellow never went to a lawyer or outside counsel while Jim Houston was on the road.

Of much the same caliber is A. T. Nelson, known to everyone on the road as "Bat." Although he retired a few years ago, trainmen still talk of Bat with tremendous respect and admiration. Bat Nelson, like Houston, was a product of the old school, with a minimum of formal education and a lifetime of practical experience. A strict disciplinarian on the one hand and a man who would fight for his men on the other, Bat represented the finest of the old M&StL tradition.

Railroaders in other days were inclined to be individualists, but no one on the road was more of an individualist than Dexter M. Denison, traffic manager extraordinary. "Deck" had neither looks, nor the polish of a higher education, but he did have personality and it was all Dexter M. Denison's. About as handsome as Will Rogers, he, like the Sage of Claremore, made friends naturally. Followed by a big smile and warm handshake, Deck's salutation to shippers big and small was: "How are you, you old so-and-so?" Many stories are told of how an occasional irate shipper stomped up to the office and complained about damage or delay in transit. If Deck was there, he'd have the enraged shipper smiling within a few minutes, and by lunch time they'd be going out together, the best of friends.

Deck was an inveterate joker and his pranks are still recalled with a chuckle by those along the M&StL. His "scientific discovery" while he was a station agent at Livermore, Iowa, probably tops them all. Things were a bit quiet in this community before a chunk of molten substance was discovered near the depot. Passersby inquired of the agent as to the strange material partly imbedded in the earth. Deck casually dropped the remark that it resembled a fallen meteor. No, it was not there yesterday —perhaps it had fallen during the night. Word got around, and the whole town became curious. The local paper carried stories on the remarkable incident. Scientific men were called... And then—well, the meteor turned out to be just a huge piece of coal burned to a "nigger-head." Deck had carefully put the large chunk of coal on his pot-bellied stove, and the flames had done the rest. It had been a simple matter to carry the fused mass outside in the evening and place it where it would attract everybody's attention the next day.

Speaking of stations brings to mind the old depot at Redwood, Minnesota, and Richard W. Sears. Back in 1886, Sears was the agent at what was then called North Redwood. One day he received a shipment of watches consigned to the local jeweler. But the jeweler refused to accept the shipment. Sears could have returned the parcel to the Chicago wholesale house from which it had come. Instead, he decided to sell the watches himself. A few letters to his fellow agents along the line, and he had convinced them he was selling good timepieces at bargain rates. In a short while Sears had disposed of the initial shipment and was ordering more. Then and there he started a mail-order business which was to become the world's largest.

At the end of that year he quit railroading to establish R. W. Sears Watch Company in Minneapolis. In 1887 the "Barnum of merchandising" moved to Chicago and continued to expand his mail-order business. He hired a watchmaker by the name of Alvah C. Roebuck, and several years later the firm became Sears, Roebuck & Company. Although Sears died in 1914, his name has become legendary. The Redwood station, with the exception of a small addition, is virtually the same as it was when Dick Sears sold tickets—and watches—there. At Lake Mills, Iowa, the agent will point out a quaint desk, cut out in the center so the operator could lean forward to see the trains from the bay window, which is at least seventy years old. "That's the desk Sears used when he worked at this depot before going to Redwood," the agent said, in much the way that the Daughters of the American Revolution elaborate on an antique bed in which Washington is reputed to have slept.

Another story, which is based on fact but which in the constant telling has become so magnified as to resemble a legend, concerns one Solon Tupper, locomotive engineer. Between his daily stints at the throttle Tupper was associated with banks at Winthrop and Morton, in Minnesota. Indeed, the engineer-banker often carried bags of currency up on the boiler-head in the cab, to save express charges. Shrewd, thrifty, and dependable, old Solon Tupper proved to be an excellent engineer, a power in rural finance, and a man of means. When the road was hard pressed for funds before the first World War, this engine-man is said to have loaned the company money on more than one occasion. Veteran trainmen aver he "helped the Louie meet the payroll," which may or may not be true, but top-ranking officials are certain he did make funds available to the railroad.

So much for the yesterdays on the M&StL. Today's employees have shown keen business ability in mutual welfare projects which are outstanding in the Midwest. The Benefit Association, *managed entirely by the employees,* started with a gift of $10,000 from the company and now has twice that sum in its treasury. It provides sickness, hospitalization, and death benefits for M&StL personnel at

243

an exceedingly low rate. The integrity of the employees is further evinced in the Credit Union, organized back in 1927, the second oldest organization of its kind still doing business in Minneapolis. It has lost less than $200 in unpaid loans during its entire existence.

With this heritage of loyalty to the company and sincere interest in the well-being of fellow workers, the road's employees face the second half of the twentieth century with confidence. A home road, always, the M&StL wisely looks to its own men and women for the stewardship of tomorrow.

Many a switchstand has flicked past my cab window since the days of the prairie and I've leaned out quite a few cabs with initials under my elbows of various roads, but the fondest memories still come from those little old cabs with that magic legend which meant you were a man of substance, a man to be trusted, a man who worked for the M & St L. The coal was rotten, the water awful, the weather horrible, but nothing mattered compared to the glory of railroading on the old M & St L.

Dennis Killeen in a letter to the author dated September 18, 1949.

20

From Woodburners to Diesels

In this day of the radio, the airplane, and the atomic bomb, human nature has not changed as much as one would think. An article which appeared not long ago in *Fortune* brought out the fact that a baby, a pretty girl, and a railroad train are still the leading attention-getters in today's advertisements. Of course the most interesting part of a train is the locomotive. So with the assurance that old favorites still have their appeal, this chapter will be devoted to the motive power development on the M&StL.

The earliest locomotives were all woodburners, named after officials and directors of the company. The first two engines were bought second-hand from the Northern Pacific in 1873 and were renamed *H. T. Welles* and *W. D. Washburn* in honor of the first and second presidents of the road. Little information is extant on these pioneer engines except that they had 16 by 24-inch cylinders, four drivers, and tipped the scales at 67,000 pounds each, exclusive of the tender. For many years their 4½-foot drivers were the smallest in the company's road service. From the available source material, they apparently were the American type (4-4-0), that is, having four leading wheels, a like number of drivers, and no trailers. On the M&StL, engines with this popular wheel arrangement were always referred to as Standards. The name was indeed fitting, for up to about 1900 the company's engines in this classification were used in both freight and passenger service—a standard locomotive for every type of road operation.

Since the M&StL had been leased by the Lake Superior & Mississippi prior to the acquisition of the *Welles* and *Washburn,* all motive power had been provided by the lessee. After the panic of 1873, the road was operated by its owners, and many locomotives were rented from the Northern Pacific. In 1877, however, the road bought its first new engines from Baldwin's of Philadelphia. Nine Baldwin locomotives were acquired that year, and the musty records indicate that they were all Standards. So sturdy were these old machines that the last one was not scrapped until 1913. While Standards predominated in the seventies, there were some four- and six-wheel switchers puffing down in the mill district. By the end of the century name plates of other manufacturers, such as Manchester, Rhode Island, Pittsburgh, and Schenectady had become familiar. The light Standards held their own, although the sturdy Mogul (2-6-0) came to supplement them chiefly in freight service and the graceful Ten-Wheelers (4-6-0) soon followed for use on the heavier passenger trains.

Unfortunately, little remains of early-day equipment data, but from the painstaking rosters of the road's motive power in *Bulletin No.* 31 of the Railway & Locomotive Historical Society and other sources, a fair cross-section of locomotive development can be gleaned. The tall-stacked Standards were, generally speaking, kept in excellent condition. Untold hours of labor went into cleaning and grooming the Iron Horses before and after the day's work. Many locomotives carried gimcracks and novelties peculiar to their enginemen. Gracing the front of engine No. 7, on the Lake run (Minneapolis to Tonka Bay), was the statue of a Negro boy. Before each run Billy Watson, the engineman, saw to it that a colorful bouquet of flowers was put in the lad's hand with the same care that he kept the brasswork of the locomotive shining like the doorknob of a nineteenth-century business house.

Being under the dominance of other roads during its earlier history, the M&StL sported engines of many companies. Coming down the tracks at one time or other were locomotives of the Lake Superior & Mississippi, the St. Paul & Duluth, the Northern Pacific, and the Rock Island. What motive power the M&StL had was typical of the era and not of the road. Aside from tall stacks, which replaced the balloon-like tops of many of the woodburners, the Louie's engines had few distinctive characteristics.

Around the turn of the century, however, the road received fifteen distinguished-looking Schenectady Moguls. These symmetrical, high-drivered machines were extensively used on fast freights and limited passenger runs. When their 64-inch drivers began to roll, railroad men reached for their watches. Then came the graceful Schenectady Ten-Wheeler, which was heralded as *the* passenger engine, and the Mogul was almost entirely given over to freight. The flexible four-wheel truck of the Ten-Wheeler held the track better while rounding curves at high speed than did the rigid, single-axle "pony" of the Mogul. For many years the Ten-Wheelers pulled the crack *North Star Limited* and the less colorful but more

249

exacting Nos. 1 and 2. Calling at all stations, the latter trains operated on a "tight" schedule between the Twin Cities and Des Moines.

Meanwhile, as the M&StL worked hand in hand with the Iowa Central, the freights became heavier and longer. Power, more power, was ever the watchword. The M&StL was slower than most roads in acquiring the Consolidation (2-8-0); however, it made up for it by ordering seven at one crack. Moguls were all right in their day, but progress and the Iowa and Minnesota hills called for the tractive effort of the Consolidation.

Down on the Iowa Central, operated in conjunction with the M&StL from 1900 to its acquisition in 1912, there was an even more varied assortment of motive power. The Marshalltown shops were 100 per cent Iowa Central. There was no infiltration of Northern Pacific or Rock Island policies. In Iowa they did things their own way.

Individuality and resourcefulness characterized the Marshalltown shops perhaps even more than Cedar Lake in Minneapolis. Look at the colorful engine No. 10. "She was a beauty," comments C. B. Rogers, an old Iowa Central man and later master mechanic on the M&StL. "A solid black walnut cab, red plush cushions on both seat boxes, and a boiler covered with Russian iron sheet metal with brass bands!" A Seth Thomas clock hung over the gauges in the cab, and a gold eagle sat proudly on the top of the sand box. The drivers were red with gold stripes. Also in gold over a panel of scarlet on each side of the cab was the name *Russell Sage,* carefully protected under glass covers. The tender, too, was something to behold, having the road's name lettered in gold with gilt water lilies embellishing the four corners.

250

Resourcefulness? Keeping locomotives in repair when one dollar had to do the work of two and rejuvenating superannuated engines far beyond their normal life expectancy was part of the day's work at Marshalltown. If a man passed muster on the Iowa Central he was trained for the exigencies of railroading anywhere! Few roads had a more precarious financial existence than the old Hook and Eye, and few roads of comparative size produced better men.

Back in the seventies a gangling youth from England came to Marshalltown for a job. He had all his earthly belongings tied in a large red handkerchief fastened to a heavy stick slung over his shoulder. Marshalltown took him in. The young Britisher worked hard when on the job, and while other employees played and relaxed at the end of the day's labor, he read textbooks on locomotives. Application to duty plus a keen native ability and what railroad men call "sand" lifted the Briton to the top position in the Marshalltown shops—that of master mechanic. When John Player could go no higher on the Hook and Eye, he turned elsewhere. He finally ended his career as master mechanic for the entire Santa Fe system.

The evolution of motive power on the Hook and Eye generally paralleled that of the M&StL. The Standard, an old faithful on the Louie, was also predominant down in the corn country. On the Iowa Central, however, there was more scrollwork and ornamentation, with a greater variety of design. For sheer beauty few engines could match those outshopped by William Mason. They had line, color, and litheness—locomotives which, as they whistled through the countryside, would make all the farm boys stare. Probably due to the stiff grades, Moguls

251

came sooner to the Iowa Central than to its sister road in the north. The same may be said for the Ten-Wheeler and the Consolidation.

All this is bygone history; what about steam locomotives which link yesterday a little closer with the present? Enter, then, the Mikado (2-8-2). Engines of this classification rolled out of the Schenectady works of the American Locomotive Company in 1915, bound for Cedar Lake; and out of its Brooks plant the following year; and again in 1921. Thirty-five in all, the so-called 600-class engines were and *are* good machines. Until the coming of the Diesels, they fitted the road like a bathing suit fits a model. Suppleness, grace, and glamor—they had all three.

From 1915 to 1938 the light Mikes, with little modification, did yeoman duty in pulling the road's time freights and heavy tonnage trains. When L. C. Sprague came along to rehabilitate the property, he promptly set out to improve the motive power. Although many of the engines were scrapped, Sprague's early experience as a locomotive engineer convinced him that the 600's were worth rebuilding. The Mikados were sent to the back shop; and when they came out, they were changed indeed. Thanks to such modern devices as feed water heaters, better superheating units, boosters, syphons, mechanical stokers, to name but a few, the tractive effort was stepped up from 46,000 to 61,300 pounds. Two of the 600's were outfitted with stainless steel jackets and partly stream-lined. The large sandboxes, lengthened to 6 feet, polished steel rods, and burnished cylinder heads, together with revamped tenders, gave them a distinctive appearance.

Another type of engine which came to the M&StL in the early twenties was the Pacific (4-6-2). The road rather

252

belatedly ordered five of these attractive locomotives from American to bolster up its passenger business when many riders were shifting from rail to highway. Although the Pacifics performed admirably, they operated scarcely over a decade before gas-electric rail motor cars began supplanting them. Passenger traffic had dwindled to such a degree that motorized service was ample to handle the remainder.

Until recently the company still had one lone Pacific on its roster, which was used to haul directors' and officials' business cars over the line. During September, 1949, this valiant old steamer, No. 502, was sent to the Chicago Railroad Fair, all shined up as in days of yore. It had the honor of appearing in the finale of *Wheels A-Rolling,* a remarkable pageant written by the late Edward Hungerford. That was the final job for engine 502.

An all-important part of the road's modernization program centers on the use of Diesel power. The first internal-combustion locomotive to see service on the Peoria Gateway Line was D-438, an eight-wheel, 600-horsepower Electro-Motive Diesel-electric switcher. It was put in operation shunting cars in Minneapolis in April, 1938—one of the earliest Diesels to appear in the Twin Cities area. With the new type of switcher came a revised method of numbering. All of the first Diesels were prefixed with the letter "D" in front of the numbers. The last two digits indicated the year put in operation, and the other numbers signified the month. This simple system of numbering is still in use, except that the Diesels ordered in recent years no longer carry the "D."

The oldest Diesel is not a striking machine, being rather squat with a cab at the end of a long business-like hood. But contrasted with steam switchers, it made a spectacular record for around-the-clock availability and the faculty of exerting its maximum power at the start. Steam, on the contrary, must undergo frequent cleaning of flues, and its maximum drawbar pull is not exerted until the locomotive is under way. In the words of one engineer, the Diesels "just get up and go." No need to take up slack, regardless of the length of train or the per cent of the grade.

Within five years the Diesel switchers took over most of the yard operations on the M&StL. The 600-horse-power units soon shared the rails with 660-, 900-, and 1000-horsepower jobs. Later came General Electric 380-horsepower engines for service in the smallest yards. In short, a Diesel for every type of switching operation. From General Electric's cab-in-the-center to Electro-Motive's cab-at-the-end, with a traditional if somewhat abortive exhaust pipe, and American Locomotive Company's compact cab-at-the-end *without* the stack, the Diesels came to stay.

When the second World War engulfed the country, traffic increased to such an extent the company felt the need for more-powerful road locomotives. This brings to mind what David P. Morgan, a keen student of motive power, calls "the M&StL's ghost articulateds." In the earlier years of the conflict an order was placed with Baldwin for five husky 2-6-6-4 simple-articulated freight locomotives. On account of wartime restrictions prohibiting new models, the engines were to be patterned after the Seaboard Air Line's R-1, 2500-series locomotives (which that road has now sold to the Baltimore & Ohio).

Although such an august authority as the *Railway Age* announced the order, the five articulateds never went beyond the blueprint stage. The hitch was the difficulty in getting additional steel to strengthen several bridges

254

for the new motive power. During that critical period the War Production Board was loath to grant permission for such projects—so the articulateds died "a-bornin'." In place of the 2-6-6-4's the road went to Electro-Motive to explore the possibilities of using a triple-unit-4050-horsepower freight Diesel. By spreading the weight over the Diesel's twenty-four wheels, as contrasted to the articulated's eighteen, the bridge-restrictions posed no problems. Once again the internal-combustion engine scored a victory when the first three-unit locomotive rolled over the M&StL rails in April, 1945.

All Cedar Lake and thousands of Minneapolis people turned out to inspect No. 445, a massive two-jointed monster, painted green and yellow with attractive red-striped wings enclosing the M&StL emblems at each end. A $400,000 engine! The 151-foot locomotive was the largest and most powerful unit ever to operate on the road.

After road tests were made and the "bugs" taken out of the new engine, it was given the task of pulling the company's fastest freights between Minneapolis and Peoria. It, together with a sister locomotive which arrived in May, blazed the trail in highballing tonnage on an accelerated schedule over the main line. Here was railroading in a truly modern manner. No backing up to take slack, no halting for coal and water, no stopping to change engines—the "three-units" barreled right through from terminal to terminal.

While there is some saving in running-time, the Diesel's chief whip hand over steam is in the elimination of fuel and water stops. On the 476-mile run to Peoria the "steamers" were obliged to halt in front of tanks or chutes at Montgomery and Albert Lea in Minnesota; Hampton, Gifford, Marshalltown, Oskaloosa, and Olds in

Iowa; and Keithsburg, Monmouth, London Mills, and Middle Grove in Illinois. Eleven stops, aggregating approximately six and a half hours! With the Diesel, however, the time freights merely tarry long enough to change crews at division points. As a result, they clipped about eight hours off the former steam schedule between Minneapolis and Peoria the very first year the three-unit engines were put in service.

With the extensive operation of 1000-horsepower road-switchers and the more recent two-unit 3000-horsepower road Diesels, steam was definitely on the way out. The old Standards had long since disappeared from the roster, but some six-wheel switchers, Moguls, Ten-Wheelers, Consolidations, and Mikados are still on the road. On the other hand, a large majority of steam engines have been scrapped or sold, and the road is expected to be completely Dieselized in 1950. Not all of the retired steam locomotives have met the cutting torch, and at the present time eight ex-M&StL Mikados are turning in a full day's work on the Algoma Central & Hudson Bay Railway. They are regularly employed in main line operation, running from Sault Ste. Marie to the heart of Ontario.

In a changing world the M&StL is keeping pace with the times. New modern Diesel shops at Cedar Lake and Marshalltown bespeak up-to-date maintenance of motive power for today and tomorrow. The weed-grown foundations of water tanks and coaling stations reflect yesterday's methods and practices. This is the day of the Diesel.

21

On Rolls the Louie

Times change and old methods and practices are replaced by new. Yesterday a boy in the prairie country
checked his horse to watch the *North Star Limited* go
puffing by. The rattle of the buggy wheels on the dirt
road was soon drowned by the roar of the train. He
couldn't get very close, because Old Dobbin shied away
from the hiss of steam and the shriek of the whistle. Today that boy is a middle-aged man and his son, in turn,
watches the train go by. Instead of a dusty country road,
however, it is U. S. 65; and in place of the buggy, he
drives a convertible. Down the track comes a long freight
pulled by a three-unit Diesel. The railroad parallels the
concrete highway, and the young man steps on the ac-
celerator to keep up with the onrushing train. He knows
it's No. 20 because it always comes through town at that
hour. That fast freight with its green-and-yellow engine
symbolizes the M&StL. The lad turns down the radio to
hear the blast of the air-horn as "20" whistles for the next
crossing.

Times change.

The railroad which once planned to reach the Pacific
found that its future lay in the Midwest. Instead of becoming a "transcontinental," it evolved into a strong bridge
line catering to transcontinental and other long-distance

traffic. Meanwhile, its mission as a local road, providing an independent outlet for the Twin Cities, has never been neglected. Eighty years of service under one name has made the Minneapolis & St. Louis an institution in the Midwest.

The growth of the M&StL went hand in hand with the development of the prairie. If the land did not yield a good crop of wheat or the corn failed to grow to its normal height, the farmer and the railroad suffered. Being locally managed and operated during most of its existence, the M&StL was in closer contact with the husbandman than was the average carrier. Its officials were and are, for the most past, recruited from the farm and the small town. Whole families "belonged" to the M&StL. The Conleys, the Hayneses, and the Munsells out of Conde; the Devenys and the Mullens from Aberdeen. It was almost heresy if a son didn't automatically hire out on the home road.

This *esprit de corps* and a good measure of Midwestern independence kept the system intact when things looked blackest. The railroad which W. D. Washburn fostered and Edwin Hawley brought into full bloom was not allowed to die. It had been up to Lucian Sprague to revitalize the historic company. And that was perhaps the toughest assignment in the whole history of the road.

For years the employees had been schooled in near poverty and the M&StL had been invariably looked upon as a weak sister among the nation's railroads. Its motive power had consisted of a decrepit lot of ancient steamers built largely during the McKinley, "Teddy" Roosevelt, and Taft eras. But beneath the shabby uniforms there had been a deep feeling of pride. One didn't just work for a railroad—one worked for *the M&StL*. The feeling

260

of self-sufficiency which flourished around the turn of the century was never entirely eradicated during the great depression and its aftermath. Better days would certainly come. Like the Mexican laborers who used to come up in droves on M&StL trains to work in the beet fields and talk about *mañana,* so the railroaders speculated on their "tomorrow." Often it was in jest, and yet no matter how flippantly they tossed off the word, the hope for the future could not be downed. Had not the Erie and the Baltimore & Ohio once been laughing stock among railroads? And from that low estate both roads had risen to become first-class carriers in every sense of the word. If such transformations could happen in the East, why not out in the prairie country?

Tomorrow did come. And with it all the promise of the future. In less than a dozen years the Louie emerged from a company of gaslight-and-buggy standards to a railroad ably equipped to meet competition in an age of jet-propelled planes and television. Indeed, the emergence of the M&StL from two decades of seemingly hopeless bankruptcy to the recognized status of a highly modern freight carrier and a sound investment is a saga in American management. It could only have happened in America.

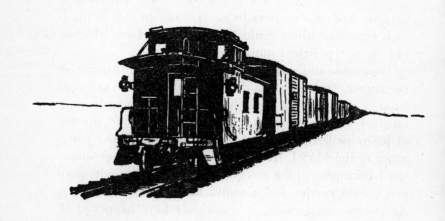

22

Time Freight 20

Minneapolis sleeps while Diesel switchers are busily engaged in making up Time Freight 20 in the Cedar Lake yard. But Cedar Lake never sleeps, for it is the very nerve center of the Minneapolis & St. Louis Railway. Down in a hollow tucked away at the extreme western rim of the city is the nineteen-track yard, the company's shops, enginehouses, and operating headquarters. True, the buildings are dark, for it will be a good three hours before the office force is at work. Not so the yard, however, for it is aglow with switchmen's lanterns bobbing up and down, to say nothing of moving headlights as yard engines come and go.

Our eastern "time" freight pulls out at 5:20, regular as a clock, every day in the year. It and its counterpart, No. 19, are the flagships of the M&StL's fleet of fast freights. They are the pride of the road—symbols of power, on-time performance, and heavy tonnage moved with dispatch. The working timetable cards them as first class— the same as passenger trains—which gives them a status rare on American railroads. Moreover, their performance is watched up at headquarters with the same interest that the New York Central lavishes on its *Twentieth Century* or the Pennsylvania on its equally renowned *Broadway Limited.* Just as everything goes "in the hole" for the *Century* and the *Broadway,* so on the M&StL all trains must take siding for Nos. 19 and 20.

While the milkmen are making their rounds and an occasional "owl" trolley casts its ray of light through the deserted streets, M&StL crews are getting cars for No. 20. Early in the evening a transfer run from St. Paul picks up cars in that capital city and at the Minnesota Transfer and then heads for Cedar Lake. All night long, yard crews bring in freight from the milling district at the Falls of St. Anthony, from the middle yard in downtown Minneapolis, and from numerous industrial sidings and interchange points. A railroad never sleeps.

Now they're getting ready to take out No. 20, for the three-unit 4050-horsepower locomotive has just come from the new Diesel house and is backing toward its train. "Twenty's on track five," Yardmaster E. H. Garlick tells us. "Better get on board and make yourself comfortable." Our yawning becomes less frequent as we walk down the tracks toward the engine. We're going to ride "20" from start to finish, from Minneapolis to Peoria, almost five hundred miles at one sitting.

Once up in the lofty cab we relax in the armchair of engine No. 147. At the throttle is Jim Cummings, a veteran who has seen "forty-three years on the Louie," and in the fireman's seat is Ted Hesch, also an old hand. Presently the car inspector shouts, "O. K. on the air," and a trainman follows this up with the highball. At precisely 5:20 we're off.

There is no taking slack with a Diesel. When all three engines roar in the flexible triplex locomotive, the whole train starts as a unit. The long freight rumbles along the double-track line, past Kenwood, the waters of Cedar Lake, and the large grain elevators at St. Louis Park.

"Yellow board," calls the fireman as the train approaches Hopkins. "Yellow board," observes the engineer, easing up on the air brake. "All lined up," shouts the man on the left, "Lined up," repeats his partner at the throttle. This is the enginemen's way of saying that the agent's signal at Hopkins is clear and the switch is set for the main stem. We leave the double track at the station, clicking by the junction of the Watertown line in doing so. Our engine veers toward the south on rock-ballasted track, laid with 100-pound rail virtually all the way to Peoria.

The sun is up and there's a fresh crispness in the air. What an ideal time to view the Minnesota River Valley and the village of Shakopee from the terrace on Chaska Hill! Interesting country, this, and an area which, geologists tell us, is filled with morainic hills deposited by glaciers eons ago. Whatever the formation, the sweep of the Minnesota River below us is always pleasing to behold. Going down Chaska Hill used to be a ticklish operation when handling a heavy freight. But Engineer Cummings just notches up his dynamic brake lever, and lo— the motors act as generators and retard the movement of the train. Gone are the days of smoking brakeshoes and screeching wheels. "Chasky" no longer holds any terrors, regardless of the length of the train.

We're soon crossing the deck-girder bridge which spans the river, then zoom southward toward the Iowa state line. The pretty falls at Jordan flit by, then the flour mills at New Prague, and the canneries at Montgomery. Farm and factory intermingle in rapid succession.

Just below Kilkenny the fireman points out Younger Brothers Crossing. This was the road over which Bob, Cole, and James Younger fled after holding up the North-field Bank in 1876. There are few people better memorialized than notorious highwaymen. Concrete may replace gravel, streets may change names, but it makes no difference—that rail and highway intersection will ever be remembered by the good folk of Kilkenny as Younger Brothers Crossing.

Waseca comes and goes as we roll along at a steady gait. Now we're "goin' through the Wapsie." If there is a hill or a vale, it has a name, and names are a tradition among railroad men. No one on the road seems to know the origin of the name of this valley or how it is spelled, but all agree it is a place to "go like hell" so as to make the summit on the other side.

After the indefinable Wapsie is passed, the grades are negligible the rest of the way to Albert Lea. At this community there's a laminated rafter works where we see boatlike ribs big enough to have fitted into Noah's Ark. Here's our first crew-change, for Albert Lea is a division point as well as a junction with the M&StL's line to Des Moines. No need to ask if we're on time; that's a foregone conclusion. As a matter of fact, we're ten minutes ahead.

There is a cardinal rule in railroading that a train must never leave a scheduled station ahead of time. There is also an unwritten understanding that a fast freight must never be unnecessarily delayed. Here, alas, is joint track from Albert Lea to Manly, track which is constantly used by two roads. In the twenty-seven-mile stretch the Rock Island owns approximately the upper half and the M&StL the lower. To make matters more involved, the Illinois Central has trackage rights from Albert Lea to

266

Glenville, nine miles. Do we lay over a full ten minutes and hope we won't be "hung up" by a Rock Island freight? Not at all. The dispatcher very adroitly annuls No. 20 from Albert Lea to Manly and substitutes an extra. The extra? That's us—same crew, same consist, same everything but the number. To make it "legal" the fireman puts up two white flags and the engineer shows white marker lights. "Displaying white" indicates we're classed as an extra and can leave as soon as we get the signal, which is now.

"Green over red," calls the fireman. "Green over red it is," acknowledges the engineer as he pulls back the throttle. Our joint track is protected by Centralized Traffic Control and there's no stopping to throw switches or get orders. Thanks to C.T.C., everything is managed from a central control board, and we roll along without let or hindrance.

At Northwood we are in Iowa and on what used to be the old Iowa Central, a road rich in history, legend, and story. That reminds us of a "poem" recounting how Conductor Frank C. (Fat) Parker missed the caboose at Kensett, the next town after Northwood. The brakemen on Parker's train, Thor E. Branstrup and Charlie Armstrong, invoked the muse in describing their conductor's sad plight and dashed off the following:

> Dear, oh dear, what shall I do?
>> There goes the Mogul and the Brownie, too.
> So here at Kensett I must stay.
>> But what the hell about the delay.
> I'll write Jones and tell him that
>> I fell from grace and just sign "Fat."
>> BUT
> If the 1167 only had those patent wings
>> To pick up fat conductors

And other clumsy things,
Those delays that make Jones worry
Would be stopped in quite a hurry—
If only the 1167 had those patent wings.

The incident occurred at the time that everyone was talking about an ingenious inventor who had rigged up a pair of wings and had tried to make a birdlike flight. Harry E. Jones was the trainmaster referred to in the verse, and the 1167, or the *Brownie,* was the caboose. So popular was the poem that a Kensett editor is said to have had it reprinted on little cards and distributed up and down the line.

When Manly is reached, the flags are taken down and we pause to get back on the time of "20." The stop is brief and before we realize it our train is thumping over the railroad crossings at Mason City, a thriving cement and meat-packing center. Just another station to us, but to the crew it's one of the many locales where a running inspection takes place. See that man at the depot giving the train the once-over? He's a car inspector peering at the slowly moving trucks as carefully as a customs officer eyes a stranger near the border. If anything is amiss, he'll phone Mason City Junction, where they will flag us down. It's check and double-check all along the line. When the enginemen stick their heads out of the windows, they're not trying to inhale fresh air. On the inside of sharp curves they invariably glance back along the train to make sure there are no hot boxes or misplaced loads. Again, at designated points on the route the head-end and rear-end crewmen are obliged to signal to each other the fact that everything is in good order.

One gets a splendid view from the full-vision windows of the Diesel and a feeling of unlimited power. The cab is clean, relatively quiet; and the whole locomotive rides with the ease of a Pullman.

The M&StL is primarily a freight road, and yet the passengers on the local trains are treated royally. Take a look at that trim $100,000 stainless steel coach on No. 7 glistening in the sun on Cameron siding. The brass-buttoned conductor gives us a friendly wave as we speed past. Big roads or small, you won't find a nicer day coach in the land—nor a more genial crew.

Our train continues across the heart of Iowa, where agriculture is king. The gently rolling countryside with field after field of newly plowed land will soon be a billowy ocean of corn stalks. Nearing Ackley, however, the terrain becomes hilly, for we are soon to descend into the Iowa River Valley. Ackley, by the way, was the terminus of the Eldora Railroad and Coal Company, the predecessor of the Iowa Central. Its pioneer line was completed from Eldora to Ackley in 1868. Over yonder stands the historic Central House, where townfolk are said to have celebrated the occasion.

By this time the engineer has one hand on the "air" and the other on the dynamic brake. Going or coming, Steamboat Rock just ahead of us is the "ruling grade."

"Come over this way and look downstream," suggests the fireman. "I think we'll be able to see 'Steamboat.' "

We lean out of the window and peer along the river until we observe a black object jutting out from the tree-lined bank.

"See it?" he shouts. "It's a rock shaped like a steamboat. Prettiest spot on the M&StL!"

It is pretty. In this picturesque area the train winds around wooded knolls and through shaded valleys. Hold on, now; we're taking the grade on the other side of Steamboat. Not so many years ago helper engines were required on nearly all freights in either direction. Now our Diesel just laughs at the hills.

Eldora, at the top of the grade, is a town characteristic of Iowa's many smaller communities. The green M&StL depot is typical of many midwestern stations. Uptown is the courthouse with its clock and tower. Here and there church steeples rise up over the trees and housetops. Trim lawns and well-kept homes abut on the right-of-way. The church, the courthouse, and the depot are plain, and yet each is distinctive in a way. All three are as much a part of Iowa as its tall corn.

We cross and recross the Iowa River before entering Marshalltown, our next division point. Here the M&StL maintains extensive car shops, one of which bears the date 1879. There's not much time to observe this industrial and railroad center, for the crews have changed, and two blasts of the whistle indicate we're on our way. A half mile down the tracks, however, we come to an abrupt halt. Why? "Hot box on the head tanker; we'll cut it off and be out of here in a jiffy," says the engineer. Even as he talks, they've uncoupled the ailing car, and a switcher shunts it onto a side track. Our head brakeman describes a circle at half arm's length, and we go back and couple up. Five minutes lost—no, it's nearer four.

For about three miles we parallel the Chicago & North Western right-of-way along which yellow streamliners race from Chicago to the West Coast. Except for a different color scheme and "southpaw" operation, many of the C&NW Diesels could easily be mistaken for those on the M&StL. Parting ways with the left-handed North Western, we again head south. Railroads? Iowa is full of them, but they generally run east and west. The Louie, on the other hand, intersects lines at frequent intervals as it cuts across the midriff of the state.

Down the road a little farther we speed over the Milwaukee at Pickering and cross the Rock Island at Grinnell. Before we come to the Route of the Rockets, however, we slow down for Grinnell College campus, which the M&StL virtually divides in half. There is always a group of lads and lassies strolling across the greensward. The University of Texas boasts that its college song is sung to the tune of "I've Been Working on the Railroad," but that's railroading by proxy. In Grinnell they have the real thing, sound effects and all.

A few years ago in Indiana an Iowa boy was listening to a football broadcast from Grinnell College stadium. The lad was from Oskaloosa, where youngsters divide their time between playing baseball and watching the M&StL trains. The former is a seasonal pastime, whereas the latter is a year-'round sport, hence very popular. At any rate, the boy's thoughts returned homeward as he listened to the "Pioneers" struggle for a goal. But when the radio announcer said, "We will now pause while an M&StL freight train passes through the campus," and when a whistle shrieked midst the sound of clanging bell and hissing steam, that was enough.

"You know that old M&StL whistle made me so homesick," he said, "I felt like packing my grip and taking the first train home."

Once again we're in the rolling, hilly country after Grinnell's spring switches are past. Our heavy freight crosses a series of ridges and then coasts down the seven-mile School House Hill. Now we're on the Searsboro-Oak Grove grade revision, and we see traces of the former road-bed zigzagging in the fields. There are still grades and curves, but the elevations are not as steep nor the bends as sharp as they were on the Iowa Central of yesteryear.

In this part of Iowa it's a safe bet that there's a river or stream in every valley—and there are plenty of valleys. More often than not, rivers like the North Fork of the Skunk (over which we cross) seem slow and motionless. But the most innocuous-looking rivulet has a way, in certain seasons of the year, of becoming a whirling, raging torrent. A few miles farther on, we cross the Skunk proper, a little wider and swifter than its neighbor to the north. In grandfather's day the Iowa Central used to run excursions from Oskaloosa to the banks of the Skunk, which was considered a first-rate picnic spot and a fisherman's paradise.

The engineer is now whistling for Oskaloosa, and there's Penn College at the edge of town. The school is named after William Penn, founder of Pennsylvania and origi-nator of one of the first plans for world government. Al-though the college is small and limited in enrollment, it has, in the true Penn tradition, sent men of good will to all parts of the globe. In 1947 one of its alumni and a former teacher, Clarence Pickett, accepted the Nobel Peace Prize for the American Friends Service Committee.

When Oskaloosans talk about Oskaloosa, sooner or later they will mention their fellow townsman and composer, Frederic Knight Logan. If you tarry a while they'll show you his home on East B Avenue. The fame of his *Missouri Waltz,* which is well known in all America, has even spread across the Atlantic.

272

To the M&StL, Oskaloosa is a vital community, a division headquarters, and a busy railroad junction. Here, and only here, does No. 20 stop to set out and pick up cars. About a third of our train will continue south to Albia, where the Wabash will highball it to St. Louis or Kansas City. There is also a cut of cars waiting for us from the M&StL's Des Moines train, as well as from other through and local freights.

While crews change and our consist is reshuffled, we stroll down to the attractive red brick station. Nine hours of continuous riding, along with the fact that we arose at 3 a.m., makes us a bit fatigued. As a result, in seeing the initials IC carved in stone on the depot, we exclaim half-forgetfully: "Illinois Central!" Right away we get a scornful look from an employee cleaning a window and then a blunt correction: "*Iowa* Central!" In Oskaloosa it's *lèse majesté* of the worst sort to confuse the two roads. The fact that the Iowa road was taken over by the M&StL in 1912 is not much solace, for a large proportion of the town once worked for the predecessor company, and the old name is a tradition.

Oskaloosa's North Yard sees a lot of activity between the time "20" arrives and the time it departs. While they are revamping our consist, yardmen are also busy making up No. 396 for Albia. Three-ninety-six is actually "Little 20," a part and parcel of our train, but for operating purposes it has to carry another number. Just as soon as our red sidebay caboose clears the yard on the way *east*, "Little 20" will leave for the *south*.

At 3:50 p.m. the engines roar, and our twenty-four driving wheels grip the rails. One hundred and eighty-six miles to go, and then Peoria! Our train is now reduced to fifty cars, a load that's child's play for the three-unit

Diesel to pull. We pass farm after farm being plowed and seeded, and everywhere the rich black soil promises good crops. The afternoon is bright and balmy and the sun glistens on the rails. The section men are proud of their track, and rightly so, for it is perfectly aligned.

Due to trackage improvements and the introduction of modern locomotives, the Peoria Gateway Line's timecard has been altered many times. In 1935, when Lucian Sprague came to the road, the best time made between Minneapolis and Peoria was 32½ hours. During Sprague's administration the elapsed time has been frequently shortened, and by 1944 it was reduced to 28 hours. When the new Diesels were put into service in 1945, they clipped it down to 17 hours 55 minutes, the present running time.

We're droning along at a comfortable rate when the fireman calls out "Skunk!" and we look for the river. No, it's the flesh-and-odor variety this time. We've been on the scent of rabbits, pheasants, and prairie chickens at various points along the line; but when the little fur-lined animal crosses *our* tracks, the scent's on us all the way to Peoria.

At Martinsburg the fireman points out an old right-of-way running parallel to our line. "That was the old M&StL route," he tells us.

"It had everything in the book," the engineer interjects. "Hairpin curves, steep grades, and spindling trestles. And crossings! We played hide and seek with the 'Q,' crossing that line at grade six times in fifty-eight miles.

"When the Burlington abandoned the branch from Oskaloosa to Winfield," he added, "the M&StL bought the Martinsburg-to-Coppock portion of it. All of us are glad we don't have to railroad over the old line, which was abandoned shortly after we began running over the 'Q'."

274

The old line had thirty-eight bridges and four 1 per cent grades.

Between Brighton and Coppock there is a pleasing succession of hills and wooded vales, clear sparkling waters, and fresh, green foliage. There's the Skunk again—the river this time—flowing rapidly toward the Mississippi. You may be sure that our enginemen frequently stick their heads out of the cab and look back over the train as we round the graceful curves in the valley.

At Winfield we pass No. 9, the westbound local freight, snug in the siding. Since we met No. 19, which is superior to us by *direction,* back in Marshalltown, all other trains must now be in the clear. Our train is "hot," and they give us the railroad. No excuses, no apologies—"20" must get through on time.

The towns of Marsh and Morning Sun go by, and then we start downward toward the bottomland of the Iowa River and the Mississippi. Before crossing Old Man River we rumble over the 1506-foot deck-girder bridge spanning Black Hawk Chute. There's a green light ahead—this is it: the Mississippi at sundown! That semaphore tells us the 233-foot vertical lift span is down and the track is clear.

Now we're on the big bridge. The nine massive spans of through-truss design are soon crossed, and we get a final view of the lordly Mississippi. It is calm and serene, blending in nicely with the purple, red, and gray sunset. Sundown on Mark Twain's river is a picture!

Here's Keithsburg, Illinois, once a division point on the Iowa Central and a port of call for nearly all the river packets. Some of its trade has gone elsewhere, but Keithsburg's charm and old-fashioned friendliness remain. Darkness soon engulfs our train, but we'll stay awake regardless

—unless, of course, the coffee gives out. Seaton...Little York...Eleanor...slip by as "20" rolls on its even, steady flight through the night.

"We're coming to Monmouth; s'far as we go," the engineer calls to us. "Get out by the door behind the portholes and wait for the caboose. The new crew knows you're to ride the 'crummy.' Have a pleasant trip!"

After leaving the locomotive we spot the fresh crew: Conductor Harry Livingston, head brakeman Harold Johnson, and rear man Charlie Hoover. We swing aboard the far end of the caboose while No. 20 slowly pulls out of the yard. The oil lamp flickers as the trucks thump over the main line of the Burlington. Also serving Monmouth is the Rock Island Southern, which we spy a little to the north, one of the few railroads with a lady president.

About sixty more miles and our long run will end. Not much to see but the moon, the stars, and our two marker lights. There's a flash of green as the agent's "board" at Nemo recedes in the background. This is an important junction with the Santa Fe where many cars are interchanged to and from distant points throughout California, Texas, and other southern and western states.

Conductor Livingston is now through checking his wheel reports, and we ask him to let us know when we cross the Spoon River, made famous by Edgar Lee Masters' *Spoon River Anthology*. Coming into London Mills he summons us to the door and we go out on the platform.

"That's it," he says, pointing to the void and then a ripple of water glistening in the moonlight. Nothing outstanding about that river, it's just as common as the everyday folks in the *Anthology*, and therein lies its fame. At Middle Grove we swish by long lines of hopper cars

276

awaiting coal from the extensive electrically operated open-pit mines north of the tracks. Then all is quiet. It is cozy inside the caboose, and our trainmen are friendly and talkative. Conductor Livingston explains to us the importance of the Peoria Gateway in expediting traffic by avoiding the congested terminals in Chicago. The road's slogan, "Between East and West M&StL Peoria Gateway Best," he tells us, is no idle boast, as the time saved to and from points in the East and the South sometimes amounts to days.

We made a few notes while glancing through the way-bills in the yardmaster's office at Cedar Lake, so let's look them over. The conductor obligingly turns up the wick and the lamp shines clear and bright. How popular is the Peoria Gateway to shippers? Well, here's a car of lumber hailing all the way from Everett, Washington, and destined clear through to Collingdale, Pennsylvania; just outside of Philadelphia. The Northern Pacific picked up the car—St. Louis Southwestern No. 38585—for the two thousand-mile haul to the NP's interchange tracks in Minneapolis. It's in our train now, a few cars ahead of the caboose. When we get to Bartlett Yard in Peoria, we'll turn the load over to the Chicago & Illinois Midland, and that road will take it to Springfield, Illinois. At Springfield it will be put into a B&O train for the one thousand-mile jaunt to Collingdale.

Some more? We've got a load of plywood originating at Eugene, Oregon, for Memphis, Tennessee. It's Nickel Plate No. 25037. The routing: Oregon Electric; Spokane, Portland & Seattle; Great Northern; M&StL; and Illinois Central. There must be a dozen cars on the train coming from West Coast and Canadian points to the East and Southeast. Probably two-thirds of the swaying cars ahead

277

of us use the Peoria Gateway Line as a bridge route, for they originate and terminate on "foreign" roads. At Peoria M&StL interchanges with thirteen important railroads for all states east of the Mississippi.Many routings, many railroads, *and* a vast saving of time.

Apart from heavy "bridge" traffic in machinery, oil, metal, and forest products, there is considerable tonnage originating along the M&StL. It's a rare day when there isn't flour from Minneapolis in the consist—or oats, malt, cement, canned foodstuff, or beverages from on-line shippers.

"Clear block," calls Brakeman Hoover, looking out the bay window on the other side of the car. We're at Maxwell, top o' the hill and only four miles from Bartlett Yard. This is the famous Kickapoo Hill mentioned so frequently by Fibber McGee and Molly, of radio fame. Both are from Peoria. Looking out from the back platform we are startled to observe a passionate lovers' embrace projected on a huge screen. It's the Bellevue Drive-In Theater—a sure sign we're coming to Peoria.

We have had a long ride through three states. We have gone the way thousands of cars are rolling and will continue to roll, to the open portal between the flourishing Midwest and the industrialized East, with a congenial crew, on an on-time run.

And now to sleep, soothed by the echo of Time Freight 20's rythmic click of wheels over rail joints as it speeds on its way, past Mileposts on the Prairie.

Acknowledgments

The comparative lack of printed matter concerning M&StL history is offset by a wealth of information in the minds of present or retired employees who were more than ready to help me. Obviously it is impossible to mention all those who have aided in writing this book, but the following are among the many who have lent a hand.

John H. Cleland, director of public relations, read the entire manuscript and gave freely of his time and knowledge in helping to prepare the copy for publication. His counsel, dry wit, and enthusiastic interest in the project made the task lighter and more enjoyable.

To William C. Knoble, treasurer and assistant comptroller, I am indebted for information regarding financial matters. Mr. Knoble's long service and his background in corporate accounting were of invaluable aid. From the start he has taken a personal interest in the history.

With George E. Brandon, land and tax commissioner, were spent many profitable hours examining old charters, stock and bondholders reports, and yellowing contracts. He has helped assemble this material and assisted in digesting it.

Merle E. Eaton, assistant to the president, aided at every turn in seeing that there was free access to the company's records and *carte blanche* to go anywhere on the 1,400-mile system.

The large collection of maps and data in the Engineering Department was put at my disposal through the courtesy of Chief Engineer C. S. Weatherill and Assistant Chief Engineer G. S. Lovering. No matter how obscure an item was, Ralph C. Haynes, clerk and photographer in that department, could

279

be depended upon to get it for me. Mr. Haynes also provided pictures, over twenty-five of which he took himself. Likewise Carl L. Johnson, valuation accountant, loaned me illustrations and offered suggestions, all of which were put to good use.

Sidelights on passenger service when the *North Star Limited* was in its glory were recounted by D. B. Ransburg, executive representative. Information on passenger operation in more recent years was provided by Walter H. Anderson and S. A. Swanson, general passenger agent and assistant general passenger agent, respectively.

E. L. Crimmen, general superintendent, William O. Rux, assistant to the general manager, and Frank H. Barry, personnel officer, all went out of their way to obtain data and significant facts on yesterday's and today's operations. Moreover, Larry Hanson, chief clerk to the vice president and general manager, was ever ready with a smile and the know-how to be of service.

Old timetables or other railway incunabula were supplied by Oscar M. Sandahl, freight traffic manager, John C. Rohner, traveling agent, Leo Burke, general car foreman, Marshall S. Needham, fuel inspector, and Hazel R. Williams, special representative. C. Leroy Fuller, traffic manager, and John W. Keller, assistant to the vice president, added greatly to my understanding of freight service.

For voluminous material on receivership proceedings and reorganization matters I had only to turn to Irene Rieke, assistant secretary of the company. Miss Rieke, one of the few lady railroad executives in the nation, gave invaluable help.

Mechanical Superintendent R. C. Goebel aided in writing the motive power chapter, and Mechanical Engineer John O. Converse assisted greatly in outlining the evolution of the M&StL's motive power. In addition, Walter C. Johnson, a clerk in the mechanical department, provided helpful material and showed a warm interest in the history. For the rare frontispiece photo I am indebted to John B. Warta, bridge and building foreman.

Henry H. Dombeck, assistant special accountant, patiently curried the personnel files for records of former employees

280

mentioned throughout the book. George T. Pierce, clerk in the accounting department and an executive in both the Credit Union and Benefit Association, explained the functions and objectives of the two employee organizations.

Of the many train and enginemen who have shared their experiences with me, conductors Fred O. Coleman, Lee L. Gillander, and Jasper Johnson, together with engineers John J. Dousette and Edward A. Eng, have been most helpful. Their reminiscences go back to the turn of the century.

An on-the-spot knowledge of the physical property is largely due to the track supervisors: C. W. Froehlich, H. E. Herington, A. L. Lechner, H. E. Olson, G. J. Svec, and J. W. Zettelmier. These gentlemen took me over hundreds of miles of line in their track motor cars while on inspection trips. They were always ready to indicate points of interest and to stop for chats with veteran agents. Whether it was the cold December ride with Section Foreman Merle Quick in looking over the historic Tracy bridge, or the balmy summer day when Section Laborer Carroll R. Reid showed me the site of the now-forgotten car-ferry landing in Keithsburg, I've found the trackmen among the most friendly of employees.

A great deal of local history together with rare illustrations have come my way, thanks to telegraphers at scattered points on the system. Among these helpful individuals are O. H. Leary of Belmond, T. W. Reynolds of Hedrick, and A. Williamson of Kanawha, all in Iowa; Howard E. Bruemmer of Minneapolis, J. H. Jorgenson of Hazel Run, and J. J. Madden of Waseca, in Minnesota; and C. L. Greimann of Keithsburg, Ill.

Most of all, however, I am indebted to President L. C. Sprague for his interest, encouragement, and helpfulness. It was he who threw open all the company records for my perusal and gave me the liberty of interpreting them as I saw fit. At no time did he tell me what to write or how to slant any phase of the road's long and checkered history. Whatever virtue the book possesses must be, in a large measure, attributed to Mr. Sprague and numerous M&StL employees; any shortcomings and errors that may appear are those of the author.

For atmosphere and tradition of the M&StL's yesterdays a great deal of credit is due to many former or retired employees. The very initials "M&StL" are an Open Sesame to hospitality, and a mere mention of the road among old timers brings on a flood of memories. A pleasant afternoon at the home of A. T. "Bat" Nelson in Des Moines, or a half day in the library of Hugh McCarthy overlooking the Mississippi in Minneapolis, brought endless stories, salty in their telling yet authentic and reliable. The Minneapolis office of W. M. Hardin, formerly general freight agent and now vice president of Colonial Warehouses, abounds with photographs of M&StL men and railroad items going back a half-century. Mr. Hardin is never too busy to push aside routine work and descant on the Louie.

The Hawley chapter would not be complete had it not been for the generous assistance of W. B. Davids, formerly treasurer and director of the M&StL. Several delightful afternoons were spent at his attractive Millington, N. J., home in quest of information. Himself a master of English, I hope Mr. Davids will some day write a comprehensive article on the little-known career of Edwin Hawley. Additional sidelights on the Hawley regime were gleaned from a scrapbook loaned to me by W. S. Crandell of Chatham, N. Y., formerly an M&StL director and an associate of the rail magnate.

In rounding out the last chapter of the book I chanced to hear of an ex-fireman on the West End, Dennis Killeen of Salinas, Calif., who is given to writing. Ere long, we were exchanging letters. He "fanned the door" of an old "Pittsburgh" engine—

"Back in the days when the prairie was rough
When nature was wild and men were tough
Where owls would hoot and coyotes yell
We went to LeBeau with the M. & St. L."

Through the courtesy of this former "ashcat" I have quoted a snatch of his letter. He is at present writing a short story on the M&StL for the *Saturday Evening Post* and has just finished a book manuscript of reminiscences out Dakota way. If the story and the book are half as interesting as his letters, they should have a ready sale.

ACKNOWLEDGMENTS

Other retired enginemen who have recited tales of their eventful years at the throttle include George Nelson of Minneapolis and Roy Graft of Oskaloosa. Mr. Nelson recalls the M&StL in the nineties, and Mr. Graft recollects events on the Iowa Central in the last days of the Sage adminstration.

To this list of acknowledgments must be added Merrill C. Wallace, mechanical draftsman of the Northern Pacific and a former M&StL man. Mr. Wallace is a student of locomotive history and has given me information concerning motive power in the days before he or I were born.

Other friendly aides have been Oscar Johnson of Minneapolis, for many years chief clerk in the office of the vice president and general manager, who supplied me with clippings collected during his long career on the M&StL; and Rev. John W. Knoble of New Haven, Conn., author of the short story titled "Oh No, Day Kann Do Dat," based on his observations while clerking in the accounting department during summer vacations. He has kindly given me permission to use a slightly modified version of the title as a chapter heading.

After being off the road for thirty-five years William Rabens, one of the crew of the "Bull Run" when the race horse escaped from that train, came from his home in Montrose, Minn., to Minneapolis just to see that my facts were straight. His interest is typical of M&StL men.

Much local color on the West End came through reminiscences of ex-Section Foreman John A. Mullen of Aberdeen, S. Dak.; and down in the corn country Edward O'Brien of Grinnell, Iowa, recounted his experience as a section boss before the M&StL took over the Iowa Central. Retired agents such as L. E. Chambard, Humboldt; P. S. Howard, Mason City; Charles S. Kruchek, Forest City; E. E. Rector, Council Bluffs; and H. A. Stevenson, Geneva, all in Iowa; and Ernest H. Willman of Waterville, Minn., provided material of historic interest.

Other individuals not associated with the M&StL aided me in countless ways.

Jack D. Andrews of Minneapolis shared many lunch hours with me reading copy, offering suggestions, and giving editorial assistance from title page to index. Long a student of busi-

283

ness history—he is at present writing the story of General Mills—Mr. Andrews generously drew on his store of knowledge in research, economics, and writing to make my path easier. His cheerful help and enthusiasm were a never-flagging incentive to me.

The attractive pen-and-ink sketches at the beginning of each chapter are the work of Franklin A. King of Duluth, a student of architecture and of railroading.

Much constructive criticism on varied aspects of the history were offered by Gilbert Burck, an editor of *Fortune;* Philip D. Jordan, professor of history, University of Minnesota; Robert S. Henry, vice president, Association of American Railroads; and James W. Lydon, advertising manager, Soo Line.

The explanation as to how "the Skally" was given that name comes from J. F. Tracy, White Bear Lake, Minn. John Mickelsen, draftsman in the NP's engineering department, and P. H. McCauley of St. Paul, a former officer on the same road, both helped clarify the relationship between the M&StL and the Northern Pacific in the eighties.

Paul Zinter of Hutchinson, Minn., provided me with an on-location description of the Minnetonka region, when he was a Great Northern section boss. Similarly J. W. Spicer and Bruce Wulff of Albert Lea, Minn., brought back memories of the community's station-hotel, once famous for its meals and its hospitality.

William Gray of Keithsburg, Ill., chauffered me around that peaceful town so I could interview nearly everyone over seventy who had a clear memory and a predilection for recalling the past. Ben Hur Wilson of Joliet, Ill., who has written many articles on the Hawkeye State's history, helped in uncovering data on the Iowa Central; and from Boston a genial Irishman, Charles J. O'Malley, forwarded anecdotes about Russell Sage. Similarly from Birmingham, Ala., Charles B. Gamble, a former official of the Minneapolis Gas Company, sent yarns concerning Jerry Moynihan.

Among others who provided pictorial or factual data are William Armstrong, Des Plaines, Ill.; Ben P. Bishman, Waseca, Minn.; M. B. Cooke, Montgomery, Ala.; Ferdinand Fink,

ACKNOWLEDGMENTS

Tonka Bay, Minn.; Robert B. Graham, St. Paul; Robert Milner, La Grange, Ill.; Paul Stringham, Peoria, Ill.; and S. R. Wood, Stillwater, Okla.

Through the courtesy of C. C. Price, yardmaster, I rode over the Northern Pacific's White Bear Lake branch with Section Foreman Ben J. Schriever as my guide. Passage on the Chicago Great Western's freight over the Cannon Valley line was arranged by Superintendent H. R. Halverson of that road; and General Superintendent L. W. Breese of the Southern Iowa Railway Company made it possible for me to cover that electric line.

Permission to quote from W. G. McAdoo's *Crowded Years* was kindly given by Houghton Mifflin Company, and Ward C. Burton granted the right to quote from Randolph Edgar's *A Record of Old Boats*. Editors of *Trains, Tracks* (the Chesapeake & Ohio Railway magazine), and *Minnesota History* allowed me to use material which I wrote for these periodicals.

Special thanks are due the librarians of the Minnesota Historical Society, the South Dakota State Historical Society, the Historical Library, State Capitol, Iowa, the Minneapolis Public Library; Joseph W. Zalusky, museum director, Hennepin County Historical Society and William J. Petersen, superintendent, State Historical Society of Iowa. Finally, an extra "thank you" to my wife, Janice, for much painstaking research, for aid in checking facts, and for general all-around help.

The Family Tree of the Minneapolis & St. Louis Railway

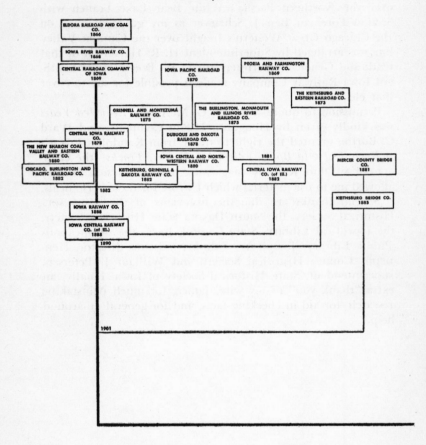

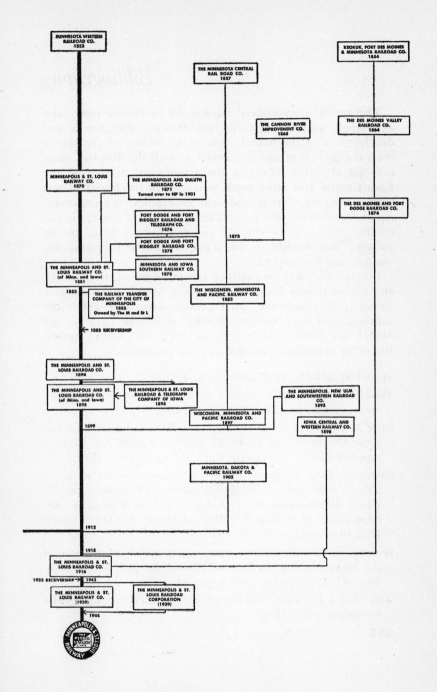

MINNESOTA WESTERN
RAILROAD CO.
1853

KEOKUK, FORT DES MOINES
& MINNESOTA RAILROAD CO.
1854

THE MINNESOTA CENTRAL
RAIL ROAD CO.
1857

THE CANNON RIVER
IMPROVEMENT CO.
1865

THE DES MOINES VALLEY
RAILROAD CO.
1864

MINNEAPOLIS & ST. LOUIS
RAILWAY CO.
1870

THE MINNEAPOLIS AND DULUTH
RAILROAD CO.
1871
Turned over to NP in 1901

FORT DODGE AND FORT
RIDGELEY RAILROAD AND
TELEGRAPH CO.
1876

FORT DODGE AND FORT
RIDGELEY RAILROAD CO.
1878

THE DES MOINES AND FORT
DODGE RAILROAD CO.
1874

MINNESOTA AND IOWA
SOUTHERN RAILWAY CO.
1878

THE MINNEAPOLIS AND ST.
LOUIS RAILWAY CO.
(of Minn. and Iowa)
1881

1878

1883

THE RAILWAY TRANSFER
COMPANY OF THE CITY OF
MINNEAPOLIS
1883
Owned by The M and St L

THE WISCONSIN, MINNESOTA
AND PACIFIC RAILWAY CO.
1883

← 1888 RECEIVERSHIP

THE MINNEAPOLIS AND ST.
LOUIS RAILROAD CO.
1894

THE MINNEAPOLIS AND ST.
LOUIS RAILROAD CO.
(of Minn. and Iowa)
1895

THE MINNEAPOLIS & ST. LOUIS
RAILROAD & TELEGRAPH
COMPANY OF IOWA
1895

THE MINNEAPOLIS, NEW ULM
AND SOUTHWESTERN RAILROAD
CO.
1895

WISCONSIN, MINNESOTA AND
PACIFIC RAILROAD CO.
1897

IOWA CENTRAL AND
WESTERN RAILWAY CO.
1898

1899

MINNESOTA, DAKOTA &
PACIFIC RAILWAY CO.
1905

1912

1915

THE MINNEAPOLIS & ST.
LOUIS RAILROAD CO.
1916

1923 RECEIVERSHIP → 1943

THE MINNEAPOLIS & ST.
LOUIS RAILWAY CO.
(1939)

THE MINNEAPOLIS & ST.
LOUIS RAILROAD
CORPORATION
(1939)

1944

MINNEAPOLIS · ST. LOUIS
THE
PEORIA
GATEWAY
LINE
RAILWAY

Bibliography

The annual stockholders' reports are by far the most valuable single source of information showing the growth and development of the M&StL. Except for fifteen of the earlier years the annual reports are intact and all the directors' minutes are available. Many of the reports and minutes of the Iowa Central and other roads now part of the M&StL, along with some construction and coal companies, are preserved. Apart from these, very few records, outside of contracts, are extant. Nearly all of the old timetables have been thrown away or were burned in the Western Avenue (Minneapolis) roundhouse fire of 1929.

Federal and state regulatory reports were also consulted, and all the county histories concerning M&StL territory were scanned. As a rule the latter contain very little about the railroad, and only volumes having significant data on the M&StL are included elsewhere in this bibliography. Among the other materials consulted are the following:

MANUSCRIPTS, DOCUMENTS, ETC.

Associated Railways Company et al. Acquisition, Abandonment, and Securities. 228 I.C.C. 277. (1938).

Brief of the Minneapolis & St. Louis Railroad Executive Defense Committee, et al. I.C.C. Finance Docket No. 10947— Application of Associated Railways Company. (1936).

Guaranty Trust Company of New York, as Trustees, et al, vs. The Minneapolis & St. Louis Railroad Company, et al. (The Minneapolis & St. Louis Railroad Company Receivership). U. S. Dist. Ct., Dist. of Minn., 4th Div. 24 vols. 1923-1944.

History of the Corporate Organization and Construction of the Minneapolis & St. Louis Railroad. By J. S. McClintock, June 17, 1921. typewritten copy. 14 p.

The M&StL Railroad Co. History. Prepared February 23, 1916. blueprint copy. 16 p.

Minneapolis & St. Louis Railroad Company. Valuation Docket No. 510. 137 I.C.C. 761. (1928).

Record of M. & St. L. and Iowa Central Equipment Owned August 1, 1888 and Acquired Subsequent Thereto.

Revised and Corrected Chart of The Minneapolis & St. Louis Railroad Company, Properties Owned and Operated...as of December 31, 1923.

Revised & Corrected History, The Minneapolis & St. Louis Railroad Company. Corrected as of June 30, 1917. Compiled by F. K. Bennett. blueprint copy. 9 p.

Scrapbook containing biographical sketches of executives and clippings concerning the M&StL, 1922-1935.

Scrapbook containing biographical sketches of executives and circulars of the M&StL, 1932-1945.

Scrapbook containing circulars and notices of the Iowa Central and its predecessor companies, 1883-1897.

Scrapbook containing circulars and notices of the M&StL, 1894-1931.

Scrapbook containing circulars and notices of the M&StL Passenger Department, 1934-1946.

Scrapbook containing newspaper clippings concerning Edwin Hawley.

BOOKS

An Illustrated Historical Atlas of the State of Minnesota. Chicago, A. T. Andreas, 1874.

Andreas' Historical Atlas of Dakota. Chicago, A. T. Andreas, Publisher, 1884.

Atwater, Isaac, ed., *History of the City of Minneapolis, Minnesota.* New York, Munsell & Co., 1893.

The Biographical Directory of the Railway Officials of America. (publisher varies) 1885-1922.

Bishop, Judson W., "History of the St. Paul & Sioux City Railroad, 1864-1881," *Collections of the Minnesota Historical Society,* vol. X, part I:399-415. St. Paul, The Society, 1905.

Boatner, V. V., and A. J. Hammond, *Report on the Minneapolis & St. Louis Railroad.* Chicago, [privately printed] 1936.

The Book of Minnesota. St. Paul, The Pioneer Press Co., 1903.

Bromley, Edward A., *Minneapolis Album.* Minneapolis, Frank L. Thresher, Publisher, 1890.

Buck, Solon J., *The Granger Movement.* Cambridge, Mass., Harvard University Press, 1913.

Cary, John W., *The Organization and History of the Chicago, Milwaukee & St. Paul Railway Company.* Milwaukee, Wis., Cramer, Aikens & Cramer, 1892.

Castle, Henry A., *History of St. Paul and Vicinity.* vol. I. Chicago, Lewis Publishing Co., 1912.

Cherington, Charles R., *The Regulation of Railroad Abandonments.* Cambridge, Mass., Harvard University Press, 1948.

Curtis-Wedge, Franklyn, comp., *History of Rice and Steele Counties, Minnesota.* vol. I. Chicago, H. C. Cooper, Jr. & Co., 1910.

Derleth, August, *The Milwaukee Road.* New York, Creative Age Press, 1948.

Donovan, Frank P. Jr., comp., *Railroads of America.* Milwaukee, Wis., Kalmbach Publishing Co., 1949.

Edgar, Randolph, *A Record of Old Boats.* Minneapolis, Ward C. Burton, 1926.

Edgar, William C., *The Medal of Gold.* Minneapolis, The Bellman Co., 1925.

Field, H. H., *History of the Milwaukee Road, 1892-1940.* [privately printed] 1941.

Folwell, William W., *A History of Minnesota.* 4 vols. St. Paul, Minnesota Historical Society, 1921, 1924, 1926, 1940.

Fuller, O. Muiriel, *John Muir of Wall Street.* New York, The Knickerbocker Press, 1927.

Goldthwait, Nathan E., ed., *History of Boone County, Iowa.* vol. I. Chicago, Pioneer Publishing Co., 1914.

Grinnell, Josiah B., *Men and Events of Forty Years.* Boston, D. Lothrop Co., 1891.

Hampton, Taylor, *The Nickel Plate Road.* Cleveland, The World Publishing Co., 1947.

Hand-Book of Minneapolis. Prepared for...American Association for the Advancement of Science, Minneapolis, 1883.

Hartsough, Mildred L., *The Twin Cities as a Metropolitan Market.* Minneapolis, University of Minnesota, 1925.

Henry, Robert S., *This Fascinating Railroad Business.* Indianapolis, The Bobbs-Merrill Co., 1942.

Hickenlooper, Frank, *An Illustrated History of Monroe County, Iowa.* Albia, Ia., [privately printed] 1896.

Historical Atlas of South Dakota...compiled by E. Frank Peterson. Vermillion, S. Dak., 1904.

History of Franklin and Cerro Gordo Counties, Iowa. .Springfield, Ill., Union Publishing Co., 1883.

History of Hardin County, Iowa...Springfield, Ill., Union Publishing Co., 1883.

History of Mahaska County, Iowa. Des Moines, Ia., The Union Historical Co., 1878.

The History of Marshall County, Iowa...Chicago, Western Historical Co., 1878.

History of the Upper Mississippi Valley...By N. H. Winchell, Edward D. Neill and others. Minneapolis, Minnesota Historical Co., 1881.

Holmes, Frank R., *Minnesota in Three Centuries.* vol. 4. [New York] The Publishing Society of Minnesota, 1908.

Hubbard, Lucius F. and Return I. Holcombe, *Minnesota in Three Centuries.* vol. 3. [New York] The Publishing Society of Minnesota, 1908.

Hudson, Horace B., ed., *A Half Century of Minneapolis.* Minneapolis, The Hudson Publishing Co., 1908.

Hungerford, Edward, *The Modern Railroad.* Chicago, A. C. McClurg & Co., 1911.

Johnson, Allen and Dumas Malone, eds., *Dictionary of American Biography.* 21 vols. New York, Charles Scribner's Sons, 1928-1944.

Kuhlmann, Charles B., *The Development of the Flour-Mill-*

ing Industry in the United States. Boston, Houghton Mifflin Co., 1929.

Larson, Henrietta M., *Guide to Business History.* Cambridge, Mass., Harvard University Press, 1948.

——, *Jay Cooke, Private Banker.* Cambridge, Mass., Harvard University Press, 1936.

——, *The Wheat Market and the Farmer in Minnesota, 1858-1900.* New York, Columbia University, 1926.

Marquis, Albert N., ed., *The Book of Minnesotans.* Chicago, A. N. Marquis & Co., 1907.

McAdoo, William G., *Crowded Years.* Boston, Houghton Mifflin Co., 1931.

Minneapolis City Directory. (title and publisher vary) 1871-1885.

Mordaunt, Frederick S. assisted by Toll Stern, *Fair Play.* Chicago, National Railway Publishing Co., 1911.

Myers, Gustavus, *History of the Great American Fortunes.* New York, The Modern Library, 1936.

Neill, Edward D., *History of Rice County*...Minneapolis, Minnesota Historical Co., 1882.

One of the Moynihans. [privately printed] 1928.

Payne, Charles E., *Josiah Bushnell Grinnell.* Iowa City, Ia., The State Historical Society of Iowa, 1938.

Pepperman, W. Leon, *Who Built the Panama Canal?* New York, E. P. Dutton & Co., 1915.

Petersen, William J., *A Reference Guide to Iowa History.* (Bulletin of Information Series: No. 17) Iowa City, Ia., State Historical Society of Iowa, 1924.

Poor's Manual of Railroads and its successor *Moody's Manual of Railroads.* (publisher and title vary) 1870-1948.

Pratt, Harlow M., *History of Fort Dodge and Webster County, Iowa.* vol. I. Chicago, The Pioneer Publishing Co., 1913.

Railway Economics: A Collective Catalogue of Books in Fourteen American Libraries. Prepared by the Bureau of Railway Economics, Washington, D. C. Chicago, University of Chicago Press, 1912.

Rasmussen, C. A., *A History of the City of Red Wing, Minnesota.* [privately printed] 1933.

Robertson, Archie, *Slow Train to Yesterday.* Boston, Houghton Mifflin Co., 1945.

Saby, Rasmus S., "Railroad Legislation in Minnesota, 1849 to 1875," *Collections of the Minnesota Historical Society,* XV:1-188. St. Paul, The Society, 1915.

Sheasgreen, Ed. E., *Switch Lights.* Minneapolis, Iron Trail Publishing Co., 1902.

Shutter, Marion D. and J. S. McLain, eds., *Progressive Men of Minnesota.* Minneapolis, The Minneapolis Journal, 1897.

South Dakota Place Names, Gold and Ghost Towns. part VI. Compiled by Workers of the Writers' Program of the Works Projects Administration in the State of South Dakota. Vermillion, S. Dak., University of South Dakota, 1940.

Spearman, Frank H., *The Strategy of Great Railroads.* New York, Charles Scribner's Sons, 1904.

Special Acts and General Laws Constituting the Charter of the Minneapolis & St. Louis Railroad Company. [privately printed] n.d.

Stickney, A. B., *The Railroad Problem.* St. Paul, D. D. Merrill Co., 1891.

Upham, Warren and Rose B. Dunlap, comps., "Minnesota Biographies, 1655-1912," *Collections of the Minnesota Historical Society,* vol. XIV. St. Paul, The Society, 1912.

Washburn, Edwin C., *The 17.* Englewood, N. J., Washburn, 1929.

Way, Clyde C., ed., *Biography and Memoirs of Thomas Asbury Way.* [privately printed] 1946.

Welles, Henry T., *Autobiography and Reminiscences.* Minneapolis, Marshall Robinson, 1899.

Werner, M. R. *Julius Rosenwald.* New York, Harper & Brothers, 1939.

Where to Recuperate During Summer Days... (The Summer Resorts of Iowa and Minnesota Reached by the Albert Lea

Route). Chicago, Rand, McNally & Co., Printers and Engravers, 1884.

Who's Who in America. Chicago, A. N. Marquis Co., 1899/1900-1948/1949.

Who's Who in Railroading. New York, The Simmons-Boardman Publishing Co., 1930-1946.

Willard, Daniel E., *The Story of the North Star State.* St. Paul, Webb Publishing Co., 1922.

Wright, Luella M., *Peter Melendy.* Iowa City, Ia., The State Historical Society of Iowa, 1943.

BOOKLETS AND PAMPHLETS

After 51 Years. (Biographical sketch of James Teyro) [privately printed] 1931. n. p.

Johnson, F. H., *Brief Record of the Development of The Milwaukee Road.* Chicago, The Milwaukee Road, 1944. 52 p.

The Minneapolis & St. Louis Railway Co. [The railway] 1943. 48 p.

Overton, R. C., *Milepost 100.* Chicago. [Burlington Lines] 1949. 64 p.

Quiz On Railroads and Railroading. Washington, D. C., Association of American Railroads, 1948. n. p.

Reference Aids for Teachers and Students on Railway Development in Iowa; 1846—Iowa Centennial—1946. Washington, D. C., Association of American Railroads, 1946. 24 p.

Shaw, Carl and Roy Graft, *In Memoriam; M. & St. L. Engineers.* [privately printed] n. d., n. p.

Truesdale, W. H., *Statement by the Minneapolis & St. Louis Railway Co., of its Position Relative to the North Minneapolis Crossing Controversy.* Minneapolis [The railway] 1888. 17 p.

The Twin Cities To-Day. Minneapolis or St. Paul, Twin City Lines, 1917. 28 p.

SPECIAL ARTICLES

"A Busy Little Railway and its Superintendent J. A. 'Jerry'

Moynihan," *Transportation and Railwayee Magazine,* 3:22 (April, 1926).

"The 'Doctors' Were Wrong," *Railway Age,* 108:1000-1006 (June 8, 1940).

Donovan, Frank P. Jr., "Doctor of Weak Railroads," Tracks 34:10-13 (March, 1949).

——, "Minneapolis & St. Louis," *Trains,* 3:32-45 (December, 1942).

——, "Passenger Trains of Yesteryear on the Minneapolis & St. Louis," *Minnesota History,* 30:232-241 (September, 1949).

——, "Time Freight 20," *Trains,* 9:40-44 (August, 1949).

"Eight Roads Propose to Take Over M. & St. L." *Railway Age,* 99:337-338 (September 14, 1935).

Fadell, Michael J., "Lucian Sprague—Horseman of the Rails," *Golfer and Sportsman,* 15:31-32 (October, 1942).

"Fare Enough," *Forbes,* 64:11-12 (August 15, 1949).

Holden, Jim, "Misery & Short Life," *Railroad Stories,* XIX: 33-39 (May, 1936).

Hubbard, Freeman H., "Out of the Red," *Railroad Magazine,* 35:46-54 (April, 1944).

"It Can Be Done," (Biographical sketch of Elliott E. Nash). *The Railwayee,* 2:6-8 (November, 1926).

Johnson, Hamilton, "The Spirit of Romance Lives: Story of the Building of the B. C. R. & N. Through Iowa," *Rock Island Magazine,* XVII:67-68 (October, 1922).

Knoble, John W., "Oh No, Day Kann Do Dat!" *Literary Supplement to the Carletonian,* LVII:3-4 (May 22, 1937).

Leonard, L. O., "The Founders and Builders of the Rock Island; Article 12—Ransom Reed Cable," *Rock Island Magazine,* XXI:19-20 (November, 1926).

"M. & St. L. Is Out of Receivership," *Railway Age,* 113:450-451 (September 19, 1942).

"M. & St. L. Rebirth," *Business Week,* 745:106-107 (December 11, 1943).

Means, O. H., "The Minneapolis & St. Louis Railroad Company," *Railway & Locomotive Historical Society, Bulletin No. 31:* 33-45 (April, 1933).

"Minneapolis and St. Louis Railroad in Marshalltown," *Progressive Marshalltown,* 1:5, 8 (August, 1930).

295

"Rejuvenation on the M&StL," *Investor's Reader,* 12:21-24 (May 25, 1949).

Sutherland, James M., "Rescued: One Railroad," *Forbes,* 50:14-15 (December 15, 1942).

"Up Comes the M. & St. L." *Time,* XLII:83-84 (November 29, 1943).

"William H. Bremner," *Transportation Magazine.* 3:8-9 (June, 1926).

Wilson, Ben Hur, "Abandoned Railroads of Iowa," *Iowa Journal of History and Politics,* 26:3-64 (January, 1928).

——, "Albert Tuston Hay," *Palimpsest,* XXVIII:193-206 (July, 1947).

——, "The Plattsmouth Crossing." *Palimpsest,* XXX:389-400 (December, 1949).

PERIODICALS AND NEWSPAPERS

The Crescent and Grip; A Journal for Commercial Travelers, September, 1905, to August, 1907.

Dacotah Magazine, 1908-1909.

Des Moines, Ia., *Tribune,* July 21, 1947.

Excelsior, Minn., *Cottager,* 1896-1897.

Fortune, November, 1947.

LeBeau, S. Dak., *Phenix,* 1908-1910.

Leola, S. Dak., *McPherson County Herald,* 1906-1907.

Minneapolis, Minn., *Journal,* 1907-1911; 1936-1938.

——, *Star,* 1936-1938.

——, *Tribune* (title varies), 1869-1878; 1907-1911; 1936-1938.

The Official Guide of the Railways & Steam Navigation Lines in the United States... (title varies), 1883-1949.

The Official Railway Equipment Register, July, 1913.

Official Railway Guide Quarterly Supplement, January, 1949.

Ohio Farmer, June 13, 1874.

Oskaloosa, Ia., *Herald,* August 21, 1926.

Railway Age (title varies), 1877-1949.

St. Paul, Minn., *Pioneer,* 1870-1871.

——, *Press,* 1870-1871.

Saturday Evening Post, February 4, 1928.

Index

"A" Mill, 52
Abbott, Howard S., 3, 4, 213
Aberdeen Chamber of Commerce, 206
Aberdeen, S. Dak., 124, 125, 127, 130, 143, 147, 218, 260
Ackert, C. H., 116, 152
Ackley, Iowa, 107, 108, 269
Adams, Cedric, 219
After 51 Years, 239
Aishton, Richard H., 174
Akaska, S. Dak., 133-135, 181, 200, 217, 218
Albert Lea Gateway, 64
Albert Lea, Minn., 21, 22, 36, 41, 50, 51, 54, 57, 67, 85, 100, 118, 139, 141, 142, 147, 151, 167-169, 203, 210, 218, 221, 227, 230, 255, 266, 267, 273
Albert Lea Route, The, 69, 139, 146, 169, 170, 173
Albia, Iowa, 36, 107, 108, 113, 116, 119, 142, 147, 155, 203, 204, 221, 230
Alden 8 mine, 119
Aledo, Ill., 114
Alert, 75
Algoma Central & Hudson Bay Railway, 256
Algona, Iowa, 163, 217
Allen, Benjamin, 17
Alton Road, *see* Chicago & Alton Railroad
American Friends Service Committee, 272
American Locomotive Co., 252-254
American type locomotive, 46, 52, 57, 73, 139, 247, 248, 251, 256
Anderson, George A., 207, 233, 234
Angus *Black Diamond,* 58

Angus, Iowa, 54, 56-60, 64, 68, 140, 217
Angus *News,* 59
Angus *Tenderfoot,* 58
Ankeny, William P., 35
Ann Arbor Railroad, 161
Anoka, Minn., 49
Appanoose County, Iowa, 153
Aquatennial, Minneapolis, 226
Armstrong, Charles W., 267
Armstrong mine, 57
Ashley, N. Dak., 130
Associated Railways Co., 200, 202, 203, 205-207
Atchison, Topeka & Santa Fe Railway, 143, 251, 276
Athens County, Ohio, 67
Atlantic, Duluth & Pacific Steamboat Line, 40
Atlantic Ocean, 156
Atwater, Isaac, 33
Austin, Minn., 11

Baker's Hollow, 27
Baldwin Locomotive Works, 74, 189, 248, 254
Baldwin, Rufus J., 33
Baltimore & Ohio Railroad, 108, 188, 254, 261, 277
Baltimore, Md., 161
Bangor, Me., 15
Banning, William L., 29, 30
Baptists, 40
Baraboo, Wis., 162
Barriger, John W., III, 202
Bartholomew, Charles L., 141, 146
Bartlett Yard, 227, 277, 278
Baruch, Bernard M., 99
Bassett, George W., 55

297

Bates car coupler, 49
Beard, Charles F., 229
Becker, George L., 17
Belden, George K., 210
Belle of Minnetonka, 72
Belmond, Iowa, 112, 163
Benefit Association (M&StL), 243
Benson, E. S., 152
Berkley, Iowa, 59
Bierd, William G., 161-163
Big Four Railroad, *see* Cleveland,
    Cincinnati, Chicago & St. Louis
    Railway
Bijou Theater, 86
Birmingham, Ala., 6, 233
Bismark, S. Dak., 125, 127
Black Hawk Chute, 275
Black Hawk mine, 119
Blair, John I., 50, 51
Bloom, Harold E., 208
Bloomington, Ill., 114, 152
Blunt, S. Dak., 125
Bode, A. H., 63
Boehme, Carl A., 207
Boehmer ranch, 134
Bohemia, 239
"Booster Clubs," 179, 181
Booth, Judge Wilber F., 193, 194
Boston Block, 67, 85, 231
Boston, Mass., 6, 11, 47, 216
Bowdoin College, 15
Bradley, S. Dak., 176
Brady, James B. "Diamond Jim," 99
Branstrup, Thor E., 267
Braun, Loella, 211
Breckenridge, Minn., 125
Bremner, William Hepburn, 172-
    174, 177-182, 184, 185, 193; bio-
    graphical sketch, 178, 179
Brennan, Thomas, 28
Brighton, Iowa, 105, 109, 275
Broad Exchange Building, 98
Broadway Limited, 263, 264
Brooks Locomotive Works, 252
Brotherhood of Railway & Steam-
    ship Clerks, 206
Brown Brothers, 88
Brown, Edward L., 164
Brown, Ross W., 121
Brown, Stewart E., 181
Budd, Ralph, 230
Buffalo, N. Y., 40, 183, 219
"Bull Run, The," 167

Bull, William L., 88, 92
Burlington & Western Railway, 109,
    110
Burlington, Cedar Rapids & North-
    ern Railway, 49-51, 64, 65, 67, 68,
    85, 98, 101, 118, 137, 139
Burlington, Iowa, 69, 139
Burlington, Monmouth and Illinois
    River Railroad Co., The, 110
Burlington Railroad, *see* Chicago,
    Burlington & Quincy Railroad
Business Week, 226
Butler, Dr. Levi, 35
Butte County homestead lands, 126

Cable, P. L., 67
Cable, Ransom Reed, 63, 64, 67-69,
    74, 79, 80; biographical sketch 67,
    68
California, 35, 140, 143, 276
California Fast Freight Line, 92
Cameron, Iowa, 269
Campbell, Alexander, 144
Camp Dodge, Iowa, 177
Canada, 130, 131, 155, 156, 159, 277
Canadian Pacific Railway, 130
Cannon Ball Express, 137, 139, 142
Cannon River Improvement Co.,
    The, 65
Cannon Valley Division, 65, 66, 95,
    240
Capital Limited, 168
Capron, Iowa, 119
Carroll, Charles, 108
Carrollton, Md., 108
Carr, S. W. W., 206
Carsons Bay, 70
Carter, Edward, 168
Carver County, Minn., 46
Carver, Minn., 25-28, 29, 30
Cataract Mill, 34
Cate, Isaac M., 109, 112
Catholics, 132
Cedar Falls, Iowa, 107
Cedar Lake, 264, 265
Cedar Lake shops, 3, 87, 175, 176,
    189, 200, 226, 227, 250, 252, 255,
    256
Cedar Lake Yard, 184, 263, 264, 277
Centerville, Iowa, 116, 120
Central America, 155
Central House, 269
Central Iowa Rail Road, 107

Central Iowa Railway Co., 107, 109-114, 153, 178
Central Iowa Railway Co. (of Illinois), 111, 113
Central Pacific Railroad, 9
Central Railroad Company of Iowa, 36, 106-109
Central Railroad Company of New Jersey, 163
Centralized Traffic Control (C.T.C.), 267
Centreville, Moravia & Albia Railroad, 115
Chaska Hill, 96, 265
Chaska Minn., 27, 28, 30, 52, 96
Chatham, N. Y., 91, 94
Chelsea, S. Dak., 176
Chesapeake & Ohio Railway, 91, 114, 146, 155
Chessie, 146
Cheyenne homestead lands, 126
Cheyenne Indian Reservation, 126
Chicago & Alton Railroad, 91, 99, 152, 153, 155, 156, 159, 162
Chicago & Illinois Midland Railway, 277
Chicago & North Western Railway, 107, 161, 162, 174, 179, 201, 203, 204, 270
Chicago, Burlington and Pacific Railroad Co., 109, 110, 116
Chicago, Burlington & Quincy Railroad, 68, 91, 114, 119, 120, 143, 179, 187, 188, 201, 204, 216, 230, 231, 274, 276
Chicago Great Western Railway, 64, 95, 101, 113, 120, 201
Chicago, Ill., 6, 11-13, 25, 38, 67, 68, 81, 82, 98, 114, 117, 125, 130, 137-139, 141, 142, 151-153, 173, 174, 195, 204, 220, 242, 270, 277
Chicago, Milwaukee & Puget Sound Railway, 130
Chicago, Milwaukee, St. Paul & Pacific Railroad, 27, 49, 52, 66, 74, 75, 98, 101, 113, 115, 119, 120, 129, 130, 163, 201, 204, 217, 271
Chicago Railroad Fair, 253
Chicago, Rock Island & Pacific Railway, 63-68, 80, 88, 92, 98, 101, 113, 118, 119, 137, 139, 141, 143, 162, 167, 178, 201, 203, 204, 249, 250, 266, 267, 271

Chicago, St. Paul, Minneapolis & Omaha Railway, 63, 80, 194, 221
China, 56
Christianson, Theodore, 144, 145
Cincinnati, Ohio, 72, 219
Circumnavigators Club (Pullman), 184
City of St. Louis, 72
Civil War, 24, 35, 106
Clark, Frank H., 22
Clearwater Lake, 141
Clerks' Adjustment Board, 207
Cleveland, Cincinnati, Chicago & St. Louis Railway, 114
Cleveland, Ohio, 40
Cleveland, Painesville & Ashtabula Railroad, 24
Cleveland, Pres. Grover, 93
Climax Coal Co., 57
Clough, Joel B., 21, 23, 24, 27, 56
Clover Leaf Road, see Toledo, St. Louis & Western Railroad
Coal Valley, Ill., 67
Coaltown, Iowa, 57
Collingdale, Pa., 277
Colorado & Southern Railway, 91
Colpitts, Walter W., 5, 192, 193, 233
Columbia County, N. Y., 91
Columbus, Ohio, 114
Conde, S. Dak., 124, 132, 147, 175, 176, 217, 260
Cone, R, L., 24
Congregationalists, 40
Conley family, 260
Consolidation type locomotive, 160, 175, 250, 252, 256
Cooke, Jay, 36, 39, 45
Coolidge, Pres. Calvin, 100
Coppock, Iowa, 216, 274, 275
Cornell, Iowa, 96
Corwith, Iowa, 230
Cottagewood, Minn., 71
Cottonwood River, 95
Coverdale & Colpitts, 5, 192, 213, 234
Crandall, S. Dak., 94
Crandell, Walter S., 94
Crawford, (conductor), 28
Credit Union (M&StL), 244
Cresbard, S. Dak., 130

Crescent and Grip, The, 169
Crocker, George, 99
Crocker, S. Dak., 175, 176
Cummings, James P., 264, 265
Cutter, A. B., 100
Cutts, Anson B., 142, 146, 179

Dacotah Magazine, 126
Dakota Construction Co., 124
Dakota Town Lot Co., 124
Dallas Center, Iowa, 228, 229
Dallas Center *Times,* 229
Dallas, Texas, 6, 216
Dallman, Gustav M., 240
Dallman, Hugo F., 240
Dallman, John A., 240
Dallman, Paul W., 240
Danville, Ill., 114
Davids, Walter B., 93, 94, 99
Davis, Frank H., 93
Dawson, Iowa, 59
Day, L Ferman, 96-98, 100, 102, 142,
    159
Dayton, Iowa, 56
Declaration of Independence, 108
Deephaven, Minn., 74, 75
DeLaittre, John, 51
Delaware, Lackawanna & Western
    Railroad, 88, 183
Delbey mine, 57
Denison, Dexter M., 179, 241, 242
Denver & Rio Grande Railroad, 143,
    164
Denver & Rio Grande Western Rail-
    road, 188
Denver & Salt Lake Railway, 161
Des Moines and Fort Dodge Rail-
    road Co., The, 64, 69, 140, 162,
    217
Des Moines, Iowa, 68, 140, 177, 179,
    200, 204, 218, 221, 229, 230, 250,
    266, 273
Des Moines River, 230
Des Moines Valley Railroad Co.,
    The, 57
Detroit, Mich., 40, 183
Deveny family, 260
Devins, John W., 232
Diamond A ranch, 125
Diamond Mill, 52
Diesel locomotives, 215, 222, 226,
    253-256
Diesel shops, 256

District Court of Hennepin County,
    84
Doan, A. C., 94
Doe, Joseph B., 17
Drake, E. F., 29, 30
Drake, Francis M., 116
Dubuque & Sioux City Railroad,
    107
Dubuque, Iowa, 112
DuFran, Phil, 127, 128, 135
Dukhobors, 131
Duluth: Minn., 12, 13, 22, 25, 28,
    37, 39, 40, 42, 45, 53, 82, 120
Duluth, Pierre & Black Hills Rail-
    way Co., 130
Dunn, Samuel A., 146
Dunscombe, John F., 57

East Minneapolis, Minn., 22
Eastern Express, 11
Eastman, William W., 34
Eaton, Merle E., 194
Eddyville, Iowa, 115
Eden Prairie, Minn., 27
Edgar, Randolph, 72
Eldora, Iowa, 107, 206, 269, 270
Eldora Railroad and Coal Co., 107,
    269
Eleanor, Ill., 276
Electric railways, 75, 86, 87, 264,
    276
Electro-Motive Division, General
    Motors Corp., 181, 253-255
Elegant Eighties, 74
England, 251
Equipment Register, 169
Erb, Newman, 155, 158, 159, 161-
    164, 167; biographical sketch 161
Erie, Pa., 40
Erie Railroad, 40, 91, 92, 261
Estherville, Iowa, 95, 176, 218, 240
Eugene, Ore., 277
Everett, Wash., 277
Excelsior *Cottager,* 140
Excelsior mine, 119
Excelsior, Minn., 64, 70, 72-74, 86,
    87, 137, 141, 143, 219

Fairfax, Minn., 206
Faith, S. Dak., 129, 130
Falls of St. Anthony, 7, 10-12, 16,
    231, 264

Farmington, Ill., 110, 119
Fast Freight (motion picture), 226
Feather River, 91
Federal Government, *see* Government, U. S.
Fehr, C. R., 198
Felton, S. M., 22
Fibber McGee and Molly, 278
First and Refunding 4% Bonds, 151
First and Refunding Mortgage, 95
First National Bank of Minneapolis, 35
First National Bank of St. Paul, 29
First State Bank (LeBeau), 135
Five Million Dollar Loan, 17
Flint Rock Creek, 129
Flor, Albert D., 210
Florence, S. Dak., 175, 176
Forbes, 186
Ford, Henry, 148, 190
Ford plant (Minneapolis), 183
Fort Dodge and Fort Ridgeley Railroad and Telegraph Co., 54
Fort Dodge and Fort Ridgeley Railroad Co., 54, 55, 112
Fort Dodge Chamber of Commerce, 206
Fort Dodge, Iowa, 54-57, 112, 140, 143, 147, 151, 167, 203, 204, 214, 217, 218, 221
Fort Madison, Iowa, 105
Fort Snelling, Minn., 10, 16, 34
Fortune, 247
Fosterdale, Iowa, 230
Franceau, Charles, 134, 135
Frankfurt, Germany, 79
Fridley, Abram M., 17
Friends, (Quakers), 35, 106, 120, 121
Frisco Lines, *see* St. Louis-San Francisco Railway
Fritch, L. C., 178
Funk, A. B., 128

Gage, Fred K., 206
Galva, Ill., 114
Galveston, Texas, 155
Gardner, Albert L., 206
Gardner, Henry A., 117, 118
Garlick, E. H., 264
Gaskell, Joseph, 239
Gates, John W. "Bet-a-Million," 99
Gay Nineties, 74, 85

Gaylord, E. W., 56
General American Transportation Corp., 229
General Electric Co., 254
Germany, 221
Gibson, Charles, 70
Gibson, Paris, 34
Gifford, Iowa, 255
Gilman, Charles C., 107-109, 112
Gilman, John S., 108
Gilman, J. W., 108
Givin, Iowa, 113, 119
Glastonbury, Conn., 14
Glenville, Minn., 267
Golden Eagle, 111
Golden, Robert N., 216
Goldthwait, Nathan, 58
Gould, George J., 154
Gould, Jay, 92
Government, U. S., 10, 11, 126, 177, 178, 180, 191; operation of railroads, 174, 177-179, 221, 225
Gowrie, Iowa, 204
Grand Opera House (Minneapolis), 86
Grange, The, 42, 47-49
Grant, Pres. Ulysses S., 9
Grasshopper plague, 47
Great Falls, Mont., 6, 228
Great Lakes, 22, 30
Great Northern Railway, 12, 70, 72, 74, 75, 86, 120, 129, 176, 188, 201, 202, 204, 277
Great Western Power Co., 91
Great Western Railway, *see* Chicago Great Western Railway
Griffin, Levi H., 30
Grinnell and Montezuma Railway Co., 112
Grinnell College, 271
Grinnell, Iowa, 106, 147, 271
Grinnell, Josiah B., 106, 107, 109, 112
Guaranty Loan Building, 85
Guiterman, Arthur, 174
Gulf of Mexico, 9, 150, 155, 156

H. T. Welles (locomotive), 247, 248
Hale, W. D., 63
Hall House, 51
Hamburg, Minn., 240
Hampton, Iowa, 112, 148, 255

Hanley Falls, Minn., 204
Harmonia Hall, 29
Harriman, E. H., 93, 154
Hastings & Dakota Railway, 27, 52
Hastings, Minn., 53
Hawley & Davis, 91, 93, 94
Hawley, Edwin, 88, 90-96, 98-102,
 118, 150-156, 159, 260; biographi-
 cal sketch, 92, 93
Hay, Abram, Tuston, 230
"Hay" steel, 230
Hayden, Charles, 177
Hayek, Edgar L., 210
Hayner, Henry Z., 17
Haynes family, 260
Hedrick, Iowa, 115
Helmbrecht, Father A. C., 132
Hennepin County, Minn., 46, 83
Hesch, Theodore P., 264
Hiawatha, 11
Hildebrandt, Fred H., 207
Hill, James J., 12, 57, 70, 72, 84, 154
History of Boone County, Iowa, 58
History of Minneapolis, 33
History of the Upper Mississippi
 Valley, 138
Hoboken, N. J., 183
Hocking Coal Co., 119
Hocking, Iowa, 119
Hollinshead, William, 17
Homeseekers excursions, 184
Hook and Eye, The, 104, 106, 120
Hoover, Charles E., 276, 278
Hopkins, Minn., 70, 74, 75, 86, 96,
 202, 203, 238, 265
Horner, Herbert F., 206
Hot Springs, Ark., 143
Houston, James P., 166, 240, 241
Houston, Texas, 228
Hoven, S. Dak., 132, 176
Hoyt, Otis, 17
Huber, David, 134, 135
Hudson River, 99
Humboldt Mill, 52
Hungerford, Edward, 253
Huntington, Clarence W., 116, 117,
 163, 164
Huntington, Collis P., 92, 93
Hutchinson, Minn., 74
Hutterites, 132

Illinois, 15, 110, 117, 118, 182, 184

Illinois Central Railroad, 101, 130,
 137, 140, 141, 143, 164, 201, 203,
 266, 273, 277
Illinois Terminal Railroad, 233
"In This Corner," 219
Indiana, 35
Indiana, Bloomington & Western
 Railway, 114
Indianapolis, Ind., 114, 219
Interborough Rapid Transit Co.,
 91, 153
Interstate Commerce Commission,
 82, 134, 202, 204, 206, 207, 209,
 218, 236
Inter-Urban Railway, 177
Iowa, 11, 14, 21, 54, 105, 106, 118,
 159, 182, 184, 250, 270
Iowa Central and Northwestern
 Railway Co., 112
Iowa Central and Western Railway
 Co., 163
Iowa Central Railroad, 106
Iowa Central Railway Co., 64, 91,
 92, 96, 99, 101, 102, 104-106, 111,
 113, 115-121, 142, 143, 151-153,
 155, 156, 160, 163, 167, 226, 250-
 252, 267, 269, 272, 273, 275
Iowa City, Iowa, 178
Iowa Construction Co., 153
Iowa Extension, 151
Iowa Pacific Railroad Co., 112
Iowa River, 270, 275
Iowa River Railway Co., 107, 108
Iowa River Valley, 269
Iowa Times, 58
Ireland, 238
Iron Mountain Railway, see St.
 Louis, Iron Mountain & South-
 ern Railway
Irwin, H. D., 213
Isthmian Canal Commission, 153
"I've Been Working on the Rail-
 road," 271

J. M. Cate (locomotive), 115
James River Valley, 132
Jay Cooke & Co., 42
Jerkwater mine, 119
Jersey Central Railraod, see Central
 Railroad Company of New Jersey
Johnson, Harold F., 276
Johnson, Pres. Andrew, 9

Johnson, Sheriff, 25
Johnson, Swan J., 240
Johnstone, Elmer J., 121
Jones, Harry E., 268
Jones Jesse H., 191
Jordan, Minn., 265
Junell, John, 193

Kalo, Jct., Iowa., 217
Kansas City, Fort Scott & Gulf Railroad, 161
Kansas City, Mexico & Orient Railway, 154, 155
Kansas City, Mo., 69, 113, 143, 151, 152, 155, 219, 273
Kansas City, St. Joseph & Council Bluffs Railroad, 143
Karlsson, Adolph, 207
Katy, see Missouri-Kansas-Texas Railroad
Keithsburg and Eastern Railroad Co., The, 113
Keithsburg Bridge Co., 111
Keithsburg, Grinnell & Dakota Railway Co., 112
Keithsburg, Ill., 105, 109, 114, 256, 275
Kelly, John B., 239
Kelly, Oliver H., 47
Kensett, Iowa, 267, 268
Kenwood, Minn., 86, 97, 264
Keystone mine, 57
Kickapoo Creek, 119, 160
Kickapoo Hill, 160, 228, 278
Kilkenny, Minn., 266
Killeen, Dennis, 246
Kimball, Robert J., 118
Kingsbury, Arthur M., 146
Knights of Labor, 58
Knoble, William C., 178
KSTP (radio station), 210

Lackawanna Railroad, see Delaware, Lackawanna & Western Railroad
Lafayette, Hotel, 70
Lake Erie, 152
Lake Kempeska, 131
Lake Mills, Iowa, 243
Lake Minnetonka, 64, 69-71, 73-76, 137, 141, 220
Lake Minnetonka Navigation Co.,

73, 75
Lake Park Hotel, 70, 73, 75, 141
Lake St. Croix, 16, 25
Lake Superior, 13, 37, 38, 81
Lake Superior & Mississippi Railroad, 9, 12, 22, 24, 25, 28, 29, 32, 36-40, 42, 45, 81, 248, 249
Lake Tetonka, 141
Leach, George E., 210
Leake, Arthur C., 233
LeBeau, Antoine, 125
LeBeau, Hotel, 128, 134
LeBeau Phenix, 126-130
LeBeau, S. Dak., 124-130, 132-135, 151, 176, 181, 218
Lehigh Valley Railroad, 162
Lemmon, S. Dak., 127
Leola, S. Dak., 124, 130, 218
Less-than-carload (L.C.L.) freight, 183, 218, 219
Less-than-truckload (L.T.L.) freight, 218
Lewis, William F., 206
Lisman, F. J., 191
Litchfield, Minn., 12
Little Cottonwood River, 95
Little York, Ill., 276
Livermore, Iowa, 54, 55, 148, 241
Livermore, Me., 14
Livingston, Harry C., 276, 277
Logan, Frederic Knight, 272
Logansport, Crawfordsville & Southwestern Railway, 80
London Mills, Ill., 182, 256, 275
Los Angeles, Calif., 6, 143, 154
"Louie, The," 120
Lowrey, Robert, 58
Lowry, Thomas, 75
Luke, Mrs. Hughie, 132, 133
Lutz, S. G., 152

McAdoo, William G., 174
McCarthy, Charley, 144
McCarthy, Hugh, 165, 166
MacKenzie, David G. "Dode," 127, 128, 135
MacKenzie, Murdo, 125, 128
McKinley, Pres. William, 93, 140, 260
McLeod County, Minn., 16
McLeod, Martin, 16
McNair, William W., 35, 64
McPherson County Herald, 124

303

McPherson County, S. Dak., 124
Maher, P., 152
Maine, 15, 34
Mallet articulated locomotive, 189
Manchester Locomotive Works, 115, 248
Manitou Jct., Minn., 70, 74, 75
Mankato, Minn., 12, 66, 95
Manly, Iowa, 266-268
Manly Jct., Iowa, 118
Maplewood mine, 119
Mark Twain, 275
Marsh, Iowa, 275
Marshall, Joseph M., 17
Marshalltown (cafe-lounge car), 184
Marshalltown, Iowa, 105, 107, 108, 114, 115, 120, 147, 165, 166, 178, 183, 240, 251, 255, 270, 275
Marshalltown shops, 200, 250, 251, 256
Martin, John, 34, 35
Martinsburg, Iowa, 105, 109, 216, 275
Mason City (cafe-lounge car), 184
Mason City, Iowa, 112, 113, 203, 218, 268
Mason City Jct., Iowa, 166, 268
Mason, William (Mason Machine Works), 251
Massachusetts, 24
Masters, Edgar Lee, 276
Matador Land & Cattle Co., 125, 128
Maxwell, Ill., 119, 160, 278
Melendy, Peter, 107, 108
Melton, James, 190
Memphis, Tenn., 277
Mendenhall, Richard J., 35
Mendota, Minn., 11
Mercer County Bridge Co., 111
Merriam, J. L., 29
Merriam Jct., Minn., 51, 56, 221; *see also* Sioux City Jct., Minn.
Merriam, Minn., *see* Merriam Jct., Minn.
Merriam, W. R., 63
Metropolitan Life Building, 85, 163, 231
Mexicans, 261
Mexico, 154
Middle Grove, Ill., 119, 204, 256, 276

Middle Grove mine, 184
Mikado type locomotive, 164, 166, 187, 189, 195, 215, 252, 256
Milwaukee & St. Paul Railway, 11, 12, 38, 39
Milwaukee mine, 57
Milwaukee Road, *see* Chicago, Milwaukee, St. Paul & Pacific Railroad
Milwaukee, Wis., 11, 12, 38
Minerva Jct., Iowa, 112
Minneapolis and Duluth Railroad Co., The, 22-26, 28, 32, 37, 39-42, 45, 46, 51, 53, 55
Minneapolis & St. Louis Defense Committee, 206, 207, 209
Minneapolis & St. Louis Executive Defense Committee, 205
Minneapolis & St. Louis Railroad Co., The, 3-5, 163-165, 167, 169, 170, 173-175, 177, 178, 181-185, 187, 189-196, 198-207, 210-213, 216, 218 220, 236, 250, 252, 254
Minneapolis and St. Louis Railroad Co., The, 75, 88, 91-98, 100-102, 118, 120, 123-132, 139-143, 146-148, 151-156, 159-162, 179, 217, 246, 250, 251
Minneapolis and St. Louis Railroad Co., The, (of Minnesota and Iowa), 163
Minneapolis & St. Louis Railway Corporation, The, 214, 215
Minneapolis & St. Louis Railway Co., 14, 18, 21-23, 26-28, 30, 33, 34, 36-38, 41, 42, 45-47, 70, 83, 112, 217, 248, 249
Minneapolis & St.. Louis Railway Co., The 5-7, 138, 214, 215, 221, 222, 225-234, 237-239, 241, 243, 244, 247, 254-256, 259-261, 263, 264, 266, 269-271, 273, 277, 278
Minneapolis and St. Louis Railway Co., The, 54, 56-58, 63-70, 72-74, 78-86, 93, 137, 240
Minneapolis and St. Louis Railway Co., The, (of Minnesota and Iowa), 55
Minneapolis & St. Paul Suburban Railway, 75
Minneapolis Board of Trade, 44
Minneapolis City Council, 50
Minneapolis Grain Exchange, 206

304

Minneapolis *Journal*, 122, 130, 198
Minneapolis, Lyndale & Minnetonka Railway ("Motor Line"),
64, 70, 74
Minneapolis Mill Co., 10, 15, 33
Minneapolis Millers, 190
Minneapolis, Minn., 5, 6, 9-14, 16,
18, 21-25, 27-30, 33-35, 37, 40,
41, 44-46, 50-53, 55, 56, 64, 67,
69, 74, 81-83, 85, 92, 96, 99-101,
139, 161, 163, 169, 175, 183, 193,
199, 200, 202-204, 207, 209, 210,
214, 218-221, 226, 230-233, 240,
242, 244, 249, 250, 253, 255, 256,
263, 264, 274, 277, 278
Minneapolis Municipal Auditori-
um, 209, 210
Minneapolis, New Ulm and Southwestern Railroad Co., The, 95
Minneapolis, St. Paul & Sault Ste.
Marie Railway, 56, 81, 130, 161,
201
Minneapolis *Star*, 219
Minneapolis Traffic Association, 207
Minneapolis *Tribune*, 8, 15, 20-24,
26, 27, 32, 40, 45, 51, 150
Minnesota, 6, 9, 15-17, 21, 30, 49,
139, 159, 184
Minnesota and Iowa Southern
Railway Co., 54, 55
Minnesota & North-western Rail-
road, 113-115
Minnesota & North-western Rail-
way, 66
Minnesota Central Rail Road Co.,
The, 65, 66
Minnesota, Dakota & Pacific Rail-
way Co., 124
Minnesota River, 10, 27, 28, 265
Minnesota River Valley, 265
Minnesota Transfer, 264
Minnesota Valley, 12, 30
Minnesota Valley Railroad, 15
Minnesota Western Railroad Co.,
15-18, 29, 34
Minnetonka Beach, Minn., 70, 72
Minnetonka Lake Park Hotel, 70
Mississippi River, 9-11, 13, 16, 26,
38, 50, 72, 105, 109-111, 275, 278
Missouri, 21
Missouri-Kansas-Texas Railroad, 91,
155, 192
Missouri Pacific Railroad, 143

Missouri River, 122-126, 129, 130,
133-135, 151, 152, 218, 230
Missouri Waltz, 272
Mitchell, Alexander, 39
Mobile & Ohio Railroad, 24
Mobridge, S. Dak., 127
Mogul type locomotive, 95, 175,
248-251, 256
Mohler, A. L., 88, 96
Moingona mine, 57
Monmouth College, 153
Monmouth, Ill., 110, 120, 182, 218,
256, 276
Monroe, Hotel, 147
Montezuma, Iowa, 112, 217
Montgomery, Minn., 211, 255, 265
Moorehead, William G., 22
Moravia, Iowa, 107
Moreau Jct., S. Dak., 129
Morgan, David, 106-108
Morgan, David P., 254
Morning Sun, Iowa, 275
Morrill, H. L., 109
Morse, Horace J., 118
Morton, Minn., 64, 66, 95, 147,
204, 243
Mossman and Gates' Turkey Track,
125
"Motor Line," *see* Minneapolis,
Lyndale & Minnetonka Railway
Moynihan, Francis V., 238
Moynihan, Francis V. Jr., 238
Moynihan, Jeremiah A., 238
Moynihan, Jeremiah J., 238
Muchakinock mine, 119
Mud Line, 56, 217
Mullen family, 260
Munsell family, 260
Murphy, James E., 175, 176
Murray, William P., 17

Nash, Elliott E., 179, 181, 184
National Exchange Bank, 35
National Grange of the Patrons
of Husbandry, *see* Grange, The
Nelson, A. T., 168, 241
Nelson, Socrates, 17
Nemo, Ill., 276
New Hampshire, 34
New Haven Railroad, *see* New
York, New Haven & Hartford
Railroad

New Orleans, La., 6, 13
New Prague, Minn., 265
New Sharon Coal Valley and Eastern Railway Co., The, 109
New Sharon, Iowa, 106, 109, 110
New Ulm, Minn., 95, 176, 210, 240
New Ulm (motor car), 181
New York Central Railroad, 263
New York, Chicago & St. Louis Railroad, 183, 277
New York, New Haven & Hartford Railroad, 162
New York, N. Y., 6, 11, 13, 33, 35, 91-93, 98, 99, 152, 153, 183, 191, 192, 225, 234
New York Stock Exchange, 91
Newburg, Iowa, 112, 181
Newsweek, 226
Newton, Iowa, 110, 120
Newton (station agent), 27, 41
Nickel Plate Road, see New York, Chicago & St. Louis Railroad
Nicollet Ballpark, 211
Nicollet House, 29
Nobel Peace Prize, 272
Noonan, D. C., 206
Norfolk & Western Railway, 161
North Carolina, 35
North Fork of Skunk River, 272
North Redwood, Minn., 242
North Star Limited, 137, 141, 142, 184, 195, 249, 259
North Western Railway, see Chicago & North Western Railway
North Yard (Oskaloosa), 273
Northern Pacific Railway, 37, 39, 42, 45, 46, 50, 53, 54, 68, 120, 125, 129, 139, 247-250, 277
Northfield Bank, 266
Northfield, Minn., 66
Northville, S. Dak., 132
Northwestern Bank Building, 226, 232
Northwestern Sanitation Association, 136
Northwood, Iowa, 36, 108, 118, 203, 267
Norwood, Minn., 204

Oak Grove, Iowa., 96, 272
O'Brien, "Billy," 55
O'Brien, John J., 234
O'Connor, E. T., 206

Ogden, Iowa, 56
Ogden, Utah, 143
Ohio mine, 57
Olds, Iowa, 255
O'Leary, L. M., 206
Oliver, E. L., 206
Ollie, Iowa, 105
Omaha, Neb., 96, 140, 143, 216
Omaha Road, see Chicago, St. Paul, Minneapolis & Omaha Railway
One of the Moynihans, 238
Ontario, 256
Oregon Electric Railway, 277
Oregon Railroad & Navigation Co., 88, 96
Orono, Me., 15
Oskaloosa, Iowa, 105, 107-110, 119, 120, 147, 160, 204, 227, 229, 230, 255, 271-274
Ottumwa, Iowa, 113-115

Pacific Division, 240
Pacific Extension, 70
Pacific Ocean, 154-156, 259
Pacific type locomotive, 184, 190, 252, 253
Panama Canal, 153
Panama Railroad, 162
Panic mine, 57
Panic of 1873, 36, 42, 47, 248
Panic of 1893, 59, 74, 87
Paoli, Pa., 86
Parker, Frank C., 267
Pearsons, George R., 55
Penn, William, 272
Pennsylvania, 35, 153, 272
Pennsylvania Railroad, 80, 86, 263
Peoria and Farmington Railway Co., 110
Peoria & Pekin Union Railway, 119
Peoria Gateway, 160, 173, 195, 203, 220, 277
Peoria Gateway Line, The, 170, 173
Peoria, Ill., 5, 101, 110, 111, 114, 119, 143, 151, 153, 160, 170, 183, 200, 203, 204, 206, 216, 218, 221, 226-228, 255, 256, 264, 265, 273, 274, 277, 278
Peoria (motor car), 181
Pere Marquette Railroad, 161
Perry, Iowa, 59, 177
Pettengill car coupler, 49

Phil Sheridan, 72
Philadelphia, Pa., 22, 25, 36, 42, 86, 216, 248, 277
Phillips Celebrated Tourist Car Excursions, 140, 143
Pickering, Iowa, 271
Pickett, Clarence E., 272
Pierce, L. E. Buffet, 134
Pierre, S. Dak., 127, 130
Pillsbury, John S., 34
Pillsbury Mills, 34
Pittsburgh Locomotive Works, 248
Plattsmouth, Neb., 230
Player, John, 251
Pond Lilly mine, 119
Porter, H. H., 63
Portland, Ore., 216
Poweshiek County, Iowa, 217
Prairie du Chien, Wis., 11
Promontory, Utah, 9
Propeller Club (Pullman), 184
Pueblo, Colo., 143
Pullman cars, 40, 113, 114, 137, 140, 143, 148, 195

Rabens, William, 168, 169
Radisson Hotel, 210
Railroad & Warehouse Commission, Minnesota, 67
Railroad Law of 1874, 48
Railway Age, 90, 158, 212, 226, 254
Railway & Locomotive Historical Society, 248
Railway Transfer Company of the City of Minneapolis, The, 178, 202, 237, 238
Raleigh, Iowa, 95
Randolph, Minn., 66
Reconstruction Finance Corporation, 191, 202
Record of Old Boats, A, 72
Red River, 16
"Red Stack, The," 120
Red Wing, Minn., 11, 65, 95
Redwood, Minn., 242, 243
Rembrandt, Iowa, 217
Reorganization Committee (1934), 5
Republican National Convention (St. Louis 1896), 140
Rhode Island Locomotive Works, 248

Rice County, Minn., 16
Rice, Henry M., 16
Rich, W. W., 56
Rio Grande Railroad, *see* Denver & Rio Grande Railroad
Rippey, Iowa, 59
River Division, 11
"Road That Runs, The," 4, 146
Roberts (switchman), 97
Rock Island & Peoria Railroad, 67
Rock Island, Ill., 79
Rock Island Lines, *see* Chicago, Rock Island & Pacific Railway
Rock Island Southern Railway, 276
Rockefeller, John D., 129
Rockets, 271
Rockford, Rock Island & St. Louis Railroad, 68, 79
Roebuck, Alvah C., 242
Rogers, Charles B., 115, 250
Rollins, John, 17
Roosevelt, Philip J., 191
Roosevelt, Pres. Theodore, 153, 260
Ross, George H., 152
Ross, W. L., 152
Russell, Roswell P., 17, 34
Russell Sage Foundation, 118
Russell Sage (locomotive), 115, 250
Russian-German stock, 131
Ruthven, Iowa, 163
Ryan, Robert E., 175, 176

Sage, Margaret Olivia, 117
Sage, Russell, 100, 114-118
St. Anthony Falls Water Power Co., 10
St. Anthony, Minn., 9-12, 14, 16, 17, 24, 34, 35, 41
St. Anthony's Church, 132
St. Benedict, Iowa, 230
St. Bonifacious, Minn., 74, 75
St. Croix River, 16, 53
St. James, Minn., 148
St. Louis & Kansas City Mail, The, 147
St. Louis and St. Paul Railroad Co., 108
St. Louis Car Co., 181
St. Louis, Hotel, 70, 74, 75
St. Louis, Iron Mountain & Southern Railway, 143

St. Louis, Keokuk & North-western Railroad, 51, 69, 139
St. Louis, Mo., 6, 13, 18, 21, 30, 50, 51, 67, 69, 72, 106, 113-115, 125, 138-140, 142, 143, 151, 152, 155, 159, 195, 219, 233, 273
St. Louis Park, Minn., 86, 265
St. Louis River, 16
"St. Louis Road, The," see Minneapolis & St. Louis Railway Co.
St. Louis-San Francisco Railway, 91, 161, 233
St. Louis Southwestern Railway, 277
St. Louis Special, 139
St. Paul & Duluth Railroad, 38, 53, 54, 249
St. Paul & Pacific Railroad, 11, 14, 26, 41, 51, 83
St. Paul & Sioux City Railroad, 12, 15, 28-30, 51, 63
St. Paul, Minneapolis & Manitoba Railway, 83, 84, 88
St. Paul, Minn., 9, 10-12, 16, 23, 29, 30, 38, 39, 50, 68, 69, 72, 75, 81, 82, 98, 106, 113, 120, 137, 139, 141, 169, 264
St. Paul Pioneer, 23
St. Paul Press, 23
San Diego, Calif., 143, 154
San Francisco, Calif., 6, 143, 155
Sante Fe, see Atchison, Topeka & Santa Fe Railway
Saturday Evening Post, 155
Saucy Kate, 75
Sauk Rapids, Minn., 12
Sault Ste. Marie, Ontario, 81, 256
Schenectady Locomotive Works, 248, 249
School House Hill, 272
Scott County, Minn., 46
Scotty Phillip, 125, 129
Seaboard Air Line Railway, 254
Sears, Richard W., 242, 243
Sears, Roebuck & Co., 242
Sears, R. W., Watch Co., 242
Searsboro, Iowa, 96, 272
Seaton, Ill., 276
Seattle, Wash., 6
Serena, Ill., 188
Shakopee, Minn., 12, 265
Sherburne County, Minn., 47
Shipstead, Henrik, 206
Shonts, Theodore Perry, 152-155,

159
Short Line, The, 11
Sibley, Henry H., 29, 30
Sidle, Jacob K., 35, 63
Silver Creek mine, 119
Sioux City Jct., Minn., 28, 30, 36, 37, 39-41, 46, 51; see also Merriam Jct., Minn.
Sioux Indian, 144
"Skally, The," 37, 38, 53, 120; see also Lake Superior & Mississippi and St. Paul & Duluth railroads
Skunk River, 272, 275
Smith, A. Hyatt, 17
Smith, Elijah, 113
Smitty (news agent), 144-146
Snelling shops, 75
"Snowbound," 174
Snyder, Frank W., "Windy," 166, 167
Solbergs Point, Minn., 73
Soo Line, see Minneapolis, St. Paul & Sault Ste. Marie Railway
South America, 155
South Dakota, 100, 125, 130, 159, 184, 204
South St. Paul, Minn., 125
Southern Pacific Co., 92-94, 143
Southern Railway, 116
Southwestern Extension, 96
Southwestern Traffic Association, 96
Spearman, Frank H., 62
Spencer, Iowa, 96, 163, 204, 217
Spink County, S. Dak., 132
Spirit Lake, Iowa, 128
Spokane, Portland & Seattle Railway, 277
Spoon River, 276
Spoon River Anthology, 276
Sprague, Lucian Charles, 5, 79, 186, 187, 189-196, 207, 209, 215, 216, 225, 231-234, 252, 260, 274; biographical sketch, 188
Spring Park, Minn., 70, 75
Springfield, Ill., 277
Springfield, Ohio, 114
Stacy, E. C., 51
Standard mine, 57
Standard Oil Co., 129
Standard type locomotive, see American type locomotive
Standing Rock homestead lands, 126

308

Standing Rock Indian Reservation, 126
State Center, Iowa, 112, 119, 181
State Fair, Minnesota, 226
Statement of the Minneapolis & St. Louis Railway Co. of Its Position Relative to the North Minneapolis Crossing Controversy, 84
Steamboat Rock, Iowa, 269, 270
Steele, Franklin, 16, 17, 29
Steinhagen, John, 240
Stephens, Bud, 128
Stickney, Alpheus B., 63, 64, 68, 113-115
Stillwater, Minn., 25, 28, 53
Stillwell, Arthur E., 155
Storm Lake, Iowa, 95, 96, 217
Story City, Iowa, 112, 120
Strategy of Great Railroads, The, 62
Strikes; Shopmen's (1922), 179; Switchmen's (1909-1910), 151
Sully, Alfred, 112, 115
Sully, Daniel J., 99
Swan Creek, 125, 135
Swedes, 37

Taft, Pres. William H., 126, 161, 260
Tara, Iowa, 57, 163
Taylors Falls & Lake Superior Railroad, 53
Taylors Falls, Minn., 53, 54
Ten-Wheeler type locomotive, 248, 249, 252, 256
Texas, 276
Teyro, George L., 239
Teyro, James, 238, 239
Theroux, Bert, 97
Third Minnesota Regiment, 35
Thompson, Horace, 29
Toledo, Iowa, 107
Toledo, Ohio, 151, 152
Toledo, St. Louis & Western Railroad, 91, 152, 153, 156, 159, 183
Tompkins, F. M., 93, 94
Tonka Bay, Minn., 70, 74, 75, 76, 141, 249
Tony (roundhouse helper), 165, 166
Topolobampo, Mexico, 154, 155
Townsend, Frank B., 173, 174, 179, 207

Tracy, Iowa, 204, 230, 231
Traffic World, 226
Trains, 226
Transportation Act of 1920, 177
Transportation Building, 163, 231
Trice, Edward, 127
Trout, William L., 194
Truesdale, William Haynes, 68, 69, 74, 78-84, 87, 88; biographical sketch, 79, 80
Tupper, Solon, 243
Turkey Track ranch, 125
Turner's Brass Band, 24, 29
Twentieth Century Limited, 263, 264
Twin Cities, 50, 57, 67-69, 81, 85, 98, 113, 115, 129, 137, 139, 142, 143, 151, 161, 183, 195, 200, 201, 204, 219, 221, 250, 253, 260
Tyler, A., 24, 26

Uintah Railway, 188, 189
Union Pacific Railroad, 9, 88, 93, 161
Union Steamboat Line, 40
United States Government, *see* Government, U. S.
U. S. News, 226
United States Railroad Administration, 174, 177
United States Railroad Labor Board, 180
United States Steel Corporation, 231
University of Minnesota, 34
University of Texas, 271

Van Cleve, Iowa, 181, 217
Van Sweringen, Mantis J., 154
Van Sweringen, Oris P., 154
Vermont, 34
Vermont Central Railroad, 24
Victory Jubilee, 209, 210, 211
Virginia, 24
Virginian Railway, 117, 164

W. D. Washburn (locomotive), 247, 248
Wabash Railroad, 113, 142, 195, 230, 273
Waconia, Minn., 86, 141
Waite, James F., 143

"Waldorf crowd," 99
Walker, Robert J., 17
Wallace, S. Dak., 176
"Wapsie, The," 266
War Production Board, 255
Ward, Herbert W., 194, 233
Warren County, Ill., 110
Waseca, Minn., 266
Washburn, Cadwallader C., 15, 52
Washburn, Elihu, 15
Washburn, Israel, 15
Washburn, William Drew, 14, 15, 18, 22, 23, 26, 28-30, 33, 36-39, 44-51, 55, 56, 63-65, 72, 81, 260; biographical sketch, 14, 15
Washington, D. C., 47, 206, 209
Watertown Express, 144
Watertown, S. Dak., 66, 67, 95, 123, 124, 131, 163, 175, 176, 206, 230, 265
Waterville, Minn., 66, 141, 147
Watson, William, 74, 144, 249
Way, Thomas A. 124, 126, 131
Wayzata, Minn., 70, 72
Webster County, Iowa, 54, 83
Welles, Henry Titus, 14, 15, 18, 22, 23, 26, 33, 36-39, 46, 63; biographical sketch, 14
West Liberty, Iowa, 68, 139
West St. Paul, Minn., 66
Westfall, W. P., 35
Wetonka, S. Dak., 131
Wheels A-Rolling, 253
White Bear Lake, Minn., 22-28, 32, 37, 39-41, 46, 49, 53
White Bear Line, *see* Minneapolis and Duluth Railroad Co., The
Whittier, John Greenleaf, 174
Wilcox, N. Greene, 17
Wilkin, Alexander, 16, 17
Wilkin County, Minn., 16

Wilkinson, Morton S., 17, 29, 30
William Crooks (locomotive), 11
William Osborn, 111
William Penn College, 272
Williams, Robert, 98
Wilson car coupler, 49
Wilson, Pres. Woodrow, 174
Winfield, Iowa, 109, 274, 275
Winona, Minn., 11
Winston-Salem, N. C., 216
Winthrop, Minn., 64, 147, 204, 214, 243
Wisconsin, 15, 49
Wisconsin Central Railway, 161
Wisconsin, Minnesota and Pacific Railroad Co., 95
Wisconsin, Minnesota and Pacific Railway Co., The, 65, 66
Woodruff sleepers, 114
World War I, 142, 148, 169, 170, 173, 174, 177, 178, 220-222, 238, 243
World War II, 219, 221, 222, 230, 254
Wright, Colin W., 213, 233
Wyoming, Minn., 53

Yahota, S. Dak., 131
Young, A. H., 84
Young, Henry, 30
Young, Robert R., 114
Younger Brothers Crossing, 266
Younger, Cole, 266
Younger, James, 266
Younger, Robert, 266
Youngstown, Ohio, 79

Zephyr Rockets, 139